POLICY CHOICES

Where there is much desire to learn, there of necessity will be much arguing . . .

John Milton

About the Editor

John F. Stack, Jr., is an associate professor and Chairman of the Political Science Department at Florida International University. He has written in the areas of ethnicity, world politics, and transnational relations. His books include; *International Conflict in an American City: Boston's Irish, Italians and Jews 1935-1944* (Greenwood Press, 1979), and *Ethnic Identities in a Transnational World* (Greenwood Press, 1981).

POLICY CHOICES
Critical Issues
in
American
Foreign Policy

John F. Stack, Jr.
Florida International University

Dushkin Publishing Group, Inc.
Guilford, Connecticut 06437
ISBN: 0-87967-442-3

To James P. Piscatori

STAFF

Jeremy Brenner	Managing Editor
Brenda Filley	Production Manager
Charles Vitelli	Designer
Libra Von Ogden	Typesetting Coordinator
LuAnn Zukowsky	Copy Editor

Library of Congress Catalogue Card Number: 83-070927

Manufactured in the United States of America

First Edition; First Printing

Table of Contents

Preface   1

Chapter 1. AMERICAN FOREIGN POLICY IN AN ERA   4
            OF TRANSITION

Chapter 2. CLASHING ASSUMPTIONS OF AMERICAN   22
            FOREIGN POLICY IN THE 1980s
            Richard Barnet, "Dancing in the Dark," *Progressive*, April 1981.
            Charles W. Kegley and Eugene R. Wittkopf, "The Reagan Ad-
            ministration's World View," *Orbis*, Spring 1982

Chapter 3. POWER AND AMERICAN FOREIGN POLICY   50
            Hans J. Morgenthau, "Six Principles of Political Realism," *Politics
            Among Nations*, Alfred Knopf, 1948
            Robert W. Tucker, "Oil and American Power, Six Years Later,"
            Commentary, September 1979
            Paul M. Sweezy and Harry Magdoff, "U.S. Foreign Policy in the
            1980s," *Monthly Review*, April 1980

Chapter 4. ECONOMIC INTERPRETATIONS OF   79
            AMERICAN FOREIGN POLICY
            Robert D. Hormats, "New Challenges in International Investments,"
            Department of State Bulletin, November 1981
            Harry Magdoff, "The U.S. Dollar, Petrodollars, and U.S. Imperial-
            ism," *Monthly Review*, January 1979
            Charles Krauthammer, "Dollar Diplomacy," *New Republic*,
            October 28, 1981

Chapter 5. THE ROLE OF SECRECY IN A   107
            DEMOCRATIC SOCIETY
            George Lardner, Jr., "Moynihan Unleashes the C.I.A.," *Nation*,
            February 16, 1980
            Ronald Reagan, "Remarks on Signing the Intelligence Identities
            Protection Act of 1982," June 23, 1982

Chapter 6. THE CONTINUING LEGACIES OF THE COLD WAR   119
            Michael T. Klare, "The Assault on the 'Vietnam Syndrome'," from
            Beyond the 'Vietnam Syndrome': U.S. Interventionism in the 1980s,
            Institute for Policy Studies, 1981
            Jeane Kirkpatrick, "U.S. Security and Latin America," *Com-
            mentary*, January 1981

Chapter 7. AMERICAN FOREIGN POLICY AND   146
            HUMAN RIGHTS
    Patricia Derian, "Human Rights and American Foreign Policy,"
    Current Policy, June 13, 1980
    Samuel P. Huntington, "Human Rights and American Power,"
    Commentary, September 1981

Chapter 8. THE UNITED STATES AND THE THIRD WORLD   162
    Barbara Ward, "Another Chance for the North?" Foreign Affairs,
    Winter 1980-81
    Peter L. Berger, "Speaking to the Third World," Commentary,
    October 1981

Chapter 9. REFLECTIONS ON NUCLEAR WEAPONS   186
    Ronald Reagan, "Nuclear Strategy Toward the Soviet Union,"
    Address to the Nation, November 22, 1982
    George F. Kennan, "Nuclear War: Confronting the Horror," Address
    at Dartmouth College, November 15, 1981

Chapter 10. THE FUTURE IS NOW   204
    James A. Nathan, "The New Feudalism," Foreign Policy, Spring
    1981
    Norman Myers, "The Exhausted Earth," Foreign Policy, Spring
    1981

Further Readings   225
Index   228

Credits

Chapter Two

Page 25. From, "Dancing in the Dark," by Richard Barnet, *Progressive*, April 1982. Reprinted by permission of the *Progressive*, 409 East Main Street, Madison, Wisconsin. Copyright ©1982, the Progressive, Inc.

Page 33. From, "The Reagan Administration's World View," by Charles W. Kegley and Eugene R. Wittkopf, *Orbis*, Spring 1982. Reprinted by permission of the publisher of *Orbis:* a journal of world affairs. Copyright ©1982 by the Foreign Policy Research Institute, Philadelphia, PA.

Chapter Three

Page 51. From, "Six Principles of Political Realism," by Hans J. Morgenthau, from *Politics Among Nations, Fifth Edition.* Reprinted by permission of Alfred A. Knopf, Inc. Copyright ©1973. All rights reserved.

Page 57. From, "Oil and American Power: Six Years Later," by Robert W. Tucker, *Commentary*, September 1979. Reprinted by permission of *Commentary*. Copyright ©1979. All rights reserved.

Page 71. From, "U.S. Foreign Policy in the 1980's," by Paul M. Sweezy and Harry Magdoff, *Monthly Review,* April 1980. Reprinted by permission of the authors and the *Monthly Review.* Copyright ©1980. All rights reserved.

Chapter Four

Page 81. From, "New Challenges in International Investments," by Robert D. Hormats, *Department of State Bulletin,* November 1981.

Page 91. From, "The U.S. Dollar, Petrodollars, and U.S. Imperialism," *Monthly Review,* January 1979. Reprinted by permission of the author and the *Monthly Review.* Copyright ©1979. All rights reserved.

Page 100. From, "Dollar Diplomacy," by Charles Krauthammer, *New Republic,* October 28, 1981. Reprinted by permission of the *New Republic.* Copyright ©1981 by the New Republic, Inc. All rights reserved.

Chapter Five

Page 109. From, "Moynihan Unleashes the C.I.A.," by George Lardner, Jr., *Nation,* February 16, 1980. Reprinted by permission of the *Nation.* Copyright ©1980, Nation Magazine, The Nation Associates, Inc.

Page 115. From, "Remarks on Signing the Intelligence Identities Protection Act of 1982," by Ronald Reagan, June 23, 1982.

Chapter Six

Page 122. From, "The Assault on the 'Vietnam Syndrome'," by Michael T. Klare, from *Beyond the Vietnam Syndrome.* Reprinted by permission of the author and the Institute for Policy Studies. Copyright ©1981. All rights reserved.

Page 132. From, "U.S. Security and Latin America," by Jeane Kirkpatrick, *Commentary*, January 1981. Reprinted by permission of the author and *Commentary.* Copyright ©1981. All rights reserved.

Chapter Seven

Page 148. From, "Human Rights and American Foreign Policy," by Patricia Derian, *Current Policy,* June 13, 1980.

Page 153. From, "Human Rights and American Power," by Samuel Huntington, *Commentary,* September 1981. Reprinted by permission of the author and *Commentary.* Copyright ©1981. All rights reserved.

Chapter Eight

Page 166. From, "Another Chance for the North," by Barbara Ward, *Foreign Affairs,* Winter 1980-81. Reprinted by permission of the author and *Foreign Affairs.* Copyright ©1981. All rights reserved.

Page 174. From, "Speaking to the Third World," by Peter L. Berger, *Commentary,* October 1981. Reprinted by permission of the author and *Commentary.* Copyright ©1981. All rights reserved.

Chapter Nine

Page 188. From, "Nuclear Strategy Toward the Soviet Union," by Ronald Reagan. Address to the Nation, November 22, 1981.

Page 197. From, "Nuclear War: Confronting the Horror," by George F. Kennan, from an address at Dartmouth College, November 15, 1981. Reprinted by permission of the author. Copyright ©1981. All rights reserved.

Chapter Ten

Page 206. From, "The New Federalism," by James A. Nathan, *Foreign Policy,* Spring 1981. Reprinted by permission of the author and *Foreign Policy.* Copyright ©1981. All rights reserved.

Page 213. From, "The Exhausted Earth," by Norman Myers, *Foreign Policy,* Spring 1981. Reprinted by permission of the author and *Foreign Policy.* Copyright ©1981. All rights reserved.

Preface

As this book goes to press five events during the last year dramatically illustrate the challenges confronting American foreign policy in the 1980s: the British-Argentine War in the South Atlantic, the Israeli battles with Syria and the Palestine Liberation Organization (PLO) in Lebanon, upheaval in Central America, the 1982 Versailles Summit of Western heads-of-state, and the peril of nuclear war. The fierce fighting in the Falkland/Malvinas Islands, and in Lebanon, as well as increasing military activities in Central America underscore the delicate balance of forces that separates war from peace—a precarious balance found in nearly every region of the world. The economic summit in Paris and President Reagan's subsequent visit to England, Italy, West Germany, and Belgium document the unprecedented levels of interdependence in economics, politics, and military affairs that bind the United States to the West, and Western Europe to America. Thus, the realities of war and peace in a world characterized by increasing patterns of mutual dependence in the West and elsewhere throughout the world suggest the crucial choices confronting the makers of United States foreign policy. In the Falklands War, U.S. diplomatic initiatives attempted to balance the geopolitical and economic significance of Latin America against traditional American cultural and political ties to Great Britain. In the case of Israel, the United States must weigh its thirty-four year commitment to the sovereignty of that state against its commitment to the political and economic stability of the Middle East. Increasing guerrilla activities in El Salvador and Honduras also raise disturbing questions about appropriate political and military involvement in a Third World country. Fear of a Soviet-Cuban Communist insurgency in Latin America and the Caribbean stand in sharp contrast to fears of a new Vietnam-like involvement in the jungles of Central America. Simultaneously, the economic summit at Versailles demonstrated that while there are no unilateral solutions to the West's problems of inflation, currency stability, and balance-of-payments, meaningful multi-lateral cooperation continues to be elusive. The complexities and ambiguities symbolized by these events are magnified ten-fold when one considers the full extent of United States global interests. The prospects of nuclear annihilation and the destruction of human civilization in the West and perhaps the world has mobilized significant segments of public opinion in the United States and Europe. But the international system constitutes only part of the foreign policy-making process.

The domestic context—both governmental and public—increases the difficulty of making comprehensive and coherent policy choices. The interests of bureaucracies, governmental officials and high-ranking advisors to the president, interest groups, Congress, the mass media and public opinion, and the prevailing ideological assumptions of the president and his national security advisors all play some role in the making of foreign policy. Indeed, the policies that emerge often reflect the extraordinary complexities of a process that includes international issues and events, domestic concerns, and the nearly constant penetration of the American political system by global issues and forces. These external forces range from the price of petroleum or the rate of inflation to questions of global survival.

Thirty years ago, it was fashionable to envision foreign policy decision-making as an almost exclusive application of domestic political policies. Many believed the United States to be immune to the currents and pressures of international politics. In 1982, no aspect of American life—public or private—escapes the influences, direct or indirect, of international politics. What we are witnessing is the steady erosion of the theoretical boundaries which separate international politics from domestic politics. The increasing internationalization of the American domestic political system intensifies patterns of interdependence which immeasurably complicate the making of foreign policy. Not only is it difficult to find a solution to contemporary global problems, it is often hard to distinguish the problem from its symptoms. It is certainly ironic that the international systems which the United States helped to shape so significantly after 1945 and during the 1950s now influence almost every aspect of our domestic political environment.

A great danger for the United States and the world is that American frustration with its inability to influence world events in the 1980s (as compared to the 1940s and 1950s) could result in a new wave of isolationism or an activism which demands American dominance or hegemony, at the expense of a more sophisticated, multilateral approach to global problem solving. While the history of American foreign policy in the nineteenth and twentieth centuries amply documents the activities of pragmatists, it also illustrates the tremendous influence that crusaders, idealists and others have exerted in shaping the destinies of the United States and the world. In this regard, many of our own political and economic successes have added to the difficulties of formulating foreign policy. We have created a domestic atmosphere which reflects America's post-industrial age. A large bureaucracy and powerful multinational corporations occupy positions of influence. Our society is increasingly penetrated and divided by transnational and international issues. These factors have intensified the traditional American vacillation between international activism and isolationism.

The goal of this book is to examine a number of assumptions which shape the framework within which contemporary foreign policy analysis is conducted. This is clearly a difficult task which can be only begun in this volume. The historic swings of American foreign policy—some would call them schizoid—transcend simple ideological differences between the left and the right, liberals and conservatives, capitalists and Marxists. The intensely divergent perspectives presented throughout this book document the con- flicts—past, present and future—which characterize the political, economic, military, and cultural transformations of the United States and much of the world during the nineteenth and twentieth centuries. From this perspective, there are no simple answers or easy solutions to the problems which confront United States foreign policy or the problems United States foreign policy creates for much of the world. There is, nevertheless, the recognition that the foreign policy of the United States—explicit or implicit, wise or imprudent, self interested or altruistic—affects in a significant manner chances for global survival in the nuclear age. While the United States cannot assume single-handed responsibility for the successful resolution of every significant global problem, American influence helps to define the world's future in more than a casual manner.

It should be noted at the outset that clashing philosophical and ideological analyses of American policy often overwhelm one's appreciation of the human factor involved in both the formulation/implementation of decisions and the human consequences of the policies chosen. Jonathan Schell's recent book, *The Fate of the Earth*, provides an inestimable service in reminding us that ideological assumptions or extant theories of American foreign policy in the nuclear age have systematically obscured basic issues concerning human survival. This is a sobering recognition especially when the vocabulary of foreign policy analysis is based on the concepts of power, dominance, secrecy, confrontation, diplomacy, and war. A central theme which runs through this book is that foreign policy choices must address the most important of all human concerns—the ability of our species to survive—if American foreign policy is ultimately to be judged a success. The central dilemma confronting students of foreign policy is that there does not exist one unambiguous way of solving multiple sets of problems let alone guaranteeing the survival of our planet.

The book's objective is to paint a large and complex picture on a huge canvas. The picture which I am attempting to draw has its legacy and receives much of its continued vitality from the forces that have shaped the history of the United States, especially since the Second World War. This is not an easy task. The danger is that the picture may be too bold in places or not vivid enough in others—distortions may result. The very imperfections of this portrait suggest the complexity of the issues and the philosophical conflicts which are debated throughout this book.

This book cannot consider every significant issue-area of contemporary American foreign relations, nor does it offer an analysis of the institutional setting of foreign policy decision-making. I have chosen to underscore three dimensions of the policy-making process: selected conceptual themes, several crucial bureaucratic actors, and a number of contemporary issues areas. I have designed each section to underscore important insights and to draw on some of the finest and most sophisticated analyses of foreign policy available. Chapter 1 provides a framework which addresses a number of the basic assumptions concerning the issues confronting contemporary American foreign policy in the 1980s.

I am pleased to acknowledge a number of debts incurred in my study of American foreign policy. John Patterson, Robert Riordan, and Richard B. Finnegan of the Department of Political Science, Stonehill College, introduced me to the study of foreign policy decision-making during the turbulent years of the late 1960s and early 1970s. Arthur N. Gilbert and the late Fred A. Sondermann of the Graduate School of International Studies, University of Denver, deepened my understanding of the historical, bureaucratic, and philosophical dynamics of U.S. foreign policy. I am grateful to Joel Gottlieb, Mark Rosenberg, Cheryl Rubenberg, and Christopher Warren for thoughtful comments on various sections of the manuscript. I am indebted to James N. Rosenau who provided important ideas on organization and substance. My appreciation for the vitality of the philosophical arguments presented in this study has been intensified by the critiques, debates, and questions posed by my students at Florida International University. Roberta McLaughlin and Judy Sheffield provided invaluable help in typing the manuscript.

Finally, I am indebted to Rick Connelly, President of The Dushkin Publishing Group, for his confidence and support. I am grateful to Jeremy Brenner for his able editorial assistance, encouragement, and enthusiasm during the writing of this study. This book is dedicated to Jim Piscatori, a great friend and colleague.

CHAPTER 1

American Foreign Policy
in an Era of Transition

American foreign policy appeared to change overnight with Ronald Reagan's election in 1980. Cold war rhetoric resurfaced with a surprising intensity and persuasiveness. Soviet aggression was portrayed as the principal challenge to American foreign policy in the 1980s. The United States suddenly realized its power was limited or declining in the world—indeed it was threatened by the Soviet encirclement in the Middle East, Africa, South Asia, and, most immediately, in Central America. Not since the 1950s and 1960s had Soviet foreign policies been placed in such a rigid cold war context by a U.S. president. It even seemed that the domino theory was being revived. The Reagan administration's increase in defense spending for both conventional and nuclear weapons was one indication of the changing foreign policy agenda. A major reinterpretation of nuclear war—including the belief that the United States might be able to win, or at least survive, a nuclear exchange—illustrated additional policy departures. President Reagan's firm belief that the United States must reassert its historic leadership in the West and revitalize existing political and military alliances further documented major ideological transformations. On a rhetorical level at least, it would seem that the central assumptions and primary goals of American foreign policy had radically changed in less than six years.

The human rights policies of the Carter administration were discredited in favor of more "realistic" strategies underscoring American power. Jimmy Carter's emphasis on the complexities of an interdependent global environment seemed irrelevant or naive in the face of the Soviet challenge. Most of all, the Reagan administration sought to distinguish itself from the Carter administration through a reliance on tough pragmatic diplomacy. Viewed from the perspective of 1982, Reagan's foreign policy seemed to be based on the attitudes of the 1950s and 1960s, before the days of detente, strategic arms limitation agreements, OPEC, and Camp David.

How can we analyze the dramatic ideological shift in contemporary American foreign policy? One way is to place the dichotomies between the foreign policies of Ronald Reagan and Jimmy Carter within a historical and analytical framework examining the divergent conceptions of American foreign policy objectives and the different styles of American foreign policy decision-making.[1] Despite the vast differences between Ronald Reagan and Jimmy Carter as presidents and, more importantly, in the articulation of their foreign policy goals, both men are the products of American philosophical and historical traditions. The apparent rejection of Jimmy Carter's foreign policy only underscores the clashing ideological assumptions that have comprised much of the history of American foreign policy in the twentieth century. To approach the study of contemporary foreign policy making without an appreciation of the historical issues that have shaped the American view of the world (whether isolationist or internationalist), is to deprive oneself of a critically important foundation. Thus, this chapter has been organized into four parts. The first emphasizes the evolution of isolationism and internationalism during the nineteenth and twentieth centuries. It argues that the distinctively American notion of "Manifest Destiny" helps us understand the dynamics of U.S. foreign policy, especially since the Second World War. The second section examines the role played by power in U.S. foreign policy during the twentieth century. It argues that Jimmy Carter's emphasis on human rights or Ronald Reagan's insistence on strength draw their vitality from long-standing philosophical traditions. The third section analyzes U.S. foreign policy from pluralist and Marxist perspectives. Finally, the fourth section examines American foreign policy decision making styles during unprecedented levels of global change.

Sources of American Foreign Policy: Isolationism and Internationalism

American foreign policy during the twentieth century often has been dominated by two seemingly contradictory forces: a retreat from world affairs (isolationism) and a zealous involvement in global politics (internationalism). Sometimes isolationism and internationalism are portrayed as mutually exclusive forces suggesting the whimsical and unstable outlook of American public opinion. Isolationism and internationalism are in fact different sides of the same coin. Isolationist and internationalist perspectives have called for radically different policy approaches to be sure. Yet, isolationism and internationalism are drawn from five aspects of U.S. history and culture: 1) a militant nationalism often expressed in the form of claims to a Manifest Destiny; 2) a historic distrust of European politics and foreign policies; 3) an explicit belief in the moral superiority of American motivations, whatever they might be; 4) a powerful sense of mission; and 5) the economic, demographic, industrial, and technological capacities to exert significant power—first in the Western Hemisphere during the nineteenth century and later throughout the world. The convergence of these five forces in U.S. history has resulted in the creation of a distinctly American approach to the formulation and implementation of U.S. foreign policy. In the interests of clarity, we will divide our analysis into four distinct periods of isolationist and internationalist activities. The first major isolationist period begins with the Declaration of Independence in 1775 and concludes with the outbreak of the Spanish American War in 1898. The period from 1898 until 1919 fostered significant internationalist activities. Isolationist sentiments reintensified from 1920 until 1941, while the years following the Second World War (1946 to the present) suggest, for the most part, an overwhelming internationalist foreign policy orientation.

Isolationism Proclaimed, 1776-1898

The roots of isolationism and internationalism are a vital part of the historic evolution of the United States.[2] Almost every aspect of the physical expansion of the U.S.—from the settlement of territories west of the Allegheny Mountains to the Louisiana Purchase of 1803, the acquisition of the Florida territory in 1819, and annexation of Texas in 1845, the establishment of title to Oregon in 1846 and the purchase of Alaska in 1867—raised diplomatic issues. The territorial expansion of the United States underscores the extraordinary appeal of the concept of Manifest Destiny for many Americans. As a moral justification for American political and economic motivations, Manifest Destiny illustrates the tremendous appeal that militant nationalism, once aroused, exerted on the American consciousness. Americans cited everything from pragmatic ambitions to mystical assertions of their God-given right to establish a new Jerusalem, to justify their territorial expansion and the accompanying conquest and extermination of the indigenous native populations. Thus, a sense of mission—itself the result of an idealization of the American religious and political experience—fused with a profoundly moralistic attitude to promote a militant nationalism. The internationalism of such twentieth-century presidents as Woodrow Wilson, Franklin D. Roosevelt, Harry Truman, John F. Kennedy, and Jimmy Carter drew heavily on assumptions of this Manifest Destiny.

The political evolution of the United States illustrated the importance of American nationalism and its fundamental difference from the European experience. Thomas Paine's *Common Sense,* while also aimed at securing French assistance, emphasized isolationist feelings by explicitly urging his fellow Americans not to become involved in European matters. The Revolutionary War, in fact, demonstrated the full extent of American dependence on European economic and military assistance, most notably from the French. However, by 1776 growing American nationalism, especially among the founders of the United States—Thomas Jefferson, James Monroe, and Ben Franklin—illustrated their ideological rejection of European political values.[3] George Washington's farewell address to Congress became an important justification for isolationism:

> Why forego the advantages of so peculiar a situation? Why quit our own to stand upon foreign ground? Why . . . entangle our peace and prosperity in the toils of European ambition, rivalship, interest, humor or caprice? It is our true policy to steer clear of permanent alliances with any portion for extraordinary emergencies.[4]

With the proclamation of the Monroe Doctrine on December 2, 1823, isolationalist sentiments found expression. By making an explicit distinction between the Old World and the Western Hemisphere, the Monroe Doctrine illustrated the depth of American fear and distain for European political and economic objectives. The Monroe Doctrine did not find practical application until after the American Civil War; even then, direct confrontations with European states over the doctrine's jurisdiction were limited during the nineteenth century. The task of building their towns and cities and forging a national consciousness absorbed Americans from 1776 until the 1890s, further reinforcing their isolationist tendencies. Indeed, the expansion of the United States from the thirteen original colonies to a country encompassing the territory between the Atlantic and Pacific oceans was a monumental undertaking. The sheer enormity of the political, economic, social, and military obstacles to building the United States as well as its geographical isolation from Europe underscored "a psychological aloofness from Europe . . . [that] led to a provincial outlook among the vast majority of Americans."[5] The physical vastness of the continental United States was conducive to isolationism, or at least illusions of independence, while the high protective tariffs imposed by the U.S. illustrated its actual self-sufficiency. Although foreign trade was only a very small part of the total overall economic picture, the United States continued to be a major market into which foreign capital flowed until the 1880s.[6] It is easy to over-exaggerate the isolation of the United States during the nineteenth century—rapid economic growth could not have taken place without significant European financial investments, and the "open door" policy to Japan (and later China) was a major diplomatic initiative. Yet, as historian Frederick Jackson Turner argued in his essay, "The Significance of the Frontier," the United States possessed the ability to begin transforming diverse European immigrants into democratically-minded citizens of an egalitarian society. The process of acculturation did not take place overnight, nor did it remove ethnic diversity, but nonetheless, the uniqueness of the

American experience underscored the gulf separating Americans from those who controlled the European states. Thus, nineteenth-century American isolationism was the outgrowth of westward expansion, the attempt to mold European immigrants into a common American nationality, and the fostering of urbanization and industrialization in the United States. In other words, the physical construction of American towns and cities was accompanied by the creation of a distinctive American identity. The concept of Manifest Destiny became more than a mere justification for westward expansion, however. It came to symbolize the triumphs of a people who escaped from European oppression, endured the hardships of immigration, conquered the American wilderness, and created a democratic system of government. The pride born of accomplishment also brought with it the self-righteousness of those who have suffered and, ultimately, prospered. Thus, a collection of motley outcasts was transformed into a nation of survivors and achievers.

Imperialism and Internationalism 1889-1919

By the 1880s the climate of isolationism began to change. Concern for the Caribbean and Central America—from economic, geopolitical, military, and cultural perspectives—increased markedly. The contradictions between the egalitarian and democratic pretentions of the Monroe Doctrine and U.S. political and economic interests intensified. By the mid-1890s, the United States explicity embraced an internationalist foreign policy. The Spanish American War of 1898 ushered in an era of unprecedented imperialist activities.* With the defeat of Spain, the United States became the dominant power in the Caribbean and Central America. In addition, the United States assumed possession of Puerto Rico and the Philippine Islands while exercising wide-ranging powers over Cuba that were legitimated through the 1901 Platt Amendment, which granted the United States the right to intervene in Cuba to preserve order and maintain its independence. U.S. activism in the Caribbean was intensified in 1904 through the proclamation of the Roosevelt Corollary to the Monroe Doctrine which conferred upon the United States the unilateral right to intervene in the internal political systems of the countries of the Caribbean and Latin America in cases of flagrant wrong-doing. The Roosevelt Corollary was applied to both the Dominican Republic and Nicaragua. In addition, American troops were dispatched to Haiti in 1915 and to several Central American, and Caribbean countries throughout the 1920s and the 1930s.

When analyzing direct American intervention in the Caribbean and Central America throughout the administrations of William McKinley, Theodore Roosevelt, William H. Taft, and Woodrow Wilson, three consequences stand out. First, the United States assumed the status of a major participant in international politics, while expanding the breadth and depth of its foreign policy interests and commitments. The shift of American foreign policy to imperialism-internationalism also can be traced to the transformation of the American political economy at the end of the nineteenth century. Rapid urbanization and industrialization brought with it the need for new sources of capital, foreign markets, and raw materials. The Monroe Doctrine provided a political justification for American intervention in Latin America. However, American involvement in the countries of Central America and the Caribbean far exceeded the political and moral spirit of the Monroe Doctrine. By 1900, an American empire had been achieved in the Caribbean and

---

*Imperialism is defined as a structural relationship of inequality in which one country dominates another through physical occupation or economic, political, military, or cultural dominance.

South Pacific. The United States "established a protectorate over Cuba, annexed Hawaii, secured a definite title to American Samoa, and acquired Puerto Rico, the Philippines, Guam, and Wake."[7] While anti-imperialist sentiments crystallized during these years, the triumph of imperialism reinforced the assertion of a new, militant American internationalism. Idealism made America's international Manifest Destiny more palatable, particularly in the face of anti-imperialist sentiments. The convergence of political, military, and economic objectives, however, complemented the rhetoric of Manifest Destiny by providing direction to American foreign policy between 1898 and 1919. The United States could never again reasonably or credibly eschew the scope or interests of its international concerns—despite isolationists' attempts in the next two decades.

Secondly, the justifications for American intervention in the Caribbean region underscored the profound significance of the projection of American nationalism into the international environment. The U.S. government and private elites argued that American humanitarian concerns and the desire to instill sound techniques of democratic government and political stability justified—indeed, demanded—intervention in the Caribbean. Therefore, the idealism of the reformer and the zeal of the evangelist partly motivated U.S. imperialism and internationalism. By the first decade of the twentieth century a new, more militant nationalism emerged. Perhaps after the conquest of the frontier and the psychological wounds of the Civil War, the United States needed a new nationalistic campaign to unite a regionally fragmented, socio-economically stratified, and ethnically diversified society confronting the upheavals of urbanization, industrialization, and continued immigration. One of the possible outgrowths of these changing values and attitudes was a new, powerful justification for an internationalist foreign policy. The actual consequences of American internationalism (or Manifest Destiny) during these years undoubtedly buttressed U.S. economic, political, and military goals. The assertions of American internationalism, especially in the Caribbean, also established a framework within which major foreign policy issues would be analyzed in following decades. Foreign policy strategies were framed not only as the pragmatic choices of a growing world power attempting to protect its sphere of influence, but as transcendent principles of truth or justice and idealizations of the American political system. Increasingly, American foreign policy goals were justified in terms of abstract dogmas or moral imperatives.[8] In other words, the guiding assumptions of American foreign policy were little more than vague restatements of traditional U.S. political values or norms. American foreign policy reaffirmed its pledge to promote self-determination, the freedom of man, or "making the world safe for democracy." U.S. police actions in the Caribbean were justified in terms of American political and economic achievements. The problem was that abstract dogmas or moral imperatives—whether based on the U.S. Declaration of Independence or the Constitution—suggested only vague policies, not the specific conditions under which the policies would be implemented.[9] Many of the basic assumptions of U.S. foreign policy can be explained by the attractiveness of such vague notions about the benefits of economic assistance to developing countries and its supposed correlation with democratic institutions. When Franklin D. Roosevelt signed the Atlantic Charter in 1941, he became part of a long-standing internationalist tradition. In the same manner, the 1947 Truman Doctrine, John F. Kennedy's proposal for the Alliance for Progress (1961), and most recently, Jimmy Carter's "absolute" commitment to human rights are examples of U.S. internationalism.

It is easy to discern the contradictions between the lofty idealism of internationalists and the more pragmatic political and economic goals of American foreign policy during 1898 and 1919. It is not at all ironic that Woodrow Wilson, perhaps the greatest idealist of them all, ordered the U.S. Marines into the Caribbean and Central America more often than had Teddy Roosevelt. One can simply view Wilson as a hypocrite, of course, but in a larger sense Wilson's actions illustrate the inherent danger of espousing goals, however worthy, that cannot be achieved reasonably. His international concerns fell far short of their target, thereby discrediting his spectacular goals. American foreign policy throughout the twentieth century, and particularly after 1946, has repeatedly raised expectations globally that it cannot fulfill. Some of the parallels between Woodrow Wilson and Jimmy Carter are particularly striking. For example, Wilson as the creator of the League of Nations called for the self-determination of the people of Eastern Europe—Poland and the nations of the Austro-Hungarian Empire—while at the same time utilizing gun boat diplomacy in the Caribbean. Jimmy Carter's human rights policy created a double standard between those countries that were important to U.S. political and military interests—Iran (before the fall of the Shah), the Soviet Union (before the invasion of Afghanistan), South Korea, and the Philippines—and those countries deemed less important to American foreign policy—Nicaragua, Haiti, Argentina, or Cambodia. It would seem that both Presidents Wilson and Carter were able to distinguish between the ideological objectives of their policies and the practical compromises involved in the implementation of these policies. A central difficulty in this kind of diplomacy is that the means and ends were not always compatible with the initial objectives. Moreover, American internationalists envisioned the formation of a global community, based on the principles of U.S. politics—a vision that is not widely shared by the rest of the world.[10]

The third consequence of American internationalist activities was that it prepared the way for American entrance into World War I. Initial U.S. reluctance to enter the war was overcome by inept German propaganda, sympathy for the British cause among members of the American elite, and, finally, by the indiscriminant use of German submarine warfare which led to the sinking of the British passenger liner *Lusitania* (May 1915) and the loss of 128 American lives.

With the American participation in the European conflict, President Wilson exploited sentiments of American patriotism to support the war effort. Wilson's rhetoric went far beyond support for U.S. soldiers fighting in Europe, however. He effectively harnessed the intensity of American nationalism in an attempt to restructure global politics after the fighting ended. In the Fourteen Points, his statement of war goals, Wilson tied the defeat of Germany to the establishment of a new international organization, the League of Nations, which he hoped would create the legal mechanisms necessary to prevent an outbreak of future global conflicts. Wilson's new role as world statesman was the ultimate expression of his conception of American Manifest Destiny. His goals were shattered by the refusal of the U.S. Senate to ratify the Treaty of Versailles ending World War I and establishing the League of Nations. Fear of entanglements in European politics as well as a sense that American sovereignty would be limited by U.S. membership in the League of Nations helped to fuel a wave of resurgent isolationism. Woodrow Wilson guaranteed his own defeat because of his unwillingness to compromise. The tragic irony was that America's greatest internationalist helped to bring about the onslaught of isolationism almost single-handedly.

The Resurgence of Isolationism, 1920-1941
The rejection of the Treaty of Versailles and the consequent refusal of the United States to enter the League of Nations set the tone for the following two decades. It is difficult to

assess the onslaught of isolationism during these years, although it seems clear that historic distrust of European political motivations was an important factor, particularly after World War I. The American public saw Wilson, the idealist, victimized by the greed of Lloyd George of Great Britain and Georges Clemenceau of France. The war "to end all wars" turned into a contest in which Britain, France, and Italy eagerly awaited the spoils of victory—enormous reparations for damages and the acquisition of German colonies in Africa, Asia, and the Pacific. Moreover, American participation in World War I was itself a disillusioning process, in which the loss of American lives and the loss of American idealism seemed quite evident. Both European and American intellectuals searched for some enduring truth or meaning to justify the deaths of millions of soldiers on both sides. Once again, it seemed that involvement with Europe brought America only suffering and tragedy. Many Americans argued that international bankers and munitions manufac-turers gained from the war, while the United States was duped into providing manpower.

Isolationist sentiments denied the importance of world politics by retreating inward. By 1924, the U.S. Congress had established the Johnson Act, dramatically limiting immigration to the U.S. from Europe and elsewhere. The pervasive sentiments of retreat are best conveyed in the literature of the period—its cynicism about human motivations, skepticism about chances for human survival, and emphasis on the destructive, animalistic aspects of human nature. There was, most of all, a sense of regret that America had lost some of its great promise through its involvement with European politics. While the United States embraced isolationism in a number of political arenas, internationalist tendencies persisted. The Kellogg-Briand Pact of 1928, outlawing war as an instrument of international politics, and the 1922 Washington Naval Arms Limitation Agreements suggest some internationalist orientations. However, the U.S. refused to undertake any meaningful or serious steps to help maintain world peace.

The Great Depression of 1928 only further reinforced isolationist tendencies. President Franklin D. Roosevelt's attempt to stabilize the U.S. economy and begin the task of reconstruction was a staggering effort. By the late 1930s, the mood of isolationism was at its zenith as evidenced by the passage of the Neutrality Acts that attempted to guarantee that the U.S. could not be drawn into a European war. With the coming of war in Europe, presidential leadership in foreign policy making was reasserted. The Japanese attack on Pearl Harbor stimulated American internationalism and sparked a new definition of Manifest Destiny for the United States.

Cold War Internationalism, 1947-1970
At the conclusion of World War II, the world was a scene of unparalleled devastation. Europe and Japan were in ruins. The Soviet Union, while victorious in battle, was itself ravaged by the costs of victory. Only the United States emerged from war relatively unscathed. The wartime economy had lifted the United States out of the Great Depression. America's industrial capacity had grown and prospered. Moreover, the United States emerged from the war as the world's creditor, possessing well over half of all gold reserves. However, the two world wars had discredited European politics in the eyes of the United States.

By 1946, the United States was ready to exercise its internationalist role. Even before World War II had ended, the United States began planning for peace. The United Nations (UN) emerged as a central political organization for the post-war world. Under U.S. guidance, the world's monetary system was restructured in the 1944 Bretton Woods Agreements to encourage free trade and to eliminate the Beggar-Thy-Neighbor economic policies of the 1930s. The International Monetary Fund (IMF) and the International Bank for Reconstruction and Development (IBRD) were also established. American dominance of the global system began to crystallize in 1946 in reaction to the expanding "menace" of Soviet communism—specifically, the Soviet takeover of the countries of Eastern and Central Europe. When Winston Churchill declared at Fulton, Missouri (March 1946) that "an iron curtain has descended across the continent," he fueled the flame of a new, powerful internationalist ideology. One year later (almost to the day) on March 12, 1947, President Harry S. Truman proclaimed the Truman Doctrine. The Truman Doctrine compared the expansion of communism to the rise of Germany and the inexorable spread of Nazi tyranny throughout Europe. By comparing Soviet objectives with those of Hitler's Germany, the Truman Doctrine erected a model of world communism that was monolithic, Moscow-dominated, and expansionistic. The notion that it was reasonable for the Soviet Union to establish a sphere of influence around its territory, especially in Eastern and Central Europe, was categorically rejected. Moreover, the Truman Doctrine dismissed the notion that communism in other nations might differ from the Russian model. Thus, it reduced the complexity of the post-World War II international system and portrayed U.S.-Soviet relations in oversimplified terms. Because communism was always monolithic and expansionistic, according to the doctrine, communist movements everywhere and anywhere were directed exclusively by the Kremlin. By using the historical analogy of German expansionism, the Truman Doctrine and its advocates conferred upon the Soviet Union not only limitless power and maneuverability, but, a historical invincibility. In other words, this philosophy maintained that the cold war was lost even before it began if the United States did not create a strategy of *containment* of world communism. Thus, the domino theory, which was based on the analogy of Nazi Germany, was launched in 1947, two years after Germany's unconditional defeat.

The roots of American hostility toward the Soviet Union are too long and complex to be analyzed here. Suffice it to say that the cold war ideology of the Truman years and the subsequent presidencies of Dwight D. Eisenhower, John F. Kennedy, and Lyndon B. Johnson overwhelmingly reinforced images of an insatiable country that was everything the United States was not: godless, tyrannical, cunning, and untrustworthy. Historical events, of course, reinforced these attitudes: Stalin's purges, the murder of antifascist non-Communist forces in Eastern Europe, the establishment of Soviet-dominated puppet regimes, the fall of Chiang Kai-shek's China, the Berlin Blockade, and the Korean War, for example. It was in many respects easy for the United States to formulate a cold war ideology which was reinforced by widespread domestic bipartisan support. As the most powerful country in the world, the United States had the resources—ideological, economic (the IMF and IBRD), political (the UN), and military (the North Atlantic Treaty Organization, 1949, and a host of regional security organizations)—to build a post-war international system based on an American conception of the world. The United States wrapped its policies in the mantle of a global Manifest Destiny and relied on moral imperatives to justify its dominance. The problem, as in the past, was that the American vision of its global role, however worthy in the abstract, was simplistic and ultimately impossible to implement in a consistent, cogent, and specific manner. As with any ideology, America's vision of the cold war was in danger of becoming a self-fulfilling prophecy. In other words, the Berlin Blockade and the Korean War confirmed American expectations of Soviet expansionism, thus doubly reinforcing the original vision of the Soviet Union as insatiable. Therefore, American idealism—as expressed in the desire to contain communism—provided the central impetus for the initial American involvement in Southeast Asia during the 1950s, and thus paved the way for the Vietnam War. The essence of American foreign policy from 1947 until the early 1970s can be expressed in four assumptions:

1. Conflict is due to Communist aggression against the free world.
2. The Communist appetite for expansion cannot be appeased and will grow without limit unless checked.
3. The United States, as leader of the free world, is obligated to act as a counterweight to aggression.
4. By fighting a small war now we avoid a bigger war later.[11]

Internationalism in the Post-Vietnam Era

Several factors converged to modify a number of cold war assumptions during the 1970s. First, the Vietnam War was a central factor because it destroyed the essentially bipartisan foreign policy consensus (from 1947 until the mid-1960s) upon which the United States based its strategy of containment. By 1970, it was clear that the war in Vietnam was one of the most bitterly divisive issues to confront the American public since the 1930s. Second, it became increasingly clear that global political relations had changed dramatically since the late 1940s and 1950s. The essentially bipolar (involving two spheres of power) confrontation between the United States and the Soviet Union had shifted to a more multipolar (involving many different actors) international environment in which neither the United States nor the Soviet Union acted as the monolithic leader of its bloc. It was clear, for example, that both China and the U.S.S.R. were offering North Vietnam different, and often competitive, support and assistance.

In the West, the countries of Western Europe, and especially members of the Common Market or European Economic Community (EEC), and Japan had distanced themselves from American economic dominance through their astounding economic growth during the 1960s and 1970s. This separation was particularly important in view of the United States' increasingly troubled economy. As early as 1960, U.S. balance of payments deficits were completely out of control, while Europe and Japan approached the level of significant economic actors. The rise of the Organization of Petroleum Exporting Countries (OPEC) to the level of an economic superpower and the expanding power of multinational corporations (MNCs) in manufacturing, banking, and marketing complicated the international environment of the 1970s. Moreover, demands for social and economic development by the countries of the Third World—many former Western colonies in the Middle East, Africa, Asia, and the Caribbean, as well as the established states of Latin America—dramatically shifted attention away from the prevailing cold war issues of the 1950s and early 1960s in the United Nations and in a growing number of international organizations. Thus, the 1970s witnessed a basic transformation in the prevailing distribution of power away from the United States and Soviet Union (except, of course, on a military and, especially, a nuclear level) as the exclusive actors, to a more dispersed environment of different types and kinds of actors ranging from the EEC, OPEC, and multinational corporations to the ideological demands of the poorer countries of the Third and Fourth Worlds (the latter including the desperately poor states of India, Pakistan, Bangladesh, Haiti, and others).

In this globally fragmented world, the central premise of the cold war—the inexorable expansion of Soviet-dominated communism—was called into question. The establishment of U.S. relations with the People's Republic of China and the recognition of the diversity of Communist regimes throughout the world laid the basis for United States-Soviet détente. The concept of détente suggested that the United States could coexist with the Soviet Union amid conflict and cooperation. Thus, the United States negotiated the first Strategic Arms Limitation Agreement (SALT I) in 1972 and the accompanying Vladivostok Accords in 1974. While President Richard Nixon and Secretary of State Henry Kissinger were always careful to underscore the fundamental differences separating U.S. and Soviet interests, the cold war attitudes and policies of the 1947-1970 period had been significantly altered.

Despite the spectacular foreign policy accomplishments of the Nixon-Kissinger years, the U.S. Congress ultimately rejected the balance-of-power and power-politics approaches of Nixon and Kissinger. Congressional resentments over the administration's handling of the Vietnam War, domestic political fallout from Watergate, and, finally, a rejection of Richard Nixon's imperial presidency in both domestic and international politics, spurred the U.S. Congress to restrict White House latitude in foreign policy making. Because a sense of morality had historically been central to American foreign policy, even America's most pragmatic (and in many ways most successful) twentieth-century foreign policy strategists, Richard Nixon and Henry Kissinger, were criticized by the U.S. Congress for their amoral policies.

With his election in 1976, President Carter eagerly searched for tangible policy alternatives to the Nixon-Kissinger-Ford years. The issue of human rights, originally identified by Congress in 1974 as an important U.S. foreign policy concern, became the Carter administration's most distinctive departure from the policies of the previous Republican administrations. Carter's foreign policy also stressed the importance of having nations consult each other on common problems while reasserting the complexity of global political, ideological, military, and economic relations. The negotiation of the Panama Canal Treaties (1978) and continued negotiations with the Soviet Union on the second Strategic Arms Limitation Treaty were intended to project a new sense of American realism in an increasingly complex and interdependent world. The fragmentation of foreign policy making within the Carter administration between National Security Advisor Zbigniew Brzezinski and Secretary of State Cyrus Vance damaged Jimmy Carter's domestic effectiveness in foreign policy making by projecting an image of inconsistency. Heightening tensions between the United States and the Soviet Union reinforced the perception that American leadership and power in the world had been reduced to its lowest point since World War II. Moreover, there was a widespread belief that the Carter administration's emphasis on interdependence and multilateral diplomacy, rather than on U.S. dominance, encouraged the Soviet Union to expand its military strength in Central Europe, to increase its repression of Soviet dissidents, and to intensify its efforts to destabilize American influence in the Middle East and Africa.[12] The Soviet invasion of Afghanistan in 1979 and the increasing threats of Soviet intervention in Poland only served to exacerbate further American skepticism of Soviet intentions.

With Jimmy Carter's defeat in 1980 and the election of Ronald Reagan, long-standing cold war policies and rhetoric were resurrected in an attempt to demonstrate a new American resolve and determination. Unlike the pragmatism of the Nixon years, the Reagan administration seemed determined to tie American foreign policy to the universal moral principles of the cold war years. The fundamental dilemma confronting Reagan's foreign policy is the real disparity between the goals of American dominance (some would call it leadership) in a world where the United States does not possess the means— ideological, political, or economic—to insure that United States' objectives are achieved.

Outside of the enormous might of the U.S. military arsenal, which is presumably unusable except in the most serious of crises, American power has declined enormously in real terms since the 1950s. In 1982, the United States cannot call upon the concrete economic, political, or even the ideological resources that it possessed in the late 1940s or 1950s. When assessing the foreign policy of the Reagan administration and other post-World War II foreign policies, it is necessary to analyze briefly the nature and scope of power in American foreign policy.

Power and American Foreign Policy

The appropriate uses of power have been a central theme in the evolution of American foreign policy during the twentieth century. Pragmatic leaders like Teddy Roosevelt or Henry Kissinger have viewed the role of power differently from idealists like Woodrow Wilson or Jimmy Carter. Indeed, the very idea of how American power is used has received sharp criticisms from realists and idealists, liberals and conservatives, pluralists and Marxists. Despite philosophical or ideological differences, the role of power is viewed as a fundamental aspect of American foreign policy.

Within this context, foreign policy is defined as the process in which external policies are formulated, implemented, and evaluated based on a country's objective/subjective needs and perceptions.[13] Our definition of foreign policy emphasizes the continual tensions between a country's domestic political environment and the broader patterns of global political relations; it also suggests that foreign policy is not shaped by purely rational decisions. The very complexity and interconnectedness of domestic and international politics make it nearly impossible for any decision-maker or policy-making group to explore every possible alternative. Our concept of foreign policy argues that specific foreign policies are defined by clashing political, economic, ideological, and bureaucratic objectives. Thus, the particular context in which a foreign policy decision is reached frequently determines both the range and scope of the policies to be used. Because of the complexity of the policy-making process, a central problem is how U.S. foreign policies will succeed in meeting a number of goals. These goals include: 1) that the policies are consistent; 2) that they are in line with both short-term and long-term policies and/or problems; 3) that the policies are creative; and, 4) that they accomplish what they are intended to achieve.

A central aspect of the foreign policy-making process, therefore, involves the notion of power. Power is defined as the ability to influence successfully the outcome of an event using either positive or negative means, or some combination of each. Power is not static, however; it can only be used by one actor *in relation* to another in an attempt to accomplish specific goals. Moreover, it is important to distinguish between the abstract uses of power and its tangible or concrete manifestations. Specific foreign policy objectives may limit the capabilities of a state's power. For example, when 52 American hostages were held for 444 days by Iranian militants, the United States could not use its superior military power, if the hostages were to be freed alive.

When evaluating American foreign policy in the twentieth century—and, especially, after the Second World War—Professor Hans J. Morgenthau perceived a clear contradiction between the United States' repeated emphasis on universal moral principles and the pragmatic concerns of an emerging superpower. In other words, American foreign policy required flexibility to meet its diverse needs and yet was tied to rigid, moralistic cold war objectives, which it could never realistically hope to fulfill. The

American emphasis on the containment of communism was a short-sighted moral crusade against evil rather than a sophisticated and pragmatic strategy to deal with a rival power. Morgenthau argued that the quest for moral imperatives tended to blind decision makers to the intentions of rivals, introduce rigidity into the foreign policy-making process, and oversimplify the complex and varied objectives of states. From this perspective, the tragic Vietnam debacle was the logical culmination of misplaced, ideological priorities.

Another area in which the nature of power needs to be addressed is the role played by modern bureaucracies as the key agents responsible for the implementation of American foreign policies. No study of the role of foreign policy making can afford to ignore the subtle yet formidable manner in which bureaucracies gather data, analyze problems, and attempt to prescribe policies. Graham Allison persuasively documents the important role of bureaucracies in his study of the Cuban missile crisis, *The Essence of Decision.* Allison demonstrates how large bureaucratic organizations, with their own parochial priorities and assumptions, often disregard the needs of the president and his explicit foreign policy objectives. The potential for bureaucratic organizations to complicate the foreign policy making process by fragmenting information, offering mediocre analyses of data or defying outright presidential decisions illustrates both the complexity of the policy-making process and the power of bureaucratic actors. To view American foreign policy as the product of the uniform rational decisions of the president and a few advisors drastically oversimplifies an immensely complex process in which central organizations (the Departments of State or Defense, the Central Intelligence Agency, and the Treasury Department to name only a few), often crucially restrict policies that presidents must confront in day-to-day decision making. In other words, bureaucracies are often the unseen, yet enormously powerful, agents of U.S. foreign policy and have substantial individual power in many issues.

Finally, our analysis of power needs to underscore both the scope and the depth of the transformation of American influence in international relations since World War II. In a real sense, the U.S. possessed nearly limitless power in world politics in the late 1940s and 1950s. As the most powerful economic and military country in the modern world, the United States essentially designed the shape of post-war political, economic, and military institutions. The host of international organizations that the U.S. constructed—the United Nations, the International Monetary Fund, the North Atlantic Treaty Organization and scores of additional organizations—are an indication of the scope of American leadership. Despite the sheer enormity of U.S. power, rapid changes in the structure of world politics challenged American hegemony. As early as 1962, tight bipolar bloc relationships, with both the United States and the Soviet Union, began to crumble. These trends toward multipolarity saw the steady fragmentation of Eastern and Western camps (especially the Sino-Soviet rift and the insistence by France that American goals were not compatible with long-run European economic, political, or military interests). What seems rather remarkable, viewed from the perspective of 1982, is the long-term stability of many U.S. military and ideological commitments. It is particularly apparent in retrospect how American cold war commitments clashed with the evolving ideological, political, and economic needs of developing countries. During the 1960s it must have appeared to many developing states that after achieving independence from their colonial masters, they confronted an even more powerful and, perhaps, more dangerous version of colonialist pretentions in the form of American foreign policy. Because of the sometimes-brutal legacies of the colonial struggle with their former Western European mother countries, the developing countries must have viewed America's emphasis on moral principles as a clever attempt to mask America's unparalleled power in political, economic, and military spheres. Non-Western analyses of American foreign policy frequently drew on a growing body of neo-Marxist assumptions in order to explain, not only America's enormous wealth and power, but also its distinctive national sense of mission and destiny.

Neo-Marxist and Liberal Explanations of American Foreign Policy

Drawing on the writings of Karl Marx and later Vladimir Lenin's theory of imperialism, neo-Marxists argued that U.S. emphasis on ideological, political, or military justifications for American foreign policy decisions deliberately obscured the fundamental economic interests of American capitalists. Imperialism is defined as a structural relationship or a system of dominance premised on the *unequal exchange* of goods or values between two actors, usually countries. Imperialism can be expressed in the blatant military occupation of a country, political dominance, or less obvious economic exploitation. In its most subtle form, imperialism, neo-Marxists argued, was transmitted through communication and technological networks, resulting in the cultural dominance of one state over another in terms of values, beliefs, perceptions, and ideas. American imperialism in the twentieth century, therefore, was the logical outgrowth of a capitalist economy and had three central goals: 1) accumulation of cheap raw materials; 2) the establishment of new, foreign export markets; and 3) the creation of lucrative foreign investments.[14]

First, neo-Marxists claimed that America's global power was the result of its acquisition of cheap raw materials from the Third World which aided U.S. technological developments. For example, the rapid development of high technology products (computers or color televisions) in the 1950s and 1960s was possible because of inexpensive petroleum and other natural resources. The importation of cheap raw material, thereby, made rapid technological development possible. The problem was that the U.S. would complete the cycle by selling manufactured products back to the Third World country at exorbitant and vastly over-priced costs. Moreover, neo-Marxists maintain that the search for raw materials assisted in the perpetuation of a worldwide American empire. The Department of Defense has stated that 80 percent of the 62 raw materials crucial for the defense needs of the United States must be imported. Thus, it is argued that the Defense Department works hand-in-hand with the corporations that supply these vital commodities to create a global empire supported by U.S. military bases all over the world.[15]

Second, according to these analyses, the quest for secure and stable export markets in which to sell American manufactured products has been a prime determinant of American foreign policy. Neo-Marxists contend that the massive economic assistance to Western Europe through the Marshall Plan (1950) was an explicit attempt to secure greater profits for America's capitalist economy, rather than a humanitarian project, as the U.S. has always claimed. The economic reconstruction of Europe served the objectives of American foreign policy by strengthening the U.S. economy, while the United States used every means at its disposal to prevent Soviet competition throughout the world, particularly in the developing countries. Cold war rhetoric and talk of American idealism only obscured the American quest for markets and raw materials, say neo-Marxists. The U.S. used its extensive networks of political alliances to encircle the Soviet Union, repeatedly resorted to military threats—including the use of nuclear weapons—and engaged in economic warfare against the non-capitalist world, contend neo-Marxists.

Third, neo-Marxists contend that the inexorable search for new sources of foreign investments since 1945 explains the dynamics of U.S. foreign policy in the developing world. American political, economic, and military power provided the vehicle whereby American-owned multinational corporations would establish subsidiaries in Third World countries. The elites of developing countries had no choice but to accept the unequal and exploitative terms proposed by American multinational firms. As an added incentive, the Third World elite were offered wealth and power to comply with the goals of American foreign policy. By cooperating with the objectives of American foreign and economic objectives, the rulers of developing countries would ensure their continued power through access to vast sums of U.S. economic assistance, U.S. military protection of their regimes from *external* and *internal* "Communist" subversion, and the most modern forms of technology (especially those technologies that could ensure the survival of local elites through the repression of internal discontent). Between 1960 and 1970 American exports increased by 133 percent while the sales from subsidiaries of U.S.-based multinational corporations increased by 400 percent.[16] The economic imperialism of American corporations is buttressed by the military might of the United States and its global network of military bases which include the most sophisticated forms of communications and transportation processes. About 50 giant corporations "control more than half of all United States foreign investments" while less than 200 corporations control more than 80 percent of the total overseas investments.[17] The concentration of economic wealth in a tiny group of corporate managers allows this capitalist class to dictate American foreign policy in a clear and consistent manner.

The fourth assumption of the neo-Marxist critique follows directly from the previous statement. The men who ultimately make foreign policy—Republicans or Democrats—are supplied by a small group of corporate executives, bankers, and lawyers that repeatedly enter governmental service for limited periods of time.[18] This process is sometimes referred to as a "revolving door" leading from business to government and vice versa. For example, former Secretary of Defense Robert McNamara was president of Ford Motor Company. After his retirement as Undersecretary of State, George Ball became an investment banker for one of the world's largest firms, Lehman Brothers. Former Secretary of Defense Melvin Laird, Secretary of State George Schultz, and Defense Secretary Casper Weinberger are tied directly to corporations with significant foreign investments. Not surprisingly, even Henry Kissinger, for all his academic achievements, was the protégé of the Rockefeller family. Thus, neo-Marxists argue that U.S. foreign policies are the result of the interests of a small, monolithic, homogeneous business class. The use of cold war rhetoric has been used very effectively to divert attention from the real objectives of foreign policy, they say. Fear of the Soviet Union, especially in the nuclear age, was used to justify presidential control, executive privilege, and excessive secrecy. Not only is the military-industrial complex a primary force in the creation of American foreign policies, claim neo-Marxists, but all major bureaucratic organizations foster similar economic goals: the Department of Agriculture promotes the interests of agribusiness while the Treasury Department assists in the coordination of far-flung American economic interests. Perhaps the most dangerous organization of them all, according to these critics, is the Central Intelligence Agency whose secrecy and subterranean contacts with all sectors of the business community (legal and illegal) can accomplish the most immoral actions without fear of public scrutiny or accountability.

The liberal response to neo-Marxist assessments emphasizes, first, the pluralist (in other words, diversified) structure of both the United States government and capitalist economic system. It argues that overlapping structures—regional, urban, rural, ethnic, racial, religious, linguistic, and cultural—diversify power in the U.S., as illustrated by shifting coalitions and an amorphous class structure. The U.S.'s democratic system of government is the ultimate confirmation of its pluralism rather than the elitism that neo-Marxists suggest.

Second, liberals argue that a capitalist ruling class simply does not exist. Millions of small businesses thrive while ownership of major corporations is spread throughout the population directly—through ownership of stocks—and indirectly—through pension funds and insurance companies.

Third, it is argued that profits are higher on investments based in the United States than those made overseas. Moreover, foreign investments are only a tiny part of the overall value of American-based corporations. Far from exploiting developing countries, contend liberals, U.S. foreign investments in the Third World are a small part of its overall investments, with most overseas resources invested in the advanced industrial countries of Western Europe. Liberals maintain the United States-owned multinational corporations provide Third World countries with needed foreign exchange, capital, and technology to assist these countries in their own economic and political development. The liberal perspective sees MNCs as a tugboat pulling poorer countries of the world to a more prosperous and secure future, rather than as agents of capitalist exploitation.

Fourth, economic interests in no way exclusively guide U.S. foreign policy, although the protection of a state's foreign economic interests—like the protection of its citizens abroad and the defense of its national security—is a legitimate foreign policy objective, maintain liberals. Geopolitical and ideological factors are more helpful in explaining the primary goals of American foreign policy, they say. American intervention in Vietnam can be neither justified nor explained in terms of economic interests, given the incredible expenditure of wealth (not to mention the number of American lives lost), during the course of that unfortunate war, argue liberals. Similarly, unidimensional and simplistic economic assumptions fail to explain continued American support for Israel in the face of long-standing American dependence on Arab oil.

Finally, liberals deny the neo-Marxist assertion that the objectives of U.S.-owned multinational corporations have defined post-war American foreign policy. U.S. foreign policies have repeatedly clashed with the economic objectives of MNCs, they point out. American-based multinational corporations established subsidiaries in Western and Eastern Europe in order to trade with Communist regimes during the height of the cold war in the 1950s—an act in outright defiance of American national security goals. More recently, MNCs have vigorously resisted U.S. attempts to tax their foreign earnings or to restrict the free flow of large amounts of capital from one part of the corporation to another. Moreover, MNCs are truly global enterprises, with multiple interests throughout the world. American foreign policies are confined to a much more restricted nationalist vision based on the legacies of political, military, ideological, and economic policies dating back to 1947. For many students of MNCs (like former Undersecretary of State, George Ball), the nationalism of states is ultimately antithetical to the international orientations of global corporations. Rather than seeing the U.S. government and foreign policy as the handmaiden of its economic interests, many managers of MNCs look forward to the day when the power of all nations will be reduced, thus ensuring a more peaceful, stable, and profitable world based on the goals and interests of cosmopolitan corporations.

The conflicting analyses of American foreign policy proposed by neo-Marxists and liberals suggest fundamentally different views of the dynamics of American political and economic institutions. The neo-Marxist perspective is important because of its rejection of traditional explanations of U.S. foreign policy—especially the assumption that Manifest Destiny and idealism helped to define American foreign policy in the nineteenth and twentieth centuries. The neo-Marxist critique rejects liberalism's assumptions of human nature and political-economic institutions. As the essays by Harry Magdoff and Paul Sweezy argue (see Chapters 3 and 4), the dynamics of expansionistic capitalism have defined the goals of twentieth century American foreign policy far more fully than political objectives. Neo-Marxists are quick to point out, however, that self-serving pronouncements (for example, the idea of making the world safe for democracy or saving the free world from the scourge of communism), are attempts to disguise U.S. economic objectives. Thus, the neo-Marxist analysis of U.S. foreign policy is unambiguous in its critique and unwavering in its solution—dismantle the capitalist elite that determines U.S. foreign policy.

The insights offered by liberalism* are equally important. Since liberalism frames the central lens in which American foreign policy is analyzed, it is sometimes difficult to discern a coherent perspective in which to assess American foreign policy. The breakdown of the post-World War II bipartisan foreign policy consensus in the late 1960s and 1970s illustrates the problem. Part of the difficulty is that liberalism is not a monolithic world view. It is, itself, divided by many different and often conflicting perspectives ranging from the right to the left of the American political spectrum. The progressive divisions among liberalism from conservatives (the right) to "liberals" (the left) make the creation of a foreign policy consensus particularly difficult.

Since 1976, two distinct foreign policy perspectives have emerged, representing some of the central assumptions of the right and left. The most significant foreign policy battles of both the Carter and Reagan administrations have been fought along these lines. Each perspective illustrates competing views of the appropriate use of American power, U.S. global responsibilities, and American-Soviet relations. The assertions of the right, typified by the Reagan administration, contrast sharply with the central assumptions of Carter's more liberal foreign policy stands, which included a more critical assessment of capitalism and, at least on a rhetorical level, some acceptance of neo-Marxist critiques.

Carter's foreign policy, largely in response to the post-Vietnam and post-Watergate periods of the mid 1970s, repudiated the idea of the containment of communism. This perspective demanded a reappraisal of the United States' role in world affairs. Central to this view was an emphasis on the need to achieve a new international standing based on cooperation and persuasion. This, Carter contended, was imperative in order to dismantle the idea of U.S. hegemony or dominance. Thus, global levels of interdependence in politics and economics dictated a new foreign policy strategy which would prevent further Vietnams in the Third World, stabilize nuclear and conventional arms races with the Soviet Union, buttress American relations with Western Europe and Japan, and help promote human rights and socio-economic development throughout the world—especially in the Third World. The Carter administration's foreign policy, therefore, was designed to insure world peace and stability while at the same time achieving economic prosperity in the United States. Supporters of the Carter administration witnessed a courageous attempt to transform American foreign policy from one of

---

*Liberalism in this broad sense, refers to the political beliefs that emphasize personal freedom from external restraint. In the eighteenth and nineteenth centuries, liberals held strongly to the principles of the free market and sought to limit government interference in business affairs. Some twentieth century liberals have turned to the government to act as a counterbalance to the power of concentrated wealth in private hands.

dominance to a more sophisticated, and more difficult, emphasis on interdependence. Richard Nixon and Henry Kissinger's attempt to link particular issues to U.S. global objectives were rejected. Proponents of the Carter administration argued that a new, more realistic, basis of American foreign policy was being formulated. This theme runs throughout the book, as Charles Kegley and Eugene Wittkopf's assessment of Carter foreign policy illustrates in Chapter 2. Patricia Derian's analysis of Jimmy Carter's human rights policies, "Human Rights and American Foreign Policy" in Chapter 7, illustrates the Carter administration's attempt to create a new foreign policy focus. Similarly, Barbara Ward's "Another Chance for the North" suggests the importance of North-South relations for the future of the Third World as well as the fate of advanced industrial societies. Finally, George F. Kennan's "Nuclear War: Confronting the Horror" illustrates many of the central assumptions of Carter's foreign policy toward the Soviet Union and the necessity of nuclear arms reductions—at least before the Soviet invasion of Afghanistan in 1979.

If the Soviet occupation of Afghanistan provoked a crisis of confidence in the Carter administration's perceptions of Soviet intentions, it confirmed President Reagan's long-standing beliefs. Indeed, the seizure of American hostages by Iranian militants amid fears of Soviet expansionism created demands for a rejection of the post-Watergate and post-Vietnam assumptions of Carter's foreign policy. For Ronald Reagan and others, it was time for the United States to assert a coherent foreign policy agenda based on military strength, global political involvements, and strong beliefs in the moral superiority of Western capitalist democracies over all other political systems, most especially communist dictatorships. Thus, the conservative wing of the U.S. foreign policy establishment became more powerful and, for many, more persuasive. A number of specific issues form the core of Reagan's foreign policy. The first is that the Soviet Union is a global aggressor as illustrated by the invasion of Afghanistan, subversive activities in Africa, and especially in Central America, as Ambassador Jeane Kirkpatrick's "U.S. Security and Latin America," (Chapter 6) illustrates. The second is the American reluctance to intervene directly in the Third World—a result of the Vietnam war. As Samuel P. Huntington suggests (Chapter 7) human rights in the Third World are dependent on active U.S. political and economic involvement. Without active American participation in world politics, the balance of power is shifted toward the Soviet Union. Thus, the constraints placed on the activities of the Central Intelligence Agency must be reduced while the American military arsenal is strengthened by both nuclear and convention weapons, as President Reagan's remarks illustrate in Chapters 5 and 9. A third area of agreement centers around a tougher, more assertive, response to Third World proposals for global economic change. The Carter administration's acceptance of Third World demands, if only on a rhetorical level, have increasingly been rejected by conservatives as Peter Berger's "Speaking to the Third World" suggests.

Because American foreign policy lacks a strong bipartisan consensus, the conflicting views of neo-Marxists, conservatives, and liberals—as presented throughout this book— are significant. Indeed, the absence of a single coherent foreign policy-making establishment illustrates the difficulty confronting the United States in the formulation and implementation of successful policies.

Conclusions: American Foreign Policy and Global Change

Perhaps the single most important factor or sets of factors confronting U.S. foreign policy in the 1980s revolves around the United States' inability to adapt to the scope and intensity of change brought about by unprecedented levels of global interdependence. Technology confers extraordinary power on different kinds of actors throughout the world. The result is a global system in which allies and adversaries are bound more closely together than ever before in history. Because of the intensity of global interdependence, political, economic, or technological developments touch every actor—states, international organizations, multinational corporations, private organizations, and individuals. The principal dilemma which bedevils foreign policy making is the absence of immediate (short-term) strategies that are consistent with long-term goals. The intensity and scope of global interdependence in 1983 makes the creation of workable, coherent, and comprehensive foreign policies all the more imperative—not only for the success of American foreign policies but also for the survival of an incredibly interdependent and fragile world. The essays, ideas, and debates that follow are an attempt to discern a future, often based on the experience of the present and the past, that is unique to the historical context of the United States and the world. The central task of foreign policy analysis, therefore, is all the more difficult *and* all the more essential to the survival of the human species.

Footnotes

1   Perhaps the most impressive analysis of an American style of foreign policy decision making is proposed by Stanley Hoffman in *Gulliver's Troubles or the Setting of American Foreign Policy* (New York: McGraw-Hill, 1968).
2   Dexter Perkins, *The Evolution of American Foreign Policy*, (New York: Oxford University Press, Second Edition, 1966).
3   *Ibid.*, p. 28.
4   *Ibid.*, p. 30.
5   *Ibid.*, p. 26.
6   *Ibid.*, p. 38.
7   Thomas A. Bailey, *A Diplomatic History of the American People*, Ninth Edition, (Englewood Cliffs, New Jersey: Prentice-Hall, 1974), p. 483.
8   Hoffmann, *Gulliver's Troubles*, p. 116.
9   *Ibid.*, p. 117.
10   *Ibid.*, p. 123.
11   Walter S. Jones and Steven J. Rosen, *The Logic of International Relations*, Fourth Edition, (Boston: Little Brown, 1982), p. 67.
12   *Ibid.*, p. 71.
13   K.J. Holsti, *International Politics, A Framework for Analysis*, Third Edition, (Englewood Cliffs, N.J.: Prentice-Hall, 1977), p. 21.
14   Johan Galtung, "A Structural Theory of Imperialism," *Journal of Peace Research*, 2(1971):81-117.
15   Jones and Rosen, *The Logic of International Relations*, p. 19-28.
16   *Ibid.*, p. 23.
17   *Ibid.*, p. 24.
18   Gabrial Kolko, *The Roots of American Foreign Policy*, (Boston: Beacon Press, 1969).

CHAPTER 2

Clashing Assumptions of American Foreign Policy in the 1980s

With the breakdown of traditional bipartisan support for the single-minded cold war objectives of American foreign policy in the 1960s, each successive administration has been subjected to searing critiques of its assumptions, values, and policies. The foreign policies of the Nixon, Ford, and Carter administrations failed to create a bipartisan consensus. Congress and U.S. public opinion became increasingly critical of the Nixon-Ford-Kissinger approach to foreign policy issues. Jimmy Carter's emphasis on human rights and North-South issues was an attempt to shift foreign policy away from the power politics of the Nixon-Kissinger years. By embracing human rights, Carter attempted to build a foreign policy consensus deeply rooted in American principles and rights. The Carter administration not only failed to create a foreign policy consensus, but unleashed a torrent of criticism focusing on its inconsistencies and the hypocrisies of its policies. Critics charged that Jimmy Carter's foreign policy resulted in an absolute decline of American power and prestige in world politics, especially in the wake of the Iranian revolution and the Soviet invasion of Afghanistan.

With Ronald Reagan's successful bid for the presidency, the outline for a new foreign policy seemed to emerge in three areas. First, President Reagan reaffirmed American involvement in international politics on a "global scale."[a] Reagan rejected isolationism, or non-involvement, in international politics—an attitude somewhat characteristic of American public opinion in the years following the Vietnam War. As Chapter 1 illustrates (p. 10), U.S. internationalism was one of the principal assumptions of American foreign policy from 1947 until the early 1970s.

Second, Reagan's foreign policy pointed to a worldwide Communist insurgency as the central problem confronting the United States and the world. Thus, he believed it was the duty of American foreign policy to use its power "to combat the spread of the Communist menace."[b] These intense fears of communism expanding throughout the world also illustrate a reliance on a cold war approach to American foreign policy. The anti-Communist beliefs of the Reagan administration disputed many of the central foreign policy assumptions of the Nixon-Kissinger-Ford and Carter administrations. The Reagan administration's anti-Communist focus also rejected a number of tenets of post-Vietnam foreign policy. Perhaps the most important of these was the reluctance to use U.S. military forces to intervene in internal Third World conflicts. For President Reagan, American impotence in the face of the Soviet invasion of Afghanistan, the seizure of American hostages in Iran, and Communist subversion in Central America resulted in further Soviet expansion throughout the world. Not only did the Carter administration's policies result in an absolute decline of American power, but they also sought to punish friendly right-wing dictatorships—for example, Iran and Nicaragua.

The third assumption of Reagan's foreign policy follows directly from its emphasis on U.S. internationalism and anti-communism. This is its contention that the Soviet Union is the central force challenging the United States throughout the world. In other words, the U.S.S.R. is the "spearhead" of a global Communist conspiracy.[c] Thus, the foreign policy initiatives of the Soviet Union must be stopped or contained throughout the world, maintains Reagan. The emphasis on Soviet-dominated Communist expansion through-out the world is a central assumption of cold war politics. Critics of the Carter administration argue that Jimmy Carter's foreign policy was naive—blinded by a moralistic vision of a better world. From this perspective, Jimmy Carter is faulted for a lack of realism. However, by 1979-1980, Carter's foreign policy toward the Soviet Union changed dramatically. Viewed from 1983, the similarities between Carter's and Reagan's foreign policy toward the Soviet Union are striking—emphasizing internationalism, anti-communism, containment, and the danger of Soviet expansion. Perceptions of the weakness of Carter's foreign policy continue to persist, however.

It is important to consider three distinct interpretations of contemporary American foreign policy. The first was exemplified by Jeane Kirkpatrick before her appointment by President Reagan as U.S. Ambassador to the United Nations.[d] Dr. Kirkpatrick argues that American foreign policy was inconsistent and hypocritical when it implemented harsh policies toward such right-wing dictatorships as Nicaragua, South Korea, and Iran while tolerating the far more brutal and oppressive left-wing dictatorships in Cambodia, Cuba, and Vietnam. When analyzing the Carter administration's double standard, Kirkpatrick and others contend that the traditional context of right-wing dictatorships—with their personalistic politics, extreme inequalities in wealth, and familial roles—are symbolically and practically offensive to the assumptions of Western liberalism. Kirkpatrick points out that many of the philosophical, ideological, and rhetorical dimensions of left-wing regimes seem more acceptable because they are "rooted in a version of the same values that sparked the Enlightenment and the democratic revolutions of the 18th century; because it is modern and not traditional; because it postulates goals that appeal to Christian as well as secular values (brotherhood of man, elimination of power as a mode of human relations), it is highly congenial to many Americans at the symbolic level."[e] Ambassador Kirkpatrick concludes that Jimmy Carter's "egalitarian, optimist liberal, Christian" philosophy was repelled by non-democratic and non-modern rulers.[f] From Kirkpatrick's perspective, Carter's emphasis on questions of global equity between the North and the South, his non-interventionist policies, his efforts at coexistence with the Soviet Union and his emphasis on human rights were inappropriate and dangerous. For Kirkpatrick, the result of such policies was a foreign policy that was inconsistent and naive. Kirkpatrick argues that a decline of American power, accompanied by the increasing expansion of a Soviet-dominated worldwide Communist insurgency, is the principal consequence of such a foreign policy.

Thus, Jeane Kirkpatrick's critique of Carter's foreign policy is based on two assumptions. First, she contends the Carter administration was blinded by the as-sumptions drawn, in part, from the Vietnam experience, particularly the belief that right-wing authoritarian dictatorships would *inevitably* fall under pressure from left-wing national liberation movements. Kirkpatrick argues that Jimmy Carter's emphasis on egalitarian and liberal beliefs made him more supportive of the rhetoric of the Left than the Right in the pre-modern, non-democratic regimes of the Third World. For Am-bassador Kirkpatrick and others, the tyranny of the Left is by far the greater political evil.

Second, Kirkpatrick maintains Jimmy Carter's reluctance to use military force in the Third World encouraged Soviet-dominated expansion and the rapid decline of American power. Consequently, Carter's foreign policy maintained there were limitations to the policies that could realistically be put in place, while emphasizing a moralistic and idealistic approach to world politics.

Without a doubt, Jeane Kirkpatrick's statements echo a number of the central ideological assumptions of U.S. foreign policy under the Reagan administration. As Dr. Kirkpatrick suggests, the traditional national security goals of American foreign policy have been to preserve American power from the encroachments of Soviet expansion. Richard Barnet's selection, "Dancing in the Dark," is a neo-Marxist critique of contemporary foreign policy under Reagan as well as many of the assumptions that Ambassador Kirkpatrick accepts as central to the successful workings of American foreign policy in the 1980s. Barnet calls for a reappraisal of American foreign policy based on fundamental questions about the nature of the United States' political economy. He also calls for a reduction in the power of the U.S. national security elite (the defense bureaucracies and defense-related industries and corporations) in shaping the goals of American foreign policy. Barnet does not see U.S. national security as being threatened by Soviet expansion throughout the world—and especially in Central America; rather, he argues that historic cold war policies have placed the Soviet Union on the defensive. He suggests that many of the Reagan administration's foreign policies (such as U.S.-Chinese detente, the beefing-up of NATO, and a rapidly escalating nuclear arms race) create a climate of fear in which the Soviet elite is increasingly isolated, thus reinforcing long-standing insecurities and paranoia. In contrast to Ambassador Kirkpatrick's demand for a strengthening of American military power and her belief in the absolute necessity of U.S. military superiority, Barnet calls for parity (approximate equality with Soviet strength) and acceptance of the U.S.S.R.'s spheres of influence and superpower status. Barnet contends that the only way a nuclear arms race can be stabilized before a nuclear holocaust occurs is for the United States to take the first step. He says that only when the Soviet leadership is persuaded that the United States is committed to working for a stable international environment, in which peace takes precedence over U.S. expansion, can the nuclear arms race be stabilized and the process of reducing arms initiated. Barnet believes that real change in the goals of American foreign policy can come only from the steadfast determination of the American public to challenge the dominance of the U.S. national security bureaucracy. In order for such changes to occur, the central socio-economic institutions of American life will have to change significantly their fundamental values and objectives, he says. Barnet emphasizes those issues affecting the quality of life in the United States—decreases in military spending, support for the nuclear freeze movement with a pledge of no first-use of nuclear weapons, and the elimination of cuts in domestic social welfare programs—to suggest that established political, economic, and social institutions in the United States can be made more responsive to more enlightened and humane politics.

References

a   Charles W. Kegley, Jr. and Eugene R. Wittkopf, "The Reagan Administration's World View," *Orbis,* Vol. 26, (Spring 1982), p. 225. Reprinted in this chapter, p. 33.
b   Ibid.
c   Ibid.
d   Jeane Kirkpatrick, "Dictatorships and Double Standards," *Commentary,* (November 1979), pp. 34-45.
e   Ibid., p. 42.
f   Ibid.

DANCING IN THE DARK

Richard J. Barnet, *Progressive,* April 1982

Richard J. Barnet is a senior fellow at the Institution for Policy Studies in Washington, DC

No one has a good word to say about Ronald Reagan's foreign policy. Liberals criticize the Administration for doing what it said it would do—promoting a mindless arms race in the name of national security, supporting murderous regimes in places such as El Salvador in the name of anti-communism, and striving clumsily to organize the world into an anti-Soviet crusade. Right-wing ideologues attack the President with rising fury because he does not do any of these things swiftly enough to suit them and has shown himself to be more "pragmatic" in some respects than they would like. The policy-making professionals, recalling Reagan's campaign promises to make "coherence" the guiding principle of his foreign policy, look on in amazement as the competing barons of the new foreign policy establishment carry on open warfare in the press.

It is easy to point to a succession of foreign policy failures, difficult to find the successes. The most immediate and conspicuous failure is in El Salvador. The Administration came into office determined to demonstrate that military force could once again be used to stem "the decline of American power." If *Pax Americana* could no longer be maintained throughout the non-socialist world, it could at the very least be enforced in our traditional backyard. The choice, the Reaganites believed, was between the sentimentality of Jimmy Carter's human rights policy and the historic dictates of the Monroe Doctrine. El Salvador seemed to provide a perfect test. It was a small country on which the Soviet Union had no claims—one that had been unmistakably in the American orbit for as long as anyone could remember. As a result of a coup in 1979 followed by a government in which some progressive Christian Democrats briefly took part, the ruling junta could be presented as a moderating voice seeking to mediate between the extreme Right and the extreme Left.

No sooner was Reagan installed in the White House than El Salvador became the war cry. Secretary of State Alexander Haig spent his early days creating headlines on the subject, sending high officials to Europe to enlist them in the new crusade against the peasant guerrillas in that tiny country. The Reaganites were confident that the American people were spoiling for a war to win—a war that would blot out the ignominy of Vietnam. Modest shipments of Soviet arms by way of Nicaragua and Cuba provided a perfect pretext for U.S. intervention. Here was a place at last where our military could demonstrate its muscle and change history.

According to the Reagan game plan, the United States could be mobilized around the El Salvador issue, and so could the allies who, conventional conservative opinion had it, would be greatly reassured by the decisions of the new Administration. In their rush to respond to the new anti-communist crusade, more nettlesome issues that divided the alliance would conveniently be forgotten. The war fever would feed the public enthusiasm for the $1.5 trillion the Administration planned to spend on the military. The headlines would focus on the brave little war in El Salvador and would crowd out the pictures of unemployed on the street, soup kitchens, and other politically burdensome aspects of the Reagan recovery plan.

But nothing worked according to plan. The situation in El Salvador proved far less tractable than the Reagan Cold Warriors had anticipated. From the outset, the Administration deceived itself—much as the Johnson Administration had in Vietnam—by underestimating the degree of popular revulsion in El Salvador against the government and by exaggerating the relatively small factor of outside aid. Just as in Indochina more than fifteen years earlier, an American government sought to legitimate its intervention into a civil conflict by arguing that it was really an international war. But instead of signaling the final victory over the "Vietnam syndrome," the Reagan Administration's call to arms in Central America proved that many Americans had, indeed, learned the lessons of Vietnam.

The El Salvador intervention has elicited the most effective public protest in the United States since the Indochina war. The opposition, which has included powerful elements of the Catholic hierarchy, became so strong that the State Department abruptly reversed itself and told the press it was making too much of the little war in Central America. From a moral standpoint, it turned out to be the worst battlefield imaginable—a tiny country run by a government that, according to the Catholic Church, has murdered 30,000 people and turned 13 per cent of the population into refugees. In Europe, El Salvador quickly captured the public imagination as Vietnam had. European leaders perceived that the Reaganites were poor practitioners of *Realpolitik*. Just as it was easy for De Gaulle to use Vietnam to dramatize France's independence from the United States, it became morally and politically satisfying for today's leaders of Holland, Germany, and France to oppose the United States on an issue in which they had so little at stake themselves.

The Administration is now caught in El Salvador. Even as the civil war intensifies, and headlines report massacres on an ever-larger scale, Washington certifies that human rights are now respected to the point that military aid can be substantially increased. Other forms of military intervention have also been announced as the United States sinks deeper into involvement in what is now a regional conflict in Central America—a conflict for which decades of U.S. policy bear heavy responsibility.

A second conspicuous failure of Ronald Reagan's first year in office was U.S. policy toward Europe. Moving quickly to convert its ideology into policy, the Administration sought to drum up support for its huge military program by invoking that old standby, the Soviet menace. But Reagan succeeded only in terrifying many Europeans about the nature of American intentions. Defense

Secretary Caspar Weinberger's posturing over the neutron bomb—he convened a press conference to inform the world we were building the weapon whether the Europeans liked it or not—and the redoubled effort to force the early deployment of European theater nuclear weapons brought more than two million people into the streets in protest. When Reagan himself speculated about the possibility of nuclear war in Europe, he was, indeed, expressing nothing more than nuclear orthodoxy, and his intent was to reassure the Europeans that the nuclear umbrella was still there. But so isolated are the nuclear theologians from popular attitudes, so little understanding do they have of the way things have changed since the days of John Foster Dulles and Konrad Adenauer, that the President was amazed when his words produced panic.

The Reagan ideology calls for delaying negotiations with the Soviet Union until the needed increments in U.S. military buildup are in place. But by the end of his first year in office, the President was forced to give a ringing endorsement to arms limitation in Europe—in the so-called Zero Options speech—to stem the rising tide of Continental protest. Negotiations have begun on an inherently non-negotiable U.S. position—a demand for the removal of all Soviet missiles in Europe in exchange for a U.S. promise not to put some in. Depending on the day and the persuasiveness of his most recent visitor, Secretary Haig favors "linkage"—conditioning arms talks on Soviet good behavior in Poland and elsewhere—or rejects the idea. . . .

This is a dangerous Administration that wishes to adopt the paranoid credo of the Committee on the Present Danger as official U.S. policy but dares not act on every irresponsible impulse. It is an Administration that can easily be ridiculed for its incompetence. But a serious critique must dig below the eccentricities of Alexander Haig, the self-pronounced "vicar" of American foreign policy, and his recent nemesis, Richard Allen, to understand that the most alarming aspect of the policy is its continuity.

I do not mean to ignore some important differences between Jimmy Carter and Ronald Reagan. Carter entered the White House with some intimations, at least, of the dangers we face, while Reagan seems to have none. Carter set some admirable goals, but failed to attain them because he was unable to explain or defend his more realistic concerns and his more sophisticated approach toward the world force of revolutionary nationalism. In the Reagan Administration, belligerent talk, the willingness to conduct a full-scale counterinsurgency war in El Salvador, dogfights with Libyan aircraft, and the preference for hectoring the Soviet Union instead of negotiating with it have all contributed to the deterioration of the international situation and to the insecurity of the American people. But it is a serious error to ascribe all these developments to the plans, prejudices, and politics of the Reagan Administration.

By the time Reagan took office, a number of his basic assumptions had already been accepted at least as working hypotheses by the Carter Administration. An arbitrary percentage increase in the military budget had been ordered, not on the basis of a new analysis of American military needs or a clearer understanding of the functions of the new weapons but as a symbolic measure to stem "the decline of American power." The assumption that there was a connection between Pentagon funding and American power to influence allies, to manage crises like that in Iran, and to prevent the Soviet Union from building up its arms preceded Reagan.

The military spending under Reagan is greater and cuts in domestic programs more severe than contemplated by Carter, but his Administration, too, had planned major additions to the nuclear arsenal. The Carter Administration had proceeded with production of the neutron bomb and deployment of theater nuclear weapons. (Indeed, the Reagan Administration has shown greater willingness to moderate its rhetoric out of deference to the European allies than Carter demonstrated at the time of the Soviet attack in Afghanistan, when he plunged ahead unilaterally with a range of sanctions the Europeans could not support.) Moderation, which Carter had shown in Nicaragua, was being abandoned in El Salvador before he left office. By Inauguration Day, the United States was once again hostage to a hopeless client.

The foreign policy of the United States is now in crisis. We face the most dangerous moment in our national history since World War II. We are heading toward an all-out arms race, the consequences of which we do not comprehend. Our Government is engaged in a massive military buildup without any sign that it has a political or military strategy that would carry out its stated objectives. A careful reading of the Pentagon budget does not show that the additional billions for "defense" will provide significant additional military capabilities. It is even less clear what new political options such new capabilities would offer.

At a time when the Soviet Union is more isolated than it has been since 1945, the U.S. Government is devoting its diplomatic energies to isolating itself. The web of relationships we have developed with the other leading industrial countries of the world in the last three decades is seriously frayed. Those relationships have been long in need of repair, but they cannot be ignored or scrapped, as some of the Reagan people seem to believe, without courting great dangers. The industrial powers of Europe and Japan are no longer clients, and cannot be treated as such.

The political problems facing the industrial world and the East-West confrontation itself are further complicated by the now-chronic economic crisis of the West. There is little hope of significant recovery of the economic momentum that characterized the brief period of *Pax Americana* (1945-1971) without fundamental reform of the world monetary system and a new set of ground rules for conducting world trade that would make it possible for billions of people in the Third World to participate for the first time in international society. There will be no prosperity for the West if the world population continues to grow but billions remain outside the economy, unable to act either as producers or consumers. . . .

A real security policy would begin with some fundamental questions—not about the Russians, the Chinese, much less the Libyans, but about ourselves. What are we trying to protect? How much protection is possible in the nuclear age? How much can we do by ourselves? What should we ask of other nations?

The purpose of our national security policy is to protect people, property, and the values we cherish. The power we need is not the power to destroy other societies, or even to remake them, but to renew our own society. That is the legitimate purpose of a national security policy. It has been clear for a long time that we cannot honor that purpose acting alone; we must have close relations with other countries, and must work with them to create the conditions in which prosperity and democracy can be maintained here. Such relationships are not built by multi-million-dollar arms deals or obsolete alliances, but by new rules of international society that can create economic and political stability.

The United States, despite its revolutionary origins, is by nature a conservative country. Despite the diffusion of power in the world, it still possesses the most powerful economy and the longest geopolitical reach. The national interest of the United States is stability. A national security policy must, therefore, aim at producing as stable an international environment as possible for the orderly evolution of American Society.

However, the concept of stability shared by both major parties and embodied in bipartisan foreign policy for a generation and a half is hopelessly obsolete. The American view remains today what it was in the time of John F. Kennedy: We will seek to support governments that are non-repressive and forward-looking; but since such governments do not exist in most places in the world, we will not hesitate to support dictatorships of the Right in order to suppress national liberation movements. The United States is prepared to abandon its stated ideals and expose itself to the world as a force favoring reaction and repression because it fears popular movements. Independence movements and social forces, which by nature are unpredictable, have been viewed consistently as threats for two reasons: First, it is assumed they will inevitably come to be dominated by the Soviet Union. This concern is not supported by a careful reading of recent history. There is overwhelming evidence that virtually every national liberation movement has sought to avoid dependence on any great power. The Vietnamese, the Angolans, and other national liberation movements have consistently sought diplomatic relations and mutually advantageous commercial relations with the United States. Vietnam has become heavily dependent on the Soviet Union, but only after hopes of entering into normal relations with the United States were dashed. It is clear that the Cubans did not and still do not desire the degree of economic dependence on the Soviet Union that the U.S. embargo has made necessary. Why should they?

A second and increasingly significant argument for our counterrevolutionary preoccupation has to do with resources. What used to be advanced by the Left as a scandalous critique of American imperialism is now routinely invoked by generals and admirals testifying before Congressional appropriations committees: that the mission of our military is to protect corporate access to raw materials around the world.

Most of the expense of the military goes not to nuclear weapons but to the "general purpose" forces whose primary function it is to keep nationalist left-wing governments from coming to power in "strategic" areas. There is a strong suggestion that where such governments come to power, U.S. investments will no longer be welcome and our country will be denied access to vital resources.

Indeed, much evidence suggests that revolutionary regimes may try to change the terms on which multinational corporations are permitted to participate, and may strike a harder bargain in selling resources—but sell them they will. A new government struggling to remake a poor country desperately needs capital, and will not reject opportunities to earn it. That Cuban soldiers were offered as guards for the Gulf Oil refinery in Angola, and that Gulf accepted them, are better indications than Reagan's rhetoric of world realities.

A serious national security policy would confront the historic moment we now face. We are at the end of a 500-year period of colonialism and imperialism. National liberation struggles have occurred and continue around the world. The United States can only temporarily prevent such movements from coming to power. Our greatest success in counterinsurgency warfare was achieved in Guatemala almost thirty years ago, and today Guatemala is engulfed in a civil war rooted in the unresolved conflicts of that time. A quarter of the country is in the hands of a guerrilla movement that regards the United States as the enemy, the sponsor of a generation of official terrorism. We should have learned something from the 1954 CIA-arranged coup: Short-term military success does not buy long-term stability.

The Reagan Administration seems unwilling to face the decisions its own policy is forcing on the nation. Quite simply, the United States lacks the military power to carry out a worldwide policy of counterrevolution. If we are to take seriously the counterinsurgency goal, even the projected military budget is not nearly large enough. To carry out such policy without conscription would be unthinkable, for the costs of maintaining a volunteer military force adequate to the security tasks this Administration has defined would be prohibitive. But the Administration wisely shies away from conscription because it recognizes that the draft would be a referendum on foreign policy, and that while fighting the "Russians" in El Salvador or Libya may be a stirring idea for Reagan's right-wing backers, it looks quite different to those who would have to go do the fighting.

A national security policy that promotes stability for the United States must rest on a fundamentally different conception of the U.S.-Soviet relationship from that put forward by the present Administration or by its predecessors. President Reagan's notion that the Soviet Union could be pressed to drop out of the arms race by a major U.S. armaments buildup is a fatuous hope. More than sixty-five years of experience suggest that the Soviet leaders are quite capable of exacting whatever sacrifices may be necessary from the Soviet people to continue the arms race, and that they have been determined since the Cuban missile crisis not to fall behind.

The Soviet Union faces some severe problems. As its top officials look out from the Kremlin, they see a net tightening around them: a U.S.-Chinese military alliance, Europe and Japan being pressed by the United States to rearm, and increasing restlessness among the nations of Eastern Europe. At the same time, the Soviet Union is a formidable military power bent on achieving the capacity to match U.S. might in virtually every sphere. It is clear that the Soviet Union cannot be threatened into reform or into withdrawal from regions it controls. It cannot be made less dangerous by playing on the paranoia of its leaders. Aiming more missiles at the Soviet Union will inevitably result in more missiles aimed at the United States.

The starting point of an American security policy must be coexistence with the Soviet Union. The alternative is war, and war would mean the end of the American experiment, if not the end of civilization or even of the species. But there can be no coexistence with the Soviet Union on any basis other than the principle of sovereign equality. The Reagan Administration's stated objective of military superiority must once more be abandoned; it is absolutely crucial that both sides recognize that military superiority is unattainable. This point can be telegraphed in many ways. Both sides should state explicitly that they will refrain from using or threatening the use of nuclear weapons except in response to a nuclear attack. (The U.S. refusal to accept a "no first use" policy heightens anxiety not only in the Soviet Union but in Europe, particularly when the President speaks openly of plans for a limited nuclear war.) A proposal to freeze further production of nuclear weapons and to ban the deployment and testing of such weapons under international agreement, subject to easy verification by satellite, would be an important contribution to stability.

The world would still be a dangerous place. The weapons stockpiles would remain, but the superpowers would have made clear to one another that they had abandoned the hope of a technological breakthrough in the arms race. The freeze would symbolize surrender of the fantasy of nuclear victory. However, the U.S.-Soviet relationship cannot be stabilized by a mere freeze; it would have to be followed by serious negotiations for radical reductions in nuclear stockpiles. There can be no stability without an end to the U.S.-Soviet arms race, which cannot be ended unless we change the internal structures within each society that keep the arms race going.

Clear political commitment in the direction of demilitarization offers the most reliable evidence of peaceful national intentions. A substantially less crowded parking lot at the Pentagon and at the Ministry of Defense in Moscow, or the conversion of military plants to civilian production, would provide more reassurance than satellite photos of missile silos, as important as they are. If Soviet consumers began to get the priority attention showered on the Soviet military-industrial complex, if Soviet tanks began to look as dowdy as Soviet hotel elevators, one could reasonably conclude that something important had happened. A serious program of conversion would require the leaders on both sides to confront powerful interests that have a bureaucratic and ideological commitment to the arms race. That in itself would be impressive evidence of a turn toward peace.

The United States and the Soviet Union must also seek equality in the order of battle. We need simple, clear rules prohibiting the further deployment of Soviet as well as American military forces outside their own borders. We need mutually agreed-upon restrictions on how each superpower can deploy its military power—rules that would outlaw future interventions of the kind we have seen in Vietnam, the Dominican Republic, Chile, Angola, Czechoslovakia, Hungary, and Afghanistan. We should offer the Soviets a broad agreement that embodies the principle of parity on which they have long insisted—a concession that sacrifices no legitimate interest of the United States. Both superpowers should accept clear ground rules that bar the use of military force by themselves or their proxies in the Third World. Unless efforts are made to isolate revolutionary struggles from U.S.-Soviet military competition, superpower confrontations in the Third World are likely to spark general war.

Finally, a new national security strategy must recognize the true sources of this nation's strength. The greatest threat to the United States is posed not by Russian missiles, much less Soviet ideas, but by our failure to manage our own society. The brutal economic medicine of the Reagan Administration inspires little confidence even among those who benefit spectacularly from the tax write-offs, subsidies, and other transfer payments from the poor to the rich. While welcoming the loopholes, subsidies, and bail-outs provided by Uncle Sam, large investors do not seem to have much confidence in the long-term prospects of the economy. The official unemployment rate (which understates the problem) is approaching 9 per cent as a national average, and is far higher in distressed areas. Most significant, neither political party seems ready to offer a plan for harnessing this nation's enormous strengths to produce a stable, prosperous society. . . .   **focus**

The clashing analyses of contemporary American foreign policy by Jeane Kirkpatrick and Richard Barnet document the vastness of the ideological gulf separating conservatives from neo-Marxists and the right from the left. In contrast to the above analysis in which there seems to be little room for compromise, in the concluding essay, "The Reagan Administration's World View" by Charles Kegley and Eugene Wittkopf, Reagan's foreign policy is placed in broader historical, ideological, and bureaucratic contexts. While critical of the explicit cold war assumptions of Reagan's foreign policy and its simplistic approach to a complex and interdependent world, Kegley and Wittkopf point to the constraints which Reagan's foreign policy confronts on the domestic scene. As Commander-in-Chief of the Armed Forces and as the central arbiter, if not initiator, of foreign policy, President Reagan's power is limited by the enormously complex machinery of often-competing government bureaucracies—the Departments of State, Defense, Treasury, and Commerce, as well as the Central Intelligence Agency, and the Arms Control and Disarmament Agency, to name only a few. Thus, the president is imprisoned by the needs, expectations, and policies that are required by frequently parochial organizations. From this perspective, the vehement cold war views of Ambassador Kirkpatrick or President Reagan are moderated by the vested interests and power of the foreign affairs bureaucracy. Kegley and Wittkopf offer a penetrating analysis of the workings of contemporary American foreign policy.

THE REAGAN ADMINISTRATION'S WORLD VIEW

Charles W. Kegley and Eugene R. Wittkopf, *Orbis,* Spring 1982
Charles W. Kegley is a professor of International Studies at the University of South Carolina. Eugene R. Whittkopf is a professor of Political Science at the University of Florida.

While the Carter administration often was accused of pursuing a consistently inconsistent foreign policy, many of its decisions were based on the conviction that the time had come for the United States to revise foreign policy assumptions prevalent since World War II and to initiate innovative approaches to rapidly changing global conditions. Energy shortages, population growth, and environmental degradation were among the global issues that rose to international prominence in the 1970s and led Jimmy Carter to argue in 1978 that "the world has been changing and our responses must change with it."

The Carter administration's new course proved difficult to implement since the problems it confronted were seemingly intractable while a series of foreign and domestic crises demanded immediate attention. Forced to respond to each problem and event as it unfolded, the administration of necessity neglected long-range goals and concentrated on short-term needs. Time and again, the nation's capacity to shape events was thrown into question, as were the competence of the administration and the wisdom of its vision. Consequently, criticism mounted and frustration grew. The "new world" that Carter believed the United States should help create seemed to pose more challenges than opportunities and to result in more failures than successes. Carter's electoral defeat was therefore perhaps predictable, and he joined the long list of postwar presidents unable to wield power for two full terms—a pattern symptomatic, perhaps, of the tendency for prevailing circumstances to victimize those who seek to manage them.

Ronald Reagan, like all aspirants to the Oval Office, campaigned vigorously against the alleged deficiencies of his predecessor's policies. He interpreted his electoral landslide as confirmation of his conviction that Carter's approach to foreign (as well as domestic) affairs should be rejected and a new approach implemented. Yet, more than a year after assuming office, Reagan has yet to lay out clearly the elements of a coherent foreign policy and the means for achieving it. The president has spoken on some issues, and other administration officials have suggested some overarching objectives. White House counselor Edwin Meese, for example, has argued that the administration's foreign policy is predicated on five principles: reviving the domestic economy, strengthening national defense, enhancing relationships with U.S. allies, improving relations with the Third World, and dealing with the Soviet Union on "a realistic basis." But Reagan himself has chosen not to lend the authority and prestige of the presidency to an explication of these principles, and one is hard pressed to find in his words a design that connects policy and tactics. Other than a consummate anticommunism that envelops a plethora of unrelated international issues, key elements of a strategy concerning the Soviet Union, U.S. allies, and nonaligned nations remain obscure or missing. "Ideology in search of a policy" is the way Raymond Aron captured this overriding characteristic of the current administration.[1]

Reagan has defended his determined reluctance to speak out on foreign policy issues with the observations that "good foreign policy is the use of good common sense" and that "we know where we are going, and we think it might be counterproductive to make a speech about it." Others in his administration have explained the low priority given to foreign policy by pointing to the high priority attached to domestic programs, particularly efforts to reinvigorate the economy. (The "bold stroke" toward launching a "new federalism" outlined in the president's 1982 state of the union address virtually ensures that foreign policy matters will remain second-order priorities during the administration's second year.) Critics can nevertheless question Reagan's unwillingness to outline his foreign policy goals, particularly considering that he promised during his campaign to have a clear and predictable foreign policy. His reluctance to define such a policy belies that promise and also conveys the impression that the Reagan administration has not yet given careful thought to foreign policy priorities. Noting that most presidents tend to establish the pattern of their foreign policy both in substance and in execution during their first four months in office, Tad Szulc pointedly criticized the contrast of Reagan's first spring:

The new team has instead shown itself to be out of touch with international realities; still grasping for form and structure, to say nothing of style; torn by internal rivalries; and surprisingly insensitive to domestic realities as they affect foreign policy.

Despite the absence of well-articulated guidelines that might structure the expectations of friends and foes, whether foreign or domestic, however, the Reagan administration's words and deeds implicitly outline its world view. Three tenets have been embraced. The tenets are far from novel; they echo assumptions that have proved remarkably durable throughout postwar U.S. foreign policy thinking:

1. The United States must permanently reject isolationism and accept responsibility for the direction of international affairs on a global scale.
2. Communism comprises the principal danger in the world, and the United States must use its power to combat the spread of the communist menace.
3. Because the Soviet Union is the spearhead of the communist challenge, American foreign policy must be dedicated to containing the expansion of Soviet influence.

The Extension of Globalism

. . . From the beginning, the Reagan administration continually has reaffirmed its commitment to an internationalist posture for the United States. In an effort to assume a high profile abroad, administration officials have consciously avoided all references to "restraint," "limits," "retrenchment," and, above all, "isolationism." Instead, they have sought to project American power abroad, demonstrating the nation's resolve to retain its global influence and to tighten its grip on global developments. Responding to the view of Jimmy Carter and others that an interdependent world has eroded the nation's ability to exercise influence, Reagan asserted, "We hear it said that we live in an era of limit to our powers. Well, let it also be understood, there are limits to our patience." By implication, America's missionary role, which had fallen into disrepute in the waste of Vietnam and Watergate, is being restored. Although Carter's foreign policy was also laced with strong moral overtones, Reagan's enthusiasm and assertiveness differ markedly from Carter's pessimism and reluctance to act. The propriety of the United States redeeming the world is not questioned; U.S. management of global affairs is to be pursued actively and accepted willingly.

Initially, the differences between Carter and Reagan were especially sharp concerning human rights. Carter stressed example over action and ideals over coercion. Reagan characteristically has chosen to let considerations of "the national interest," and not concern for ideals, predominate. Accordingly, the Reagan administration announced early on that violations of human rights in other countries were not an overriding concern of the United States. Instead,

Secretary of State Haig proclaimed that "international terrorism will take the place of human rights in our concern," a proclamation followed by the claim that the Soviet Union is the sponsor of international terrorism—an assertion that has proved embarassingly difficult to substantiate. Since then, however, the administration has moved somewhat closer to the Carter position, as indicated by the appointment of Elliott Abrams, a former Senate aide with a reputation as a conciliator, as assistant secretary of state for human rights and humanitarian affairs.

Another departure from Carter policy is the Reagan administration's greater reliance on market mechanisms to deal with other nations economically. The administration has reaffirmed the Republican party's traditional emphasis on the principle of free international trade (although in practice it has supported protectionist measures, as for the auto industry), and it has emphasized that Third World nations must learn to help themselves rather than relying on U.S. economic assistance to realize their economic development goals. . . . Corollaries of this thrust include skepticism toward multi-lateral assistance, based on the argument that the United States is better able to control the use of its funds if they are allocated on a bilateral basis. The preference for bilateralism reflects the administration's desire to make foreign aid an instrument for the realization of U.S. political objectives; it implies a greater reliance on security-supporting assistance (that is, aid designed for political or security purposes within the recipient nation) and a diminished role for economic development aid.

Although the Reagan administration understandably has tried, through its pursuit of globalism, to convey the impression that U.S. foreign policy has been reoriented, its convictions, like those of the Carter administration, reflect Zbigniew Brzezinski's assumption that the U.S. "commitment to international affairs on a global scale [has] been decided by history. It cannot be undone, and the only remaining question is what its form and goals will be."[2] The alternative thrusts of the Carter and Reagan presidencies indicate that differing perceptions of the intentions of potential adversaries will affect the form that global involvement assumes. . . .

Anticommunism in U.S. Policy

President Carter did little to displace the anticommunist focus of U.S. foreign policy. At least initially, however, he did challenge the obsession with communism and the corresponding tendency to reduce complex international affairs to simplistic, Manichaean terms. The often quoted passage from Carter's 1977 Notre Dame address—"We are now free of that inordinate fear of communism which once led us to embrace any dictator who joined us in our fear"—epitomizes the initial thrust of Carter's efforts to dethrone the anticommunist icon. But as events unfolded (especially the Soviet inter-vention in Afghanistan), the penchant for seeing developments as part of a struggle between the forces of communism and the supposedly free world reasserted itself. Carter's foreign policy ended up being distinctive more in emphasis than in essence.

The anticommunist bias in U.S. foreign policy has intensified even further during the past year. Nearly every international development faced by the Reagan administration has been viewed through the distorting prism of anticommunist ideology; each event that has threatened to disturb the global status quo has been traced to the revolutionary activities of a supposedly coordinated communist conspiracy. Whether it has been insurrection by the left against their oppressors or rightist terrorism by nationalists pursuing national causes, the interpretation is the same: communism is responsible.

It is only a short step from here to accept repressive regimes that deny freedom to their own people but voice opposition to Marxist principles. Thus, administration spokesmen have dismissed the denial of basic rights to people in South Africa, Argentina, Chile, South Korea, and elsewhere as beyond the purview of Washington's concern. "The message is clear to the dictators and would-be tyrants of the world," syndicated columnist Carl Rowan has written. "If you claim to be anticommunist, the Reagan administration is not going to give you any trouble." Yet such a policy is likely to exacerbate the polarization of left and right within those societies, virtually ensuring a virulently anti-American posture among those who perceive themselves as victimized by the American-backed ruling regime. It thus seems likely that a product of the administration's posture will be the reinforcement of oppressive governments in other nations as well as eventual communist victories—the very result that is most feared.

Contradictions are also apparent in the administration's policies toward governments already within the communist orbit. Ideological anticommunism necessarily inclines the administration toward the nationalist Chinese government of Taiwan, but the proclivity to continue playing "the China card," as the Carter administration did so willingly, has been shown nowhere more starkly than in the decision to sell lethal weapons to the Beijing government. Coping with the prolonged Polish situation has also proved ticklish. Thinly veiled threats against Soviet intervention were frequent, but the record now shows fulfillment of the expectation of many that the United States is not in a position to affect materially the course of events in Eastern Europe. The imposition of martial law by the Polish military was not anticipated—direct Soviet intervention seemed more likely—and the imposition of economic sanctions against the Soviet Union in retaliation for their alleged complicity sounds a hollow ring, particularly given the administration's unwillingness to embargo grain, America's most important export product. Even as sympathetic an observer as Henry Kissinger lashed out against the administration's reaction to the Polish situation: "[F]reedom-loving Poles who looked West saw dithering procrastination, sophisticated justifications for impotence, or rhetoric incapable of rising to serious action."[3]

If the administration has a new wrinkle in the old anticommunist approach, it is the argument that communism is a transitory historical phenomenon whose time has passed. Speaking at Notre Dame University in May 1981, Reagan argued that in the years ahead "the West will not contain communism; it will transcend communism. We will not bother to denounce it. We'll dismiss it as a sad, bizarre chapter in human history whose last pages are even now being written." A few weeks later the president branded communism an "aberration—it's not a normal way of living for human beings," while his secretary of state charged that the Soviet Union was suffering from "spiritual exhaustion" and showing "clear signs of historic decline." Haig added: "Moscow has an unenviable present and an extremely gloomy future. A list of formidable problems confront it, ranging from the hostility of China to the difficult Polish situation, from economic failure to ideological sterility."

The administration's purpose in downgrading Soviet communism appears to be to lower the image of communism and the Soviet Union in the eyes of other nations—many of which see international circumstances through less ideologically tinted lenses. By boasting of the virtues of the American way of life, the administration also has given its blessing to the long-standing tendency of the United States to pursue its foreign policy objectives with crusading zeal. Yet is it wise to challenge so boldly the nation's historic adversary? Might not the Soviet Union adopt an even more aggressive posture simply to disprove the administration's charge of weakness? As others have also argued, the dangers of provoking the Soviet bear are all the more ominous since, whatever its other weaknesses may be, the Soviet Union has managed to build enormous military might.

Ultimately, then, the administration's rhetorical posturing raises the specter of open conflict with the Soviet Union itself. National Security Council staffer Richard Pipes dramatized the danger by declaring that the Soviets would have to choose either "peacefully changing their Communist system . . . or going to war." His prediction that "it could go either way" is hardly reassuring.

The Issue of Containment

For more than three decades, rivalry with the Soviet Union has dominated American diplomacy, coloring all other aspects of foreign policy. That focus has been challenged by some policymakers. It has also been challenged by significant new issues in world politics that either do not involve the Soviet Union or require cooperation with it—such as the North-South split, the energy predicament, resource scarcities, balance-of-payments deficits, resurgent nationalism, and the rise of powerful nonstate actors—all of which demand attention and a reordering of foreign policy priorities.

The Carter administration sought to understand and cope with many of these challenges. But the fact that it temporarily chose to expand its foreign policy agenda to face the problems of an increasingly interdependent world does not obscure the continued emphasis it placed on relations with the Soviet Union. That containment of potential Soviet expansionism remained a central goal of the Carter administration, as of all previous postwar administrations, was underscored in Carter's 1978 address at the Naval Academy in which he posed alternative means to the same end. "The Soviet Union can choose either confrontation or cooperation—the United States is adequately prepared to meet either choice."

Confrontation has been the choice of the Reagan team. Opportunities to collaborate in areas where U.S. and Soviet interests intersect have been approached cautiously and reluctantly, as in the area of European theater-nuclear arms limitations (where in fact there have been few visible signs of forward momentum), and almost daily the United States has gone to new lengths in pursuing an unremittingly militant, confrontational posture toward the Soviet Union. The bitter antagonism that punctuated America's approach toward the Soviets from the end of World War II until the 1962 Cuban missile crisis has returned, along with some of the toughest cold-war rhetoric since the Eisenhower and Kennedy years.

Belief in the Soviet menace stands behind the Reagan administration's efforts to project (for domestic as well as foreign consumption) the image of a resolute and unswerving policy toward the Kremlin. "The Soviet Union underlies all the unrest that is going on," declared President-elect Reagan shortly before his inauguration, adding, "If they weren't engaged in this game of dominoes, there wouldn't be any hotspots in the world." In granting the Soviet Union "most favored enemy" status, the administration's verbal assaults express its fears while simultaneously reaffirming a belief that has undergirded U.S. foreign policy for decades. Haig echoed this philosophy: "A major focus of American policy must be the Soviet Union . . . because Moscow is the greatest source of international insecurity today . . . and the greatest danger to world peace." Haig explained what would later become the administration's position at the 1980 Republican national convention: "Clearly, the task ahead for this vital decade before us will be the management of global Soviet power."

If the goal is unoriginal, the means selected to accomplish it are likewise unimaginative. Two tactics have been outlined. First, the administration has pledged to resurrect Kissinger's linkage strategy. U.S. behavior toward the Soviet Union was to be tied directly to Washington's assessment of Moscow's activities anywhere in the world; cooperation on such issues as arms control, trade expansion, and the like was to be contingent upon the willingness of the Soviet Union to curb what Washington sees as its expansionist appetite. In a speech before the Foreign Policy Association in July 1981, Haig described the administration's position on arms-control negotiations when he noted:

> We . . . seek arms control bearing in mind the whole context of Soviet conduct worldwide. . . . Soviet international conduct directly affects the prospects for success in arms control. . . . Such "linkage" is not the

creation of U.S. policy. It's a fact of life. A policy of pretending that there is no linkage promotes reverse linkage. It ends up by saying that in order to preserve arms control, we have to tolerate Soviet aggression.

As one approach toward containment, linkage is based on the conviction that it yields leverage. Concessions can be extracted, supposedly on a quid pro quo basis, through peaceful competition. In return for Soviet restraint and an end to Soviet exploitation of regional conflicts, Haig promised on another occasion "a broader relationship of mutual benefit" in which the United States would be prepared to offer specific rewards:

"We offer a reduction in the tensions that are so costly to both our societies."

"We offer diplomatic alternatives to the pursuit of violent change."

"We offer fair and balanced agreements on arms control."

"And we offer the possibility of Western trade and technology."

In practice, however, linkage has been applied selectively, and perhaps abandoned. Minimally, the appearance of vacillation is counterproductive. The imposition of economic sanctions (admittedly more symbolic than real) against the Soviet Union in retaliation against martial law in Poland, for example, combined with the administration's willingness to proceed with European arms-limitation talks, contributes to the image of an internally inconsistent foreign policy.

Besides linkage, a second tactic for restraining the Soviets, which remains intact, is to confront them with preponderant military strength, thereby challenging the Soviet Union with force and with the risk of devastation. The essence of this spirit was captured by Secretary of Defense Weinberger's claim that "we have to be prepared . . . to exploit the aggressor's weaknesses, wherever we might find them." The implication is that conflict with the Soviet Union will not remain localized. If the Soviets attack in the Middle East, for example, the United States might choose to retaliate in any number of other locations, depending on the risks and options available. The restoration of the two-and-a-half-conventional-wars posture prevalent during the Johnson and Kennedy years (the belief that the country must be prepared to fight two-and-a-half conventional wars simultaneously) reinforces the militant posturing—even while the specter of U.S. troops on foreign soil facing enemy fire once again seems all too possible.

"The only thing the cause of peace has to fear is fear itself. We must build peace upon strength. Only if we are strong will peace be strong." These simple ideas, uttered by Reagan shortly after his election, underlie the administration's preference for a military approach to what is fundamentally a political problem, namely, the containment of Soviet influence. The centrality of the ideas is noteworthy as a manifestation of the extent to which the assumptions of political realism have permeated the foreign policy thinking of the administration. "Military strength is . . . the backbone of diplomacy," is the way Undersecretary of Defense Fred C. Iklé put it. The proposition reflects the lessons of the past embraced by the president himself: "The lesson of history is that among the great nations only those with the strength to protect their interests survive." . . .

The administration's stress on military preparedness includes increases in U.S. arms destined for those perceived to need or otherwise be willing to pay for them. "Where, in the fashionable vernacular, money was once thrown at problems, weapons now seemed to be."[4] Jimmy Carter's 1976 campaign characterization of the United States as "the arms merchant of the world" has thus gained renewed relevance, as has the presumption that political influence can be purchased by supplying arms to others. As articulated by Undersecretary of State James L. Buckley, arms sales abroad are to "complement and supplement our own defense efforts and serve as a vital and constructive instrument of American foreign policy." Arms transfers are also to be an instrument to "face up to the realities of Soviet aggrandizement." Arms sales have thus become "perhaps *the* major instrument for action overseas short of the direct use of U.S. armed forces."[5] Unhappily, the administration seems to have missed the lesson of Iran—that pumping billions of dollars' worth of sophisticated military equipment into a developing country ensures neither peace nor the survival of the client regime.

In conformity with the martial thrust of Reagan's foreign policy, the administration has shown little hesitation in expressing its willingness to employ military instruments other than arms sales to protect U.S. interests overseas, as Colonel Qaddafi learned. "Those who live by the sword can expect to die by it," UN Ambassador Jeane Kirkpatrick has warned. The administration's decision in 1981 to send U.S. military advisers to El Salvador was consistent with this and other views it espouses, inasmuch as the decision was based on the conviction that "outsiders," not domestic injustice, were the instigators of Central American turmoil.

Such a view is intimately linked to the logic of containment and to the perceived threat of a communist conspiracy subservient to the Kremlin's wishes, if not always dictated by Moscow's hand. Lurking in the background is the shadow of Vietnam. Acting Assistant Secretary of State John Bushnell in 1981 invoked a Hispanic version of the domino theory once prevalent in justifying U.S. involvement in Southeast Asia: "I know these guerrillas are committed to fight tomorrow in Guatemala and the next day in Honduras." A year later Thomas O. Enders, assistant secretary of state for inter-American Affairs, sounded a similar theme in testimony before Congress: "There is no mistaking that the decisive battle for Central America is under way in El Salvador. For if after Nicaragua, El Salvador is captured by a violent minority, who in Central America would not live in fear? How long would it be before major strategic interests—the Panama Canal, sea lanes, oil supplies—were at risk?" What might the United States do to ensure defeat of the leftist guerrillas? According to Haig, "whatever is necessary." . . .

Whatever the ultimate consequences of the administration's policies, the assumptions regarding military might and interventionist means have been reaffirmed as a part of the nation's postwar policy based on the trilogy of globalism, anticommunism, and containment: strength produces peace, might yields influence, superior firepower can both deter and compel, power can be purchased, the capacity to destroy is the capacity to control, and political problems are susceptible to military solutions. Corollaries include the beliefs that superior firepower ensures victory in war, that arms supplied to an ally will guarantee its abiding loyalty, that the dispersion of weapons promotes international stability, and that the price of military preparedness is never too high. The president thus seeks to undo Carter's modest changes in the nations' preference for military might and interventionist means and to rekindle the consensus that emerged in the late 1940s to contain Soviet influence through a global strategy based on such premises. Time-worn foreign policy goals have been embraced enthusiastically and the past agenda has been given new life.

The Sources of U.S. Foreign Policy

When we look beyond the rhetoric and deeds of the administration and inquire into the sources of U.S. foreign policy, there is little on the horizon that leads one to believe Reagan will not be successful in perpetuating the patterns of globalism, anticommunism, containment, military might, and interventionist means, for the administration's own world view is clearly compatible with the interests and values underlying these tenets of postwar U.S. foreign policy. Furthermore, the combination of internal and external factors that influence that policy—including stimuli from the external environment, the characteristics of American society as they impinge on foreign policymaking, the structure of the government that manages it, the roles that shape the behavior of individuals occupying positions within the policymaking arena, and the personal predispositions of the individuals who occupy policymaking roles—interact with one another in such a way that radical departures from past foreign policy patterns are rare and typically short-lived. While the factors that influence foreign policy will thus restrain Reagan's excesses, the compatibility of the administration's world view with the persistent patterns of postwar American foreign policy will promote continuity with the past rather than encourage deviation from it. . . .

The selection of key personnel on the basis of their ability to conform and to demonstrate loyalty as team players was the administration's approach to overcoming potential bureaucratic intransigence—control it before it develops. But loyalty to the president's concept has not prevented the inevitable struggle for power among ambitious men and the consequent adverse effects on the coherence, consistency, and effectiveness of the nation's foreign policy, which Reagan ridiculed so vehemently during his campaign for the presidency.

Haig's threat to resign when Vice President Bush was made chief of crisis management was an early sign of ensuing, less publicized jurisdictional struggles. Haig's expectation that he would become the foreign policy "vicar" lies in shambles as the presence of Edwin Meese and Caspar Weinberger looms large.

Weinberger in particular has consistently spelled out the guidelines of the administration's policies in a manner normally reserved for either the secretary of state or the president himself. (Meese, meanwhile, occasionally appeared to have assumed the role played by the national security adviser in previous administrations, as witnessed by his management of the flow of information to the president when Navy pilots downed two Libyan fighters and when the North Koreans allegedly tried to shoot down a high-flying U.S. spy plane. Whether William P. Clark will effectively pre-empt Meese's position is possible but not ensured.) As Tad Szulc notes, Weinberger's associates have defended the secretary's initiatives by saying that the line between defense and foreign policy is thin and blurred, and that an activist secretary of defense cannot be expected to deny himself the right to speak out on problems concerning his department.[6] But the fact that the administration has so far failed to develop the National Security Council (NSC) system into an effective mechanism for coordinating discordant voices and implementing coherent policies exacerbated these feuds over bureaucratic turf.

Whether Reagan's decision earlier this year to replace Richard Allen with William P. Clark as his national security adviser and to give Clark, unlike Allen before him, direct access to the president and to cabinet-level officials will produce greater coherence and consistency in the administration's policies remains to be seen. Minimally, the decision is an apparent recognition of the need to upgrade the role of the national security adviser and his staff.

In the absence of a strong national security adviser, an informal version of the NSC—sometimes referred to as the National Security Planning Group— reportedly emerged as the forum for the secretaries of state and defense to present their arguments to the president on various foreign policy issues. Within this framework, Weinberger, a close personal friend of the president, appears to have enjoyed greater influence. It was Weinberger, for example, who favored the decision to proceed with production of the controversial neutron bomb, while Haig, more sensitive to the concerns of the nation's European allies, reportedly urged a delay in the decision. Thus, the Pentagon has emerged as a significant competitor to the State Department in the formulation and execution of foreign policy, adding to the latter's historic competition and conflict with the White House itself.

Reagan's ultimate success, of course, will be influenced by the nature of the government he has been elected to run. His plans for the creative destruction of the federal bureaucracy have probably raised exaggerated expectations about his ability to reduce, streamline, and manage the government. The vow to "get government off the backs of people" will be circumscribed by the fact that:

> Bureaucrats do not climb onto the people's backs without a boost from interest groups and members of Congress. They do not write regulations because they are malevolent but because someone wants those rules on the books. . . . Congress, in the interest of appearing responsive to public revulsion with large and complicated government, may tinker a little here and streamline a little there, but the basic structure of alliances will remain intact.[7]

Reagan himself provided an apt description of the impact of governmental forces on his policies and programs: "Government is like an ocean liner, not a speedboat. If you turn the wheel a few degrees, it must come around gradually, lest it capsize. So, though we shall move deliberately, with clearly identified goals, we won't do so in haste."

While Reagan appears to be sensitive to the impact of the federal bureaucracy on his proposals, his skill in persuading Congress to implement the initial elements of supply-side Reaganomics was masterful. Some even likened Reagan to Lyndon Johnson, whose handling of the legislative branch contributed immeasurably to realizing his vision of the Great Society.

On foreign policy matters, however, Reagan's early record has been markedly less impressive. Many key foreign policy positions remained unfilled well into the new administration partly, as noted earlier, because of Reagan's role conception, but also because of his unwillingness to do battle with conservative elements in Congress (especially "Secretary of State" Helms) over the issue of whether potential appointees are sufficiently conservative. The Foreign Relations Committee's overwhelming disapproval of Ernest Lefever's State Department nomination was unprecedented in recent memory. Congressional rumblings led the administration to postpone its plan to supply Saudi Arabia with sophisticated AWACS planes—only to face formidable congressional opposition once the decision to proceed was made. Victory was finally achieved by making the presidency itself the issue at stake. And the president still faces stiff resistance to his strategic weapons program—from those on the right who believe Reagan has done too little to close the elusive "window of vulnerability," and from those on the left who believe the proposals are either unnecessary or fundamentally flawed.

Ultimately Reagan's ability to work his will on Congress will be influenced by the support he enjoys among the American people. For just as Congress provides different federal bureaucracies with influential friends and allies, its generally parochial viewpoint makes it particularly sensitive to pressure from constituents. Indeed, the potential influence of societal forces is especially great in an interdependent world, for under conditions of interdependence "intermestic" issues often dominate the agenda, and foreign policy often becomes little more than an extension of domestic policy. Different groups within society are therefore driven to attempt to influence the shape of foreign policy, and presidents are tempted to take foreign policy positions primarily for their domestic impact.

Despite the fact that Reagan entered office with an electorate favorably disposed to him and his avowed goals, American society still poses formidable obstacles to his policies. Single-issue public-interest groups continue to press their causes, and public opinion, always fickle, may turn against the president as the costs of his more ambitious programs continue to be felt. It is significant that not only has the president experienced the same general erosion of popularity as did his predecessors, but also that the number of Americans who disapprove of the way the president is handling his job has run consistently higher than is normally the case in presidential popularity contests. In a December 1981 Gallup Poll, 41 per cent of the American public disapproved of Reagan's job performance, while 49 per cent approved. The approval rating was 8 percentage points below Carter's in December 1977, while the disapproving proportion was 14 percentage points higher. The data suggest that Reagan's policies may be contributing to a dangerous polarization of American society.

Also relevant is that while internationalist attitudes may appear now more dominant than at any time since the Vietnam debacle,[8] an assertive foreign policy mood does not necessarily signal the rebirth of a domestic consensus paralleling the pre-Vietnam consensus. Questions sparked by Vietnam about the wisdom of conflict and cooperation as strategies for coping with the external environment remain significant undercurrents in the attitudes of the American people[9] that can be expected to surface periodically in policy debates, as they did during the Saudi Arabian AWACS controversy last year.

Reagan's plan to engineer the nation's economic recovery makes him especially vulnerable to attack. Although Americans generally favor lower taxes, the massive budget cuts projected by the president have already encountered stiff opposition, even among his Republican supporters. Furthermore, the combination of massive cuts in social programs with unprecedented increases in defense spending poses a serious risk. The projected increase in military spending would be three times as large as the increase during the Vietnam War and seems virtually guaranteed to stimulate an inflationary spiral that may threaten the entire economy.[10]

If the past is any guide, the probability that Reagan's defense-spending projections will be realized "is less than one in a million. The actual chances are probably less."[11] The real odds are illustrated by the fact that since the Korean War defense spending has never risen during more than three consecutive years. Increases invariably have been followed by reductions. The lesson is that guns and butter are incompatible in the long run, that one can be obtained only at the expense of the other. If Reagan's plans to spend lavishly on the defense establishment thus seem doomed to failure by a combination of finite economic resources and limited political patience, the likely scenario is a revision of the ambitious goals. Instructively, Reagan's effort to realize new cuts in the fiscal 1982 budget to reduce a deficit projected by the administration to be more than $40 billion resulted in a minimal trimming of projected defense expenditures. With additional increases in defense spending in the offing, and with budget deficits now projected by the administration near $100 billion during the remaining years of Reagan's term, more trimming of the defense budget can be expected, perhaps effected by Congress, where many seem to recognize that economic security is essential to national security, even if, as some charge, the administration does not.

The influence of the external environment on U.S. foreign policy remains formidable, and it will likely increase as the United States becomes more dependent on foreign resources and vulnerable to the political, economic, and military challenges posed by other nations. Reagan may wish to reduce that vulnerability, but the inescapable fact is that the United States is no longer the unchallenged, pre-eminent superpower; its power no longer automatically commands awe and respect from others. It has a limited ability to shape events elsewhere, events that in any case have a way of unfolding regardless of the wishes of the United States. It is instructive to note, for example, that while the Reagan administration focused on the domestic economy as its first priority, tensions in Poland, strife in Lebanon, Israel's attack on Iraq's nuclear facility, South Africa's march into Angola, and other developments thrust upon the administration the apparently unwanted task of spelling out its foreign policy posture toward issues heretofore ignored.

Interestingly, few of these developments fit neatly into the East versus West, communism versus capitalism mold that delineates the administration's world view. The administration nevertheless has persisted in defining its approach in terms that often bear little resemblance to external international realities. The fact is that many others disagree with Reagan's basic ideas. Many in the Western community, for example,

> don't think every disruptive development in the world is caused by the Kremlin's decision. They don't think government controls are the main obstacle to economic growth. They don't think that turning the world over to private enterprise and individual initiative is a universal solution. Reiteration of these ideological themes by the new administration creates new domestic political problems made in America for every allied leader.[12]

Preaching the virtues of individualism and the private sector has not been confined to the First World, as noted earlier. The president himself has urged others to try Reaganomics, urging Third World nations to rely on the "magic of the marketplace" to promote economic growth. Although the president did not utilize the Cancún North-South summit to quash the Third World's drive for a round of global negotiations designed to further its goal of a new international economic order (NIEO), as many had expected, it is now clear that no massive transfer of resources from rich to poor will take place. "A strategy for growth that depends on a massive increase in the transfer of resources from the developed to the developing countries is simply unrealistic," Haig asserted at the UN. Instead, private investment and free trade are to be emphasized and promoted, as illustrated in the Caribbean Basin initiative unveiled earlier this year. The agenda of the NIEO may have been dead in any event, but such burial tactics are unlikely to endear the preacher to the mourners.

The administration's inaction on other issues is felt by others affected by global interdependence. Not only do excessive interest rates adversely affect the domestic housing industry; but also the appreciation of the dollar they propel reduces the competitiveness of U.S. goods overseas, with a probable impact on the nation's trade and payments balances not unlike those precipitating the dollar crises of the 1970s.[13]. .

Prospects for U.S. Foreign Policy

Whether the premises that have guided American foreign policy since World War II and that have been reaffirmed by the Reagan administration remain appropriate in the current international context is questionable and will certainly be challenged domestically as well as internationally.

The revitalization of anticommunism and containment as the twin pillars on which to rebuild a domestic consensus about the nation's appropriate world role—which appears to be the underlying purpose of much of Reagan's behavior—is particularly troublesome. Liberal internationalists in particular will recoil from the administration's militant tone because of the consequences that could flow from it. Carter articulated the concern in a speech delivered to the Council on Foreign Relations in late 1981: "A one-sided attitude of belligerence toward the Soviet Union may be politically attractive for a time, but it is not an adequate basis for American policy, because it precludes cooperation and generates fear among those who would avoid a superpower confrontation." James Chace has argued more broadly that a foreign policy posture that forces everything "into a hard-line Soviet mold would be ineffective at best and dangerous at worse." Consequently, "the kind of broad consensus that obtained during the postwar era and which became a shibboleth of American foreign policy may no longer be possible to resurrect short of war. American interests are too diverse and American power now much less predominant."[14]

Conservative internationalists, on the other hand, fear the consequences of being any less militant. To them, Nixon's détente and Carter's human rights initiatives were no more palatable as rallying cries around which to rekindle the pre-Vietnam internationalist consensus than is anti-Sovietism to liberal internationalists.[15] To them, the shibboleths of the past are not conventional wisdoms but time-worn truths. The Soviet Union is the present danger. Failing to heed it not only is irresponsible but also courts disaster. The argument that the Vietnam War was lost not on the battlefield but rather in the councils of government as leaders anticipated the resolve of the American people is relevant to the present.

As noted earlier in our discussion of globalism, differences about the nation's world role turn fundamentally on differing perceptions of the intentions of others, and on the correspondingly appropriate mix of conciliatory and conflictual strategies for protecting and promoting the nation's interests. Even in the absence of consensus, however, the persistence of the premises of postwar American foreign policy is noteworthy. To a considerable extent the resilience of the assumptions made by U.S. policymakers in the immediate aftermath of World War II derives from the constraining impact of individual, role, governmental, societal, and external influences on foreign policymaking. Consequently, even though our changing times may seem to call for a new U.S. foreign policy, the persistence and continuity that have marked that policy for so long will likely remain undisturbed. The Oval Office is now occupied by a president who shares the essential premises of this policy tradition. Reagan's tasks may be made easier as a consequence, and the long-standing traditions of U.S. foreign policy will likely find reinforcement not only from those factors that influence the making of foreign policy but also from the man toward whom those influences are frequently directed. Differences over how the nation's interests are best pursued may persist, but globalism, anti-communism, and containment, supplemented by a faith in military might and interventionist means, will remain the parameters defining the debate.

What is lacking is the recognition that the problems foreign policy leaders must tackle are defined not only by them, by powerful domestic interest groups—or even by the Soviet Union. The agenda is also set by external forces over which a no-longer pre-eminent superpower does not have sole control or even dominant influence. Reasserting American pre-eminence may alter the order of priorities, but the agenda itself will continue to be influenced by a combination of political and nonpolitical actors and forces understood by few and mastered by none. In such an environment, the need remains for a U.S. foreign policy that applies to the present principles informed by the past that will also ensure a peaceful and prosperous future. A nostalgia for the past alone is not sufficient. Perhaps the Reagan administration may yet rise to the challenge.

References

1 Raymond Aron, "Ideology in Search of Policy," *Foreign Affairs*, vol. 60, no. 3, pp. 503-524.
2 Zbigniew Brzezinski, *Between Two Ages* (New York: Viking, 1970), p. 306.
3 Henry Kissinger, "Poland's Lessons for Mr. Reagan," *New York Times*, January 17, 1982.
4 Thomas L. Hughes, "Up from Reaganism," *Foreign Policy*, Fall 1981, p. 10.

5   Andrew J. Pierre, "Arms Sales: The New Diplomacy," *Foreign Affairs*, Winter 1981/1982, p. 282.
6   Tad Szulc, "Dateline Washington: The Vicar Vanquished," *Foreign Policy* Summer 1981, p. 181.
7   Ross R. Baker, "Outlook for the Reagan Administration," in Gerald Pomper et al., *The Election of 1980* (Chatham, N.J.: Chatham House 1981), p. 142.
8   See Lloyd Free and William Watts, "Internationalism Comes of Age . . . Again," *Public Opinion*, April/May 1980, pp. 46-50; and Daniel Yankelovich and Larry Kaagan, "Assertive America," *Foreign Affairs*, vol. 59, no. 3, pp. 696-713.
9   Eugene Wittkopf and Michael A. Maggiotto, "Since Vietnam: Public Attitudes Toward American Foreign Policy in the 1970's," paper delivered at the annual convention of the International Studies Association, Cincinnati, March 24-27, 1982.
10   See Lester Thurow, "How to Wreck the Economy," *New York Review of Books*, May 14, 1981, pp. 3-8.
11   James Fallows, "The Great Defense Deception," *New York Review of Books*, May 28, 1981, p. 17.
12   Hughes, "Up From Reaganism," p. 15.
13   C. Fred Bergsten, "The Costs of Reaganomics," *Foreign Policy*, Fall 1981, pp. 24-36.
14   "Is a Foreign Policy Consensus Possible?" *Foreign Affairs*, Fall 1978, p. 15.
15   For Empirical evidence supporting this reasoning, see Wittkopf and Maggiotto, "Since Vietnam . . ."; Wittkopf and Maggiotto, "Elites and Masses, A Comparative Analysis of Attitudes Toward America's World Role," paper delivered at the annual convention of the International Studies Association, Philadelphia, March 18-21, 1981; Maggiotto and Wittkopf, "American Public Attitudes Toward Foreign Policy," *International Studies Quarterly*, December 1981, pp. 601-631; Ole R. Holsti, "The Three Headed Eagle: The United States and System Change," *International Studies Quarterly*, September 1979, pp. 339-359; and Ole R. Holsti and James N. Rosenau, "The Three Headed Eagle Revisited: Who are the Cold War Internationalists, Post Cold War Internationalists, and Isolationists?," paper delivered at the annual convention of the International Studies Association, Philadelphia, March 18-21, 1981.   **focus**

The three perspectives discussed in this chapter present many of the most basic concerns confronting American foreign policy in the 1980s. These views are even more important because of their underlying ideological assumptions. Kirkpatrick's analysis of Soviet expansionism and the failures of Jimmy Carter's foreign policy suggest a pessimistic view of human nature—akin to the works of Machiavelli, St. Augustine, and Hobbes—in which the pursuit of power and the self-aggrandizement of the individual are the key dimensions of human motivation. Richard Barnet, on the other hand, emphasizes the perfectability, or at least potential for self-growth, of man. Both Kirkpatrick and Barnet prescribe a number of ways to achieve their views of a better world.

For Kirkpatrick, the necessity of self-preservation demands the acceptance of right-wing dictatorships, whose political and social policies are often offensive to American ideals and practice. However, the growing threat of the expansion of Soviet totalitarianism demands American vigilance, she contends. Barnet's vision calls for the people of the United States to restructure some of their most powerful political, social, and economic institutions in order to secure more stable and just domestic and international environments. Kegley and Wittkopf embrace a middle-ground, recognizing the limitations of power politics in an extraordinarily interdependent world while admitting the difficulty of bringing about significant changes within the United States and abroad. Each of the three approaches presented above evaluates American foreign policy from different standards and with different values. This absence of a stable, bipartisan consensus illustrates both the wide range of assumptions and values and the dynamic nature of foreign policy issues in the 1980s.

CHAPTER 3

Power and American Foreign Policy

Perhaps no term is more synonymous with the actions of states and their foreign policies than power. The history of post-World War II international politics illustrates the importance of power, defined in terms of military capabilities—especially nuclear weapons. However, power also involves economic resources, technology, the force of ideologies (communism, nationalism, anti-colonialism, and anti-imperialism) and any combination of incentives (rewards) and disincentives (sanctions) which are used to obtain political ends. Notions of war or peace, instability or equilibrium, harmony or disharmony, diplomacy or conflict, all spring from the crucial role played by power. The use of nuclear weapons at Hiroshima and Nagasaki in August 1945 transformed the military power of the United States, and eventually that of the Soviet Union, as never before in history. Not only did nuclear weapons constitute a qualitative change in military capabilities, but the evolving political, economic, technological, and ideological might of the two superpowers transformed world politics from an arena in which there were several great powers with different resources into one dominated by two global actors. The continued evolution of the post-World War II international environment eventually created a situation in which the awesome military power that nuclear weapons conferred on the United States and the Soviet Union would remain unusable in all but the most desperate circumstances. The 1950s, 1960s, and 1970s witnessed further transformations which challenged 19th and 20th century concepts of world politics. The process of decolonization created a world in which a European-dominated state system was transformed into a global one, where the vast majority of states were non-Western, poor, and struggling to avoid internal dissolution.

A crucial aspect of power, both within states and throughout the global environment, centered upon technological resources (transportation and communication networks), economic capabilities, and the force of prevailing ideologies. The growing assertiveness of the Third World and the increasing fragmentation of the American and Soviet spheres from the 1950s onward provided an opportunity for the growth of non-Western ideologies and justified the redistribution of political, economic, technological, and military resources from the superpowers and their allies to the developing countries of the world. In this context, the international politics were being challenged and, in some cases, changed.

It is fitting, therefore, to consider the role played by power in American foreign policy both because it is such a basic element of world politics and because the traditional dynamics of the 19th century state system have been greatly modified. The three articles presented below—Hans J. Morgenthau's "The Six Principles of Political Realism," Robert W. Tucker's "Oil and American Power—Six Years Later," and Paul M. Sweezy and Harry Magdoff's "U.S. Foreign Policy in the 1980s"—suggest distinctive approaches to the uses of power.

Perhaps no post-World War II student of international politics exerted more influence on the study of global politics than the late Hans J. Morgenthau. When his masterpiece

Politics Among Nations first appeared in 1948, his emphasis on the role of power in international politics and foreign policy was greeted by scholars and politicians as an intellectual tour de force. Morgenthau attacked the idealism and utopianism of the 1920s and 1930s, arguing that the survival of the state and the preservation of international politics created an arena in which the struggle for power transcended all other motivations. Looking back on the history of the 20th century, in which two world wars inflicted horrendous damage on all mankind, Morgenthau concluded that the Anglo-American idealism demonstrated in the Kellogg-Briand Pact of 1928, the Washington Naval Arms Limitations Agreements of 1922 and the American isolationism of 1919 to 1941, helped to create an environment in which aggression would flourish. During these years, the United States withdrew from active involvement in world politics (with the exception of Latin America). The absence of an active American presence in world politics, Morgenthau contended, helped to create a void in which German and Japanese aggression flourished. *Politics Among Nations* was an exhaustive analysis of the history of world politics. Morgenthau's assumptions were drawn largely from that body of philosophy in which the dark side of human nature and human behavior was emphasized—that of St. Augustine, Machiavelli, and Thomas Hobbes, among others. Morgenthau's study of world politics illustrated how states, like individuals, resort to power in order to insure their survival and prosperity, and defined the pursuit of power and national interest as the central maxim of foreign policy. It should be noted that American perceptions in the late 1940s and 1950s of the rising tide of a worldwide Communist conspiracy led by the Soviet Union convinced many of the inherent validity of Morgenthau's vision of human nature and the behavior of states. As the cold war intensified, Morgenthau's emphasis on power politics and the pursuit of the American national interest became even more appealing. "The Six Principles of Political Realism" embodies the essence of Morgenthau's thought, and the principles described have remained essentially unchanged since the publication of the first edition of *Politics Among Nations.*

SIX PRINCIPLES OF POLITICAL REALISM

Hans J. Morgenthau, *Politics Among Nations,* 1948

The late Hans J. Morgenthau was Albert A. Michelson, Distinguished Service Professor of political science and modern history at the University of Chicago.

Six Principles of Political Realism

1. Political realism believes that politics, like society in general, is governed by objective laws that have their roots in human nature. In order to improve society it is first necessary to understand the laws by which society lives. The operation of these laws being impervious to our preferences, men will challenge them only at the risk of failure.

Realism, believing as it does in the objectivity of the laws of politics, must also believe in the possibility of developing a rational theory that reflects, however imperfectly and one-sidedly, these objective laws. It believes also, then, in the possibility of distinguishing in politics between truth and opinion—

between what is true objectively and rationally, supported by evidence and illuminated by reason, and what is only a subjective judgment, divorced from the facts as they are and informed by prejudice and wishful thinking.

Human nature, in which the laws of politics have their roots, has not changed since the classical philosophies of China, India, and Greece endeavored to discover these laws. Hence, novelty is not necessarily a virtue in political theory, nor is old age a defect. . . .

For realism, theory consists in ascertaining facts and giving them meaning through reason. It assumes that the character of a foreign policy can be ascertained only through the examination of the political acts performed and of the foreseeable consequences of these acts. Thus we can find out what statesmen have actually done, and from the foreseeable consequences of their acts we can surmise what their objectives might have been.

Yet examination of the facts is not enough. To give meaning to the factual raw material of foreign policy, we must approach political reality with a kind of rational outline, a map that suggests to us the possible meanings of foreign policy. In other words, we put ourselves in the position of a statesman who must meet a certain problem of foreign policy under certain circumstances, and we ask ourselves what the rational alternatives are from which a statesman may choose who must meet this problem under these circumstances (presuming always that he acts in a rational manner), and which of these rational alternatives this particular statesman, acting under these circumstances, is likely to choose. It is the testing of this rational hypothesis against the actual facts and their consequences that gives theoretical meaning to the facts of international politics.

2. The main signpost that helps political realism to find its way through the landscape of international politics is the concept of interest defined in terms of power. This concept provides the link between reason trying to understand international politics and the facts to be understood. It sets politics as an autonomous sphere of action and understanding apart from other spheres, such as economics (understood in terms of interest defined as wealth), ethics, aesthetics, or religion. Without such a concept a theory of politics, international or domestic, would be altogether impossible, for without it we could not distinguish between political and nonpolitical facts, nor could we bring at least a measure of systematic order to the political sphere.

We assume that statesmen think and act in terms of interest defined as power, and the evidence of history bears that assumption out. That assumption allows us to retrace and anticipate, as it were, the steps a statesman—past, present, or future—has taken or will take on the political scene. We look over his shoulder when he writes his dispatches; we listen in on his conversation with other statesmen; we read and anticipate his very thoughts. Thinking in terms of interest defined as power, we think as he does, and as disinterested observers we understand his thoughts and actions perhaps better than he, the actor on the political scene, does himself.

The concept of interest defined as power imposes intellectual discipline upon the observer, infuses rational order into the subject matter of politics, and thus makes the theoretical understanding of politics possible. On the side of the actor, it provides for rational discipline in action and creates that astounding continuity in foreign policy which makes American, British, or Russian foreign policy appear as an intelligible, rational continuum, by and large consistent within itself, regardless of the different motives, preferences, and intellectual and moral qualities of successive statesmen. A realist theory of international politics, then, will guard against two popular fallacies: the concern with motives and the concern with ideological preferences. . . .

Good motives give assurance against deliberately bad policies; they do not guarantee the moral goodness and political success of the policies they inspire. What is important to know, if one wants to understand foreign policy, is not primarily the motives of a statesman, but his intellectual ability to comprehend the essentials of foreign policy, as well as his political ability to translate what he has comprehended into successful political action. It follows that while ethics in the abstract judges the moral qualities of motives, political theory must judge the political qualities of intellect, will, and action.

A realist theory of international politics will also avoid the other popular fallacy of equating the foreign policies of a statesman with his philosophic or political sympathies, and of deducing the former from the latter. Statesmen, especially under contemporary conditions, may well make a habit of presenting their foreign policies in terms of their philosophic and political sympathies in order to gain popular support for them. Yet they will distinguish with Lincoln between their "*official* duty," which is to think and act in terms of the national interest, and their "*personal* wish," which is to see their own moral values and political principles realized throughout the world. Political realism does not require, nor does it condone, indifference to political ideals and moral principles, but it requires indeed a sharp distinction between the desirable and the possible—between what is desirable everywhere and at all times and what is possible under the concrete circumstances of time and place.

It stands to reason that not all foreign policies have always followed so rational, objective, and unemotional a course. The contingent elements of personality, prejudice, and subjective preference, and of all the weaknesses of intellect and will which flesh is heir to, are bound to deflect foreign policies from their rational course. Especially where foreign policy is conducted under the conditions of democratic control, the need to marshal popular emotions to the support of foreign policy cannot fail to impair the rationality of foreign policy itself. Yet a theory of foreign policy which aims at rationality must for the time being, as it were, abstract from these irrational elements and seek to paint a picture of foreign policy which presents the rational essence to be found in experience, without the contingent deviations from rationality which are also found in experience. . . .

3. Realism assumes that its key concept of interest defined as power is an objective category which is universally valid, but it does not endow that concept with a meaning that is fixed once and for all. The idea of interest is indeed of the essence of politics and is unaffected by the circumstances of time and place. Thucydides' statement, born of the experiences of ancient Greece, that "identity of interests is the surest of bonds whether between states or individuals" was taken up in the nineteenth century by Lord Salisbury's remark that "the only bond of union that endures" among nations is "the absence of all clashing interests." . . .

Yet the kind of interest determining political action in a particular period of history depends upon the political and cultural context within which foreign policy is formulated. The goals that might be pursued by nations in their foreign policy can run the whole gamut of objectives any nation has ever pursued or might possibly pursue.

The same observations apply to the concept of power. Its content and the manner of its use are determined by the political and cultural environment. Power may comprise anything that establishes and maintains the control of man over man. Thus power covers all social relationships which serve that end, from physical violence to the most subtle psychological ties by which one mind controls another. Power covers the domination of man by man, both when it is disciplined by moral ends and controlled by constitutional safeguards, as in Western democracies, and when it is that untamed and barbaric force which finds its laws in nothing but its own strength and its sole justification in its aggrandizement. . . .

The realist parts company with other schools of thought before the all-important question of how the contemporary world is to be transformed. The realist is persuaded that this transformation can be achieved only through the workmanlike manipulation of the perennial forces that have shaped the past as they will the future. The realist cannot be persuaded that we can bring about that transformation by confronting a political reality that has its own laws with an abstract ideal that refuses to take those laws into account.

4. Political realism is aware of the moral significance of political action. It is also aware of the ineluctable tension between the moral command and the requirements of successful political action. And it is unwilling to gloss over and obliterate that tension and thus to obfuscate both the moral and the political issue by making it appear as though the stark facts of politics were morally more satisfying than they actually are, and the moral law less exacting than it actually is.

Realism maintains that universal moral principles cannot be applied to the actions of states in their abstract universal formulation, but that they must be filtered through the concrete circumstances of time and place. The individual may say for himself: "*Fiat justitia, pereat mundus* (Let justice be done, even if the world perish)," but the state has no right to say so in the name of those who are in its care. Both individual and state must judge political action by universal moral principles, such as that of liberty. Yet while the individual has a moral right to sacrifice himself in defense of such a moral principle, the state has no right to let its moral disapprobation of the infringement of liberty get in the way of successful political action, itself inspired by the moral principle of national survival. There can be no political morality without prudence; that is, without consideration of the political consequences of seemingly moral action. Realism, then, considers prudence—the weighing of the consequences of alternative political actions—to be the supreme virtue in politics. Ethics in the abstract judges action by its conformity with the moral law; political ethics judges action by its political consequences. . . .

5. Political realism refuses to identify the moral aspirations of a particular nation with the moral laws that govern the universe. As it distinguishes between truth and opinion, so it distinguishes between truth and idolatry. All nations are tempted—and few have been able to resist the temptation for long—to clothe their own particular aspirations and actions in the moral purposes of the universe. To know that nations are subject to the moral law is one thing, while to pretend to know with certainty what is good and evil in the relations among nations is quite another. There is a world of difference between the belief that all nations stand under the judgment of God, inscrutable to the human mind, and the blasphemous conviction that God is always on one's side and that what one wills oneself cannot fail to be willed by God also. . . .

[I]t is exactly the concept of interest defined in terms of power that saves us from both that moral excess and that political folly. For if we look at all nations, our own included, as political entities pursuing their respective interests defined in terms of power, we are able to do justice to all of them. And we are able to do justice to all of them in a dual sense: We are able to judge other nations as we judge our own and, having judged them in this fashion, we are then capable of pursuing policies that respect the interests of other nations, while protecting and promoting those of our own. Moderation in policy cannot fail to reflect the moderation of moral judgment.

6. The difference, then, between political realism and other schools of thought is real, and it is profound. However much the theory of political realism may have been misunderstood and misinterpreted, there is no gainsaying its distinctive intellectual and moral attitude to matters political.

Intellectually, the political realist maintains the autonomy of the political sphere, as the economist, the lawyer, the moralist maintain theirs. He thinks in terms of interest defined as power, as the economist thinks in terms of interest defined as wealth; the lawyer, of the conformity of action with legal rules; the moralist, of the conformity of action with moral principles. The economist asks: "How does this policy affect the wealth of society, or a segment of it?" The lawyer asks: "Is this policy in accord with the rules of law?" The moralist asks: "Is this policy in accord with moral principles?" And the political realist asks: "How does this policy affect the power of the nation?" (Or of the federal government, of Congress, of the party, of agriculture, as the case may be.)

The political realist is not unaware of the existence and relevance of standards of thought other than political ones. As political realist, he cannot but subordinate these other standards to those of politics. And he parts company with other schools when they impose standards of thought appropriate to other spheres upon the political sphere. It is here that political realism takes issue with the "legalistic-moralistic approach" to international politics. . . .

This realist defense of the autonomy of the political sphere against its subversion by other modes of thought does not imply disregard for the existence and importance of these other modes of thought. It rather implies that each should be assigned its proper sphere and function. Political realism is based upon a pluralistic conception of human nature. Real man is a composite of "economic man," "political man," "moral man," "religious man," etc. A man who was nothing but "political man" would be a beast, for he would be completely lacking in moral restraints. A man who was nothing but "moral man" would be a fool, for he would be completely lacking in prudence. A man who was nothing but "religious man" would be a saint, for he would be completely lacking in worldly desires.

Recognizing that these different facets of human nature exist, political realism also recognizes that in order to understand one of them one has to deal with it on its own terms. That is to say, if I want to understand "religious man," I must for the time being abstract from the other aspects of human nature and deal with its religious aspect as if it were the only one. Furthermore, I must apply to the religious sphere the standards of thought appropriate to it, always remaining aware of the existence of other standards and their actual influence upon the religious qualities of man. What is true of this facet of human nature is true of all the others. No modern economist, for instance, would conceive of his science and its relations to other sciences of man in any other way. It is exactly through such a process of emancipation from other standards of thought, and the development of one appropriate to its subject matter, that ecnomics has developed as an autonomous theory of the economic activities of man. To contribute to a similar development in the field of politics is indeed the purpose of political realism. . . .   **foCus**

Morgenthau's six principles of political realism offer a coherent and logical explanation of how foreign policy should be approached. However, his approach is limited by its emphasis on the rationality of decision-makers. However logical, careful, and prudent a state's chief foreign policy decision-makers are, a number of crucial factors lie beyond their control. Perhaps the most important is the often subtle, but powerful, impact of a state's central foreign policy bureaucracies. As was pointed out in Chapter 1, the bureaucracies possess significant power to influence decisions, such as: fragmenting information, failing to carry out fully direct orders by the president or his subordinates, frustrating policies by indecision or non-decision, and jealously guarding their turf through parochial goals and priorities. During the Cuban missile crisis, for example, both John F. Kennedy and Nikita Khrushchev were in many significant respects the hostages of their respective national security bureaucracies. Morgenthau's emphasis on the fundamental importance of wise leadership and decision-making is, of course, vital. While the role of the individual decision-maker is crucial in crisis situations, constraints on presidential action (in the case of the United States) cannot be ignored, as Kegley and Wittkopf suggest in Chapter 2. In attempting to divorce the study and practice of American foreign policy from the realm of subjective ideological assumptions, Morgenthau's analysis is valuable and insightful. A fundamental weakness of this analysis, however, is that it requires superhuman rationality and objectivity on the part of the individual decision-maker. Moreover, Morgenthau tends to oversimplify the concept of power in the relationships between individuals and groups, as well as complex organizations, including bureaucracies, states, and ideologies. The assumption that power is central to world affairs is based on an explicit and consistent belief about human nature, as well as theory about the behavior of individuals and the institutions with which they must interact. Because Morgenthau's essay includes logic, rationality, and the calculated pursuit of self-interest among its six principles of political realism, it restricts the range of the "acceptable" behavior of individuals and states in world politics. As long as individuals determine the foreign policies of states and complex hierarchical bureaucracies are central agents of government, Hans Morgenthau's theory of realism has limited universal applicability.

For all the limitations of Morgenthau's world view, his notion that the national interest can be defined as power continues to constitute an important justification for the actions of states. The following essay by Professor Robert W. Tucker illustrates the continuing influence that Morgenthau's emphasis on political realism casts on the analysis of contemporary American foreign policy. Tucker's article was published in 1979, and it attacks a number of central assumptions of Jimmy Carter's foreign policy. Central to Tucker's analysis is his belief in the Carter administration's unwillingness (Tucker calls it passivity) to act decisively in behalf of American interests. Tucker objects to a world view that places responsibility on the United States for some of the supposed ills of the contemporary international environment—in particular, economic inequalities between the wealthy developed capitalist states of the North and the impoverished developing societies of the South. Like Morgenthau, Tucker argues that American power must be exercised or it will decline or atrophy. Professor Tucker's analysis of why American foreign policy is under seige abroad and how it has been assaulted by the Carter administration's incorrect and damaging vision of power should be considered in light of the analysis of Reagan foreign policy provided by Charles Kegley and Eugene Wittkopf in Chapter 2.

OIL AND AMERICAN POWER—
SIX YEARS LATER

Robert W. Tucker, *Commentary*, September 1979

Robert W. Tucker is a professor of international relations at Johns Hopkins University.

It will soon be six years since the Organization of Petroleum Exporting Countries (OPEC) raised the price of its oil fourfold. Shortly thereafter the noted oil economist Walter J. Levy declared: "Rarely, if ever, in post-war history has the world been confronted with problems as serious as those caused by recent changes in the supply and price conditions of the world oil trade." At the time Levy wrote, his opinion was widely shared by knowledgeable observers. By 1976 and 1977, however, it appeared a distinct exaggeration to many. Now, in the late summer of 1979, it once again expresses the prevailing outlook. The relative optimism that characterized the years 1976-78 has suddenly given way to a pessimism in some respects more marked than the outlook of 1974.

In retrospect, the preceding years appear as a prolonged Indian summer, and a period during which preparations for winter were not undertaken or, for that matter, even generally acknowledged as necessary. Not surprisingly, the realization that the crisis brought on by the oil cartel has not passed, that it is a continuing one, and that its current phase holds out prospects even more serious perhaps than those anticipated in 1974, has resulted in a remarkable display of retrospective wisdom. Unfortunately, the wisdom is only retrospective. At that, much of it remains suspect. Doubt must surely persist whether the lessons of a recent past—a past that has cruelly betrayed one expectation after another—have been properly assimilated.

It is instructive to recall the earlier phases of the continuing crisis. The initial period began in the late fall of 1973 and ended in the early spring of 1975. Throughout 1974 the experts, through whose eyes most of us came to view the crisis, were divided between those who were persuaded that the oil cartel's actions would not hold, either because the cartel itself would fall apart or because the market would inevitably force a break in price, and those who, largely accepting the staying power of OPEC and the effectiveness of the new price structure, worried about devising a satisfactory means for settling the huge transfers of claims that loomed ahead. By the early months of 1975, the optimism of the former group was already beginning to wear thin. Although it was apparent that a cartel made up of sovereign states necessarily operated under considerable difficulties, and that these difficulties—above all, of allocation—would markedly increase in an easy market, it was equally apparent that OPEC showed little signs of breaking up. Indeed, as between the major producers and the major consumers, it was clearly the producers who had shown greater solidarity.

At the same time, however, the fears of the pessimists had begun to recede, and would continue to do so in the period immediately to follow. For the dangers that had so aroused the apprehension of the pessimists, and in terms of which most of them had largely defined the crisis, had not come to pass. What had seemed very nearly impossible at the outset, a solution whereby consumers continued to receive at least minimally necessary supplies of oil while the claims of producers were met in a manner satisfactory to them, now appeared possible and even quite manageable. To be sure, the solution was admittedly not without its vulnerable features. It depended upon the avoidance of further exorbitant price increases (though rises in nominal, as opposed to rises in real—i.e., inflation-adjusted—oil prices were expected). It also depended upon a continuing high level of imports by the producer countries, together with a system of recycling the still very considerable surplus of petrodollars in such a manner that the weaker countries— developed and developing—could continue to borrow in the capital markets of the stronger in order to meet their oil-related deficits. Any of these conditions was subject to change and thus to the reemergence of fears widely entertained at the outset. But with the passage of time, a considerable measure of confidence grew over arrangements that were never more than fragile.

Thus the apparent easing of the crisis by the spring of 1975 largely followed from the manner in which the crisis had been defined by expert consensus. On this definition, the great and immediate question was, how could the world pay for OPEC oil? A technical question, to be answered by technical means, it reflected the view that the transfer of wealth now to be exacted by the cartel was secondary in importance to the ways by which this wealth might be transferred without dangerously disruptive effects.

The answer emerged, or seemed to emerge, in the developments of late 1974 and 1975. Of these developments, the worst recession since the 1930's proved critical. By markedly reducing the demand for OPEC oil, the sharp economic downturn insured that the real world price of petroleum would remain relatively stable and, as it turned out, even decline moderately. The cost of this insurance proved very high, however. What is more, it was an ominous harbinger, for it indicated that in the absence of new non-OPEC sources of oil of sufficient magnitude to supply the incremental needs of consumers, the movement toward resumption of substantial growth would sooner or later run up against either the constraints on supply imposed by the cartel or—even should supply constraints be moderately relaxed—by the constraints of sharply rising prices.

The pervasive tendency among experts to see the crisis in predominantly economic terms accounts for what now must appear as the rather unguarded optimism of the years 1976-78. That optimism sprang for the most part from the assumption of continued price stability. Even among the less optimistic, it was assumed that the world oil price would remain relatively stable until sometime in the middle 1980's when demand would rise beyond a level that could be met by world supply, OPEC and non-OPEC. At this point, the conditions of 1973 would be repeated, and though the pressures would be less severe than on an earlier occasion, they were still expected to result in a major unilateral price rise by the cartel. Until that time, the world could expect relative price stability. . . . The powerful economic counterforces OPEC had called into being—counterforces of conservation, of rejuvenation (whether of coal, oil, or gas), and of development (oil, natural gas liquids, and natural gas)—would correct the energy disequilibrium of the early 1970's.

Have the optimists been discredited by the events of the past eight months? Not necessarily. It may be argued—as, indeed, some do now argue—that the recent OPEC price increases, though admittedly unexpected, will only serve to give added momentum to those counterforces already set in motion, that what had been happening as a result of the incentive provided by $13 per barrel will happen all the more rapidly given the incentive of $20 per barrel. Setting this argument aside for the moment, the point remains—and it is an all-important one—that the very large price rise was unexpected prior to the persisting cutback in Iranian production. Even after it was apparent that the cutback would result in a major unilateral price action by the cartel, the eventual size of the increase came as a surprise. And we may not yet have seen the end of this year's increase.

The experts are not to be criticized for failing to have foreseen what most of the political analysts who should have been sensitive to the trend of events in Iran nevertheless failed to foresee. But they are to be faulted for their persistent failure to have grasped the broader significance of the actions taken by the OPEC states in 1973-74. It was this failure that led to the unwarranted confidence in continued price stability, at least for the immediate years ahead. Price stability could not be considered apart from the political framework conditioning OPEC actions and Western responses. That framework, however, had been profoundly altered by actions which called into question the issue of secure Western access to Persian Gulf oil.

In taking the actions they did, the cartel members not only asserted a right to determine the price of their oil and to maintain the price by refusing to produce in excess of a certain level. They also asserted a right to deny access to an indispensable source of energy for reasons and in circumstances of their choosing. Such denial is implicit in the act of price setting itself, which of course necessitates the restriction of supply. In a broad sense, then, the very raison d'être of OPEC has been the denial of access in order to increase the market value of its members' oil reserves over what they would have been in the absence of the cartel. This is why the argument that was once heard—that our differences with OPEC were simply differences over "prices"—was either obtuse or disingenuous. For the prices could not be separated from the means taken to maintain the prices, and the means—principally restriction of supply—constituted a form of denying access.

Still, it is in a more conventional sense of the term that denial of access is understood and employed. In this sense, it is identified with what are considered to be specifically political circumstances and motivations. This was the meaning of the 1973-74 embargo, and though that particular denial was little more than symbolic in its effects, the assertion of the right together with the absence of a clear challenge in response were significant.

In the years between the 1973-74 embargo and the revolution in Iran, the question persisted whether the Western states had through word and action legitimized the claimed right to denial of access. If the answer appeared unclear prior to the fall of last year, events since that time have gone quite far toward removing former doubt. Western passivity before the total cutoff of Iranian production during the brief period of intense political upheaval and, of much greater importance, continued passivity in response to the decision of the new regime to limit production severely for the present and indefinite future, prompt the conclusion that the claimed right has now been legitimized. . . .

[I]t is clear that the third, and present, phase of the continuing crisis that began with the revolution in Iran differs from the preceding phases in that it was brought on almost entirely by a political event *par excellence*. That event has already had, and will continue to have, momentous economic consequences. It has already led to a price rise of between 50 and 60 per cent, a rise that has evoked anew the question asked at the outset of the oil crisis: how can the world—and particularly the developing states—pay for OPEC oil? It has condemned the industrial countries to at least several years of very slow growth (and to no growth at all in the following year for the American economy), with all the attendant side effects. It has for the time being relieved the OPEC states of dealing with the difficult problems of allocation. Most important, perhaps, it has pointed up a lesson to the principal members of the cartel that they may well be expected to heed in the future—namely, that short of pushing the industrial West into sheer economic chaos, and thus bringing the entire international system down, their best course of action is to produce only so much as they need for sound development, to stretch out the life of their reserves, and to operate on the assumption that oil kept in the ground is a better, and safer, investment than dollar deposits. There was a time when expert opinion inclined to the view that this strategy carried considerable risk for the producers and would likely prove self-defeating. Now, there is much less assurance on this score.

These consequences, to repeat, have followed from the signal event of political revolution in Iran and the subsequent decision of the new Iranian government to keep oil production to approximately half of its former level. They are the direct result of the loss of access suffered by the major industrial consumers in 1973-74. A major producer has chosen to assert a claim the West no longer appears to contest.

Thus attempts to explain the current phase of the continuing crisis as one of supply, thereby laying the blame for the price rise on the West (and particularly on this country), are simply misplaced. There was no problem of supply prior to last fall. Instead, there was a problem—for the cartel—of a continuing surplus which, though modest, was quite sufficient to compel moderation and frustrate the desires of the price hawks. The measures of energy conservation taken by the consumers, the reduced rate of growth that followed upon the recession, and the bringing onstream of new sources of non-OPEC energy, combined to limit the demand for OPEC oil. But the Iranian cutback suddenly altered this emergent pattern and presented the cartel with a golden opportunity. It is ludicrous to see that opportunity as the result of growing scarcity of supplies, brought about in turn by a profligate America that refuses to curb its wasteful consumption of energy. Supplies, both OPEC and non-OPEC, were not becoming more scarce, despite a modest increase in demand between 1973 and 1978, but marginally greater. The explanation of growing scarcity of supply induced by ever rising consumption no doubt serves the purpose of Saudi Arabia's Ahmed Zaki Yamani, but it remains a mystery why this explanation should be accepted by so many in the West who have every reason to know better.

The American government's response to the latest actions of the oil cartel has followed, in the main, a now familiar pattern. The Carter administration, in the manner of its predecessors, can find no effective way for the present to challenge the power of OPEC. Indeed, until very recently, the President could not bring himself even to the point of voicing criticism of the cartel. One was almost led to believe that he considered OPEC, as have many others since 1974, a kind of blessing in disguise to the extent that it served to drive home the lesson that we must mend our wasteful ways and, even more, we must seriously consider the dangers confronting societies which make material growth their overriding imperative.

President Carter recently returned to this theme in his much-heralded address to the nation on the energy crisis, when he identified America's crisis of confidence largely with our tendency to "worship self-indulgence and consumption" and our sudden realization that "piling up material goods cannot fill the emptiness of lives which have no confidence or purpose." It does no harm to be reminded that man does not live by bread alone. But it seems doubtful that the contrary belief is at the root of America's present crisis of confidence, assuming such to exist. If there is a crisis of confidence today, it is in large measure owing to the fact that a society committed to constant improvement in its standard of living—what President Carter chooses to term "piling up material goods"—now finds this commitment increasingly elusive of achievement. One reason it does so is the inability of successive administrations, including the present one, to act effectively and with dispatch to meet the challenge of the oil producers' cartel.

This inability has been openly and repeatedly conceded by the President and his subordinates. If anything, President Carter has gone out of his way to emphasize our impotence at present, and for many years ahead, to break the cartel's power over the world oil market. As late as February of this year, he dismissed as an "idle hope" the view that the United States might somehow break up or intimidate the cartel and thereby drive down the price of world oil. . . .

But the taking of effective and speedy action internally has been rejected by President Carter. In his energy program he accepted neither a market solution nor an administered solution for a substantial and immediate reduction in the amount of gasoline consumed by the public. At the same time, the prospect of taking effective action externally, which can only mean serious confrontation with the cartel, remains as far from the consideration of this administration as it was from preceding administrations. The President may at last believe the "vivid statement" he has quoted to the nation from his correspondence— "Our neck is stretched over the fence and OPEC has a knife"—but he has shown no disposition to consider any action against OPEC which, even if it would not remove the knife altogether, might at least cause it to be held at a greater distance. Although the policy of appeasing OPEC that has been followed for nearly six years clearly has not worked, and shows no prospect of working, Washington remains as committed to it as ever in everything but its rhetoric.

What has changed in the American, and Western, response to OPEC's actions is the manner in which these actions are now increasingly viewed. In contrast to 1974-75, the challenge of the cartel is now seen less in terms of a new egalitarianism to which many American, and Western, elites in varying degree only recently subscribed and more in terms of a conventional contest of states for wealth and power. The initial sympathy evidenced here and in Europe for the ostensible ends of OPEC actions reflected a preoccupation with what were considered unjust and even dangerous international in-equalities of income and wealth. And while this preoccupation was never marked among the governing elites of the major Western states, and clearly not in the administrations of Richard Nixon and Gerald Ford, it is a matter of record that a substantial number of those appointed to high office in the Carter administration did once entertain views which might readily have found in OPEC the historic agent, however imperfect, for giving momentum to a great and necessary transformation. The emphasis on North-South rather than East-West relations, the insistence that North-South relations required a "world-order" politics in place of a balance-of-power politics, and the conviction that equality—individual and collective—was the overriding desi-deratum of global politics in the late 20th century, inclined the present administration to look on OPEC with tolerance and even sympathy.

There is something of this outlook left in the Carter administration, but not much. The continued appeasement of OPEC cannot be traced today to sympathy for a more egalitarian international system. Nor can it be attributed to any lingering sense of contrition for the past sins of the West. The disastrous effects of the cartel's actions on the non-oil-producing developing countries have dampened egalitarian sentiments, just as the effects of the cartel's actions on Western economies have sobered those who once justified OPEC's depredations in the name of atonement. What is left today in the response to the cartel is simply appeasement.

Moreover, it is appeasement destitute even of the pragmatic justification that is normally put forth in defense of such a policy. For there is no evidence that in this instance the policy has either bought needed time or has led to moderation on the part of those demanding change once their initial demands were met. Instead, after a brief period, and when the opportunity again arose, these demands were merely escalated.

The erosion of American power that has resulted from OPEC's actions seems so apparent as scarcely to warrant comment, for its signs are everywhere. Indeed, a persuasive case may be made to the effect that it is the oil cartel, and not the rising military power of the Soviet Union, that has formed the greatest threat in the 1970's to the structure of American interests and commitments in the world. Quite apart from the specific constraints on American power (e.g., in the Middle East) that have been consequent upon our passivity before OPEC, there is the general, and altogether critical, constraint consequent upon the loss of credibility before allies and adversaries.

Yet there persists a strong disposition to question the gravity of the cartel's challenge to the American global position. In this respect, as in others, there is a marked parallel between the responses made to the twin challenges presented by OPEC and by the Soviet Union. In both instances, the challenge has been seen either as grossly exaggerated or, to the extent it is acknowledged, as rooted in our own shortcomings as a nation. In the case of the Soviet Union's relentless military build-up, the emphasis has been on the exaggeration of the threat by the "alarmists" among us who are unwilling to confront the "fact" that the utility of military power has markedly declined. In the case of OPEC, it is presumably our almost willful failure to change a way of life that continues to hold us in thralldom to the cartel. In either case, the result is to rationalize the abandonment of power and position, since it is only slightly less difficult to effect a sudden transformation in a nation's way of life than it would be to create a world in which military power might be discounted to the extent that certain advocates now equate with reality.

But the main erosion of American power which the challenge of the oil cartel has effected is to be found in the challenge itself and, of course, in this nation's general reaction to it. It was the absence then and now of an effective American response to the actions of OPEC that has signaled as no other event of the preceding decade the erosion of American power. The power of nations is commonly measured by their capacity and willingness to vindicate interests regarded as vital to their security and well-being. There is no question that access on reasonable terms to a source of energy indispensable to this nation and its major allies constitutes a vital interest. Since 1974 the security of this interest has at the very least been a matter of serious doubt. Yet the United States has consistently maintained a posture of passivity before each successive challenge to this interest.

It is only to labor the obvious to point out that there is an inescapable linkage drawn by friend and foe between our credibility, or rather the lack thereof, for employing power in this instance and in other situations, yet to arise, where our interests may be threatened. Whereas the American response to OPEC has given our major allies further reason to distinguish their interests from ours, it has given the Soviet Union reason to believe those interests more vulnerable to inroads than it had once thought.

If the price attached to the main erosion of American power consequent upon our passivity before OPEC's actions has yet to be paid, the same cannot be said of the subsidiary erosion of that power. The effects of a weakened domestic economy and of an equally weakened dollar on the American capacity to act effectively in the world are daily apparent.

Less apparent, though no less real, are the effects of the loss of American power to influence events in the Middle East. Having abandoned the direct search for a comprehensive settlement of the Arab-Israeli conflict in favor of a separate peace between Egypt and Israel, in the hope that out of such a peace a comprehensive settlement will emerge in time, the administration now finds itself unable to obtain support for its new policy from either Saudi Arabia or Jordan. This failure is perhaps the clearest measure of the erosion of our power and influence in the region. In the case of Jordan, a small client state has simply rejected American overtures that it enter into the broader negotiations dealing with the status of the Palestinians in the West Bank. In the case of Saudi Arabia, the principal supplier of imported oil to this country has not only declared its open opposition to the Egyptian-Israeli peace but has taken measures to give this opposition effect.

In southern Africa too, American policy reflects a sense of growing vulnerability to the power of a major OPEC supplier. Nigeria provides approximately 10 per cent of our current imports. The government in Lagos has declared that it will not tolerate American—or British—recognition of the new government in Rhodesia or the lifting of sanctions and that, in the words of General Obasanjo, if such actions are nevertheless taken they will be "met with an appropriate response"—presumably an oil boycott. The Nigerian government lacks the delicacy and diplomatic finesse of the Saudi Arabian government, whose leaders are adept at putting their threats in the guise of rewards for desired behavior—always a more palatable bargaining tactic. In either case, however, the results have been to place serious constraints on American policy. Nor are the merits of policy in the Middle East or in southern Africa of relevance here. Whatever the merits of policy, the point of significance is the extent to which American freedom of action has been compromised by virtue of the fear entertained of OPEC oil power.

To ask whether the erosion of American power can be stopped, if not reversed, is in effect to ask whether there is a satisfactory resolution of the continuing crisis. Few doubt that there is a resolution in the long run, when we will have become much more efficient than today in the use of energy and when we will have found major new sources of energy. But these developments, we are told, will not come to pass before another decade has elapsed and perhaps not even then. If this is the case, the problem is what, if anything, can be done in the interim. Is there any promising way of satisfactorily resolving—or, at least, materially easing—the crisis in the immediate years ahead? . . .

The major alternative strategy, rejected by the President, is one that would seek an immediate reduction of imports. The reduction might be achieved either through the mechanism of the market or through rationing. In either case, it would probably run in the neighborhood of 10 per cent. Even if we assume a slightly higher reduction of one million barrels a day, the question remains whether this would, as its advocates insist, tame OPEC. One may reasonably doubt that it would. After all, the cartel weathered a far more substantial cutback in consumption during the recession of the mid-1970's, and there is no apparent reason for assuming it could not do so again. Moreover, the optimism that regularly attends advocacy of a strategy of an immediate cut in imported petroleum must be tempered by the events of the past eight months. Having unexpectedly experienced the beneficial effects of a tight market, brought on not by the play of economic forces but by a political event, the cartel members may well redouble their efforts in the future to subordinate the law of supply and demand to political decision. No doubt, a strategy designed for the immediate reduction of imports can easily be justified as desirable in its own right. Taken alone, however, it is not an action whose effects the cartel would find difficult to absorb.

Does a different and more optimistic conclusion emerge if we add to the effects of this strategy the pressures on OPEC that some expect to result from the increasing supplies of non-OPEC oil (and gas)? In the years between 1973 and 1978, world oil consumption rose 1.5 million barrels per day. During the same period supplies of oil from non-OPEC sources rose almost 3.5 million. The need for OPEC oil thereby decreased by some 2 million. The Iranian cut in exports of 3 million changed an oil market from one of glut to one of scarcity (the shortage estimated between 1 and 1.5 million barrels per day). These figures suggest, and some would argue they demonstrably show, that in the absence of the unexpected in Iran, the world oil market was clearly moving in the direction of displacing OPEC from its role as supplier of first resort to that of last resort. They are seen to presage a time that is not far removed when OPEC will no longer have the power to set the world price for oil and, no longer enjoying this power, will itself founder. Iran interrupted this development. But despite the interruption, and the economic dislocation caused by the resulting increase in world prices, the trend toward replacing OPEC as supplier of first resort is expected to continue and even quicken under the impetus of $20-per-barrel oil. . . .

Whether in the year immediately ahead or in the longer four- to five-year period, then, the expectation is that the cartel will encounter the glut it did in the years 1975-77. And should this happen, the cartel will again be confronted with problems of allocation, this time more difficult to deal with than before. Whereas in previous years the major oil companies still assumed the task of allocation for the cartel members, today their role has been very substantially reduced. The members themselves must agree on their respective shares of a smaller market and unless the Saudis are willing to absorb most of the cut—which is considered doubtful—the failure to allocate shares will eventually give rise to serious rifts in the cartel and to competitive selling and price cutting. If in these circumstances the American government were to impose a strict quota on OPEC imports or, even better, to institute a system of sealed bidding on such imports, the stage would be set for breaking the cartel's hold on the world price.

In brief outline, this is the optimistic view of how the crisis may be resolved before those long-range developments have proceeded sufficiently to yield a more permanent solution. For all its apparent optimism it still entails a very stiff price and holds out not inconsiderable dangers. Our deliverance from OPEC is to be achieved by at least five very lean years and quite possibly a considerably longer period. What may transpire politically in the United States during these years is anyone's guess.

Serious as they are, it is not these considerations that engender the deepest skepticism with respect to the above view. Nor is it the heated and unresolved dispute over whether the Soviet Union will continue to export oil and, if so, how much, or turn into an importer by the mid-1980's. The future role of the Soviet Union in the world oil market might well be a factor of major importance in the evolution of the crisis. For our purposes it may be set aside (though not without noting that it introduces yet another element of uncertainty). What cannot be set aside, let alone taken as given, are some of the inarticulate assumptions on which the above view implicitly rests. One such assumption is that the cartel members have learned very little in recent years about the necessary conditions for maintaining their hold on the world oil market. But what evidence we have would seem to indicate they have learned a good deal, perhaps more than the hapless consumers. Recent experience has taught them that if they can concert their actions, the kind of decreases in demand they will have to face can be made up, and perhaps more than made up, by reducing their exports and maintaining a tight market. In the bargain, they will also be able to stretch out the life of their reserves, a prospect that appears—with good reason—increasingly attractive to them. Nor does this assessment depend upon Saudi Arabia's willingness to bear the brunt of a reduction alone. Others—Iran, Kuwait, Libya, perhaps even Iraq—may show a willingness to reduce exports if and when necessary to maintain price. Given the strength of the cartel's position today, there are a number of members able to reduce their output without enduring financial pain.

What is essentially a market solution to the continuing crisis also must, and does, pass over in silence the crucial problem of security of access to Middle Eastern oil. What happened in Iran this past year may happen in Saudi Arabia next year (and not because Saudi Arabia is "another Iran," which it obviously is not, but because Saudi Arabia has its own sources of instability). There are any number of possibilities for the disruption of Persian Gulf oil supplies, quite apart from the possibility of overt or covert aggression that is Soviet-inspired and supported. If Iran taught us anything, it is that the principal—though not the sole—threat to security of access comes from the purely indigenous forces of the region, whether these forces are confined within the borders of a state or operate across state boundaries.

If these considerations have merit they can but point to one conclusion. There is very little prospect in the decade ahead for stopping, let alone reversing, the steady erosion of American power consequent upon OPEC's actions—so long as we persist in viewing the crisis as an economic event and continue seeking its resolution by economic means.

This view of the oil crisis as an economic event has been the great and persisting illusion that has marked the American response from the outset. If we have failed to resolve the crisis, the reason is not simply our failure to take the right economic measures, but our failure to face the fact that economic measures are by themselves insufficient. It would be foolish to deny that we might have pursued a number of domestic measures which, had they been acted upon immediately, would by this time have substantially alleviated our plight. But it is important to realize that impressive corrective measures have nevertheless been made. In the past six years there has been a decline of energy consumption in relation to real GNP of approximately 10 per cent. In addition, the rejuvenation of what had been no more than marginally productive sources of oil and gas, together with the search for new sources, adds up to no mean record, particularly in light of a government policy that has held out many disincentives to such ventures. In spite of all this, the crisis remains, and even given a much better record at home in the past six years, it would still have been with us.

Today it appears less likely than ever that there is in the short run a satisfactory, or even a tolerable, economic solution to the continuing crisis. And it is, to repeat, the short run with which we must be above all concerned, if only for the reason that we can know little of the long run and that even if we knew as much as some would pretend, it is only through enduring in the short run that we may reach the long run.

If there is no satisfactory economic solution to the crisis that has erupted again with greater force than almost anyone expected, it is because, like it or not, we are dealing with issues which are quintessentially political. As such, they can be resolved, if at all, only by political means. Until recently it has almost unquestioningly been accepted that we can and must avoid a confrontation with OPEC. But for many, this view has been predicated on the assumption that confrontation was quite unnecessary, that there were distinct limits to the transfer of wealth and power which would accrue to the cartel members, and that this transfer would not place serious constraints on growth at home and policy abroad. What that assumption really came down to was the belief that we could beat OPEC at its own game, whether because we were intrinsically superior at playing the game or because we still held, after all, the trumps. But this belief has now been exposed as hollow. Indeed, the administration has conceded that at the level we have played the game to date, and this is the level at which it is still resolutely committed to playing, we do not have any effective trumps—at least, none that can be played for a number of years to come. The continued avoidance of confrontation with OPEC now holds no other prospect than further concession to its demands.

It is difficult to see the present resignation persisting indefinitely. If nothing else, the events of the past few months have rudely torn the veil of illusion that has obscured our true position and revealed it for what it is. This is why more serious consideration is already being given to the prospects of confrontation. These prospects are not exhausted by the employment of military power. The insistence that they are is more often than not motivated by the desire to do nothing at all. But they cannot exclude the possible use of military power without compromising their effectiveness from the start. The logic of political confrontation over interests as great as those at stake in the oil crisis can have no rigidly prescribed limits and it serves no useful purpose to pretend otherwise.   **fOCUs**

Robert Tucker's critique of Carter's foreign policy and OPEC's real potential to limit the United States' access to oil challenges a world view that envisions the Third World nations as the victims of historical Western colonialism and economic imperialism. Tucker's analysis, however, overlooks two crucial questions. First, Tucker's emphasis on the necessity of maintaining America's status as a superpower fails to recognize the absolute reductions of American power which have resulted from increasing global interdependence. This diminishing power is illustrated by the U.S. dependence on OPEC oil as well as the chronic balance of payments deficits since the early 1960s. Second, Tucker presumes that the United States possesses the capabilities (and one must conclude that Tucker ultimately means military capabilities) to force OPEC to provide the U.S. and the West with access to its oil. How could the U.S. guarantee access to OPEC oil? The only answer might be the invasion and occupation of the Middle Eastern oil fields themselves. Moreover, advocating a military solution implies the president has the ability to secure the consent of Congress, which is by no means a foregone conclusion in the wake of Vietnam and Watergate. Yet, it was Jimmy Carter who, following the Soviet invasion of Afghanistan, endorsed the right of the United States' intervention in the Middle East.

The inconsistencies in the Carter administration's foreign policy remain troubling. For many Americans, as Robert Tucker's essay illustrates, Jimmy Carter's outlook was naive and dangerous. For example, his emphasis on human rights and openness to the Third World demands for the creation of a new international economic order demanded a change in the fundamental interests and values of American foreign policies. In order for a new, more equitable global system to emerge, the United States had to take the lead in helping to restructure *traditional patterns* of power politics. Thus, on a rhetorical and symbolic level, American foreign policy changed course between 1977 and 1978. Jimmy Carter proposed an alternative to the Nixon-Kissinger emphasis on power politics. The

Panama Canal Treaty, negotiations for the second Strategic Arms Limitation Agreement (SALT II) and Carter's human rights policies seemed to be new departures for American foreign policy.

Jimmy Carter's vision of a complex interdependent world changed abruptly in 1979, however. With the Soviet invasion of Afghanistan and the seizure of American hostages in Iran, Carter became obsessed with the decline of American power. President Carter withdrew the SALT Treaty in protest over the situation in Afghanistan before the U.S. Senate voted on its ratification. The Soviet Union had already ratified SALT II. The Carter administration proposed a 25 percent increase in the U.S. defense budget while developing plans for the deployment of the huge MX missile system in the southwestern United States. President Carter ordered the establishment of a Rapid Deployment Force of 100,000 troops in order to protect vital American interests overseas—for example, the Middle East oil fields. The Carter administration initiated the mechanisms to create military conscription. Reagan foreign policy has continued to follow most of the policies initiated in the last two years of the Carter presidency.

What accounts for the transformation of Carter's foreign policy between 1977-1978 and 1979-1980? Three sets of factors help to explain the sudden shifts. First, growing fears of expanding Soviet power were expressed among the leaders of American public opinion: the mass media, members of Congress, and the foreign policy elite. Second, there were at least three competing visions of what American foreign policy should become. The competition among Secretary of State Cyrus Vance, National Security Advisor Zbigniew Brzezinski, and U.S. Ambassador to the United Nations Andrew Young hampered Jimmy Carter's effectiveness in presenting cohesive and consistent foreign policies. Cyrus Vance's middle-of-the-road position was often undermined by Andrew Young's emphasis on Third World issues and Zbigniew Brzezinski's power-politics approach to East-West issues. By attempting to reconcile such divergent perspectives, Jimmy Carter's authority in foreign policy making was compromised. An aura of indecision and non-decision permeated Carter's foreign policy, particularly in the wake of the Soviet invasion of Afghanistan and the crisis in Iran. Third, many of the *initial assumptions* of Carter's foreign policy called for fundamental alterations in longstanding goals and values. Jimmy Carter's emphasis on human rights and Third World issues could not be implemented in a consistent manner without reversing the political, economic, and military goals which have characterized U.S. foreign policy since World War II, as Chapters 7 and 8 will illustrate. Thus, the Carter administration was handicapped by a lack of realism concerning Soviet intentions and bureaucratic in-fighting over appropriate policies. Despite Jimmy Carter's hard-line stand toward the Soviet Union in 1979 and 1980, the public's perceptions of his inconsistency and naivete drastically limited public acceptance of the goals and achievements of Carter's foreign policy.

The third essay by Paul M. Sweezy and Harry Magdoff, "U.S. Foreign Policy in the 1980s," written in April 1980, suggests a radically different perspective from that presented by Robert Tucker. For Sweezy and Magdoff, the power of American foreign policy is not rooted exclusively in nuclear capabilities, but in the direction of the world's capitalist system. Hence, Sweezy and Magdoff have noted a progressive decline in the absolute power of both the United States and the Soviet Union since the zenith of cold war antagonisms in the mid-1950s. With the gradual but progressive fragmentation of the American-dominated sphere of influence and its Soviet counterpart, Third World countries have increasingly resisted domination by the superpowers. American foreign policy, therefore, remains only as strong as the capitalist economic forces which structure or shape the political, ideological, and cultural conflicts which emerge. The national liberation movements which challenge U.S. economic and political interests can be seen as the most menacing political developments facing U.S. foreign policy.

U.S. FOREIGN POLICY IN THE 1980's

Paul M. Sweezy and Harry Magdoff, *Review of the Month,* April 1980

Paul M. Sweezy and Harry Magdoff are the editors of the Monthly Review.

The trouble with most discussions of U.S. foreign policy, on the left as well as on the right, is that they are placed in a totally inappropriate framework of assumptions and preconceptions. The most important of these is that the United States and the Soviet Union are locked in a gigantic superpower struggle for world supremacy. This is seen as *the* number one contradiction in the world today to which all other contradictions and conflicts are subordinate. From this premise it is assumed to follow that a gain by either side is, directly or indirectly, a loss for the other. In other words, the superpowers are playing what is called a zero-sum game: a plus for one is cancelled out by a minus for the other; it is impossible for both to gain or lose at the same time.

Into this theoretical framework there is inserted an empirically observed trend, namely, that the curve of U.S. power and influence in the world has been declining ever since it reached an historic peak at the end of the Second World War. The obverse of this, derived from the underlying theory but rarely subjected to any sort of empirical scrutiny, is that the curve of Soviet power and influence has been rising during the same period. The supposed coexistence of these closely interrelated trends, taken to be the dominant characteristic of the whole postwar period, has gradually assumed the status of a self-evident axiom which forms the starting point of all reasoning about gross politics and international relations.

The most consistent expression of this view is the well known Chinese doctrine—which clearly constitutes the actual premise of Chinese policy— that there are two imperialisms in the world today, the American and the Russian, and that the former is in decline and on the defensive while the latter is in the ascendency and on the offensive. Exactly the same thought, though of course couched in different terms, has long figured in the shaping and execution of American policy, most notably in the aftermath of the Soviet invasion of Afghanistan. It is hardly an exaggeration to say that the reaction to this event in the United States*—at the governmental level as well as in the

---

*A typical example of this reaction appears in a letter to the editor of the *New York Times* (March 12th): "In his appearance before the Senate Foreign Relations Committee on Feb. 27, Ambassador George Kennan accused the Carter administration of overreacting to the Soviet invasion of Afghanistan. . . . The ambassador expresses concern over what he perceives as a developing war psychology. But surely he must recognize, better than most, that Russia's unimpeded advances have been encouraged by the perceived indifference and lack of will and capacity of the United States. Now we are at the point of recovering both our awareness and our resolve. We are starting to combine our resolve with that of others into an effective force for peace."

realm of public opinion—would be totally incomprehensible except in the context of this theory of the two imperialisms, one declining and one rising.

There are two basic flaws in this interpretation of the post-Second World War period. First, there is no reason for the *a priori* assumption that the superpower game is of the zero-sum variety. Logically they could both gain or lose at the same time: it is a question of fact, not of theory. And second, a serious examination of the record clearly points to the conclusion that during the last two decades *both* superpowers have in fact been losing power and influence. In the case of the United States this is obvious; indeed, as mentioned earlier, the decline begins much sooner, certainly no later than the collapse of the Chiang Kai-shek regime in China and the victory of the Communists in 1949. Interestingly, the decline in Soviet power and influence also begins with the "loss" of China, made definitive by the Sino-Soviet split of 1960. Since then the Soviet Union has had successes and failures in the international arena, but the failures have outweighed the successes and the overall trend has been down. This is the conclusion of a sober, factual investigation by the Washington-based Center for Defense Information.** So important are the findings of this study that we reproduce here the complete summary as presented in the document itself:

Defense Monitor in Brief

• American fears of Soviet geopolitical momentum strongly affect U.S. foreign and military policy.

• A comprehensive study of trends of Soviet world influence in 155 countries since World War II does not support perceptions of consistent Soviet advances and devastating U.S. setbacks.

• Outside Eastern Europe, Soviet influence has lacked staying power. Inability to accumulate influence in foreign countries over long periods is a dominant feature of Soviet world involvement.

• Starting from a very low base of political, economic, and military involvement, the Soviets have increased their influence around the world. Starting with influence in 9 percent of the world's nations in 1945, they peaked at 14 percent in the late 1950s, and today have influence in 12 percent of the world's nations. Of the 155 countries in the world today, the Soviets have influence in 19.

• The Soviets have been successful in gaining influence primarily among the world's poorest and most desperate countries.

• Soviet foreign involvement has to a large extent been shaped by indigenous conditions, and the Soviets have been unable to command loyalty or obedience.

**"Soviet Geopolitical Momentum: Myth or Menace—Trends of Soviet Influence Around the World from 1945 to 1980," *The Defense Monitor* (January 1980), published by the Center for Defense Information, 122 Maryland Ave., NE, Washington, DC 20022. Copies of this issue of *The Defense Monitor* can be obtained from Halcyon House, Inc., 67 Byron Rd., Weston, MA 02193 at $1 for single copies.

● Soviet setbacks in China, Indonesia, Egypt, India, and Iraq dwarf marginal Soviet advances in lesser countries.

● Temporary Soviet successes in backward countries have proved costly to the Soviet Union. They provide no justification for American alarmism or military intervention. U.S. policies should emphasize our non-military advantages in the competition for world influence.

The most significant of these conclusions is not the one relating to the number and proportion of countries in which the Soviet Union is judged to have influence but rather the next to the last item calling attention to the large and important countries in which the Soviet Union has *lost* influence during the last two decades. This record, on the face of it, is simply not compatible with the belief in a rising and aggressively successful Soviet imperialism. Nor is there any reason to believe that current efforts of the Soviet Union to expand its influence in such areas as Indochina, the Horn of Africa, and Southern Africa are meeting with significantly more success than similar efforts have achieved in the past.

It is very important to understand this, since it relates to the present and future rather than simply to what happened in the past. It is easy for the Soviet Union to get involved in almost any area of the Third World you may care to designate. In all of them without exception complex national and class struggles are in process. In terms of money and arms the contending forces are weak and needy, and the Soviet Union is an ample source of both. Political and ideological barriers prevent some of the contestants from approaching or accepting aid from the Soviet Union. This applies mainly to defenders of the status quo who find the United States a better and more congenial source of supply. But nationalist and revolutionary forces, whether on the offensive or defensive, rarely have scruples of this kind and eagerly accept Soviet aid, usually without giving or indeed being able to give anything concrete in return. The result is that the Soviet Union frequently gets into situations in which it plays an important role for a time but from which it derives no lasting benefit or influence and from which indeed it may be unable to extricate itself without serious economic and political costs.

A classic example of this kind is provided by the Horn of Africa. As long as Ethiopia was a U.S. client state, the Soviet Union gave aid to the Eritrean independence struggle and to Somalia which had territorial claims on Ethiopia's Ogaden area, in the latter case actually getting naval-base facilities and perhaps hoping for the same in Eritrea later on. But when Haile Selassie was overthrown by a popular upheaval, Moscow apparently decided it could gain more by shifting its support to the new nationalist regime in Ethiopia. The latter, once assured of Soviet support, rejected Soviet efforts to mediate the Eritrean conflict and instead launched an all-out war to crush the revolutionary Eritrean People's Liberation Front (EPLF), in the process dragging the Russians (and the Cubans who had unwisely followed the Soviet lead) deeper and deeper into a sordid counter-revolutionary adventure. Latest reports at the time of writing indicate that after initial setbacks for the Eritreans, the tide has turned in their favor and that the situation in Ethiopia is seriously deteriorating. . . .

It looks as though Ethiopia may come to share the privilege so far monopolized by China as a country which has been "lost" twice, once by each of the superpowers.

For present purposes there is no need to analyze the Soviet position in Indochina or Southern Africa. Suffice it to say that the situations are very different, but that neither looks at all promising from the point of view of Soviet power and influence. Given a gravely weakened economy and debilitating entanglements in the affairs of its Cambodian and Laotian neighbors, Vietnam may cling for a long time to its alliance with the Soviet Union, but it is hard to see what strategic, let alone economic, benefits the Russians can expect to get out of it. From their point of view, the prospects in Southern Africa are certainly much more favorable. By helping the nationalist and revolutionary forces in Angola, Mozambique, and Zimbabwe, the Russians appear at their best before public opinion in the Third World and the international left generally. But it is something altogether different to claim or imply, as Americans and Chinese persist in doing, that the Russians are somehow penetrating the area and establishing permanent power positions. The truth is that after a century of ruthless colonial oppression, no genuine nationalist or revolutionary movement in Africa is going to settle for a new foreign overlord. To be sure, Africa still has a long way to go to gain economic independence, but that is a problem which concerns Africans and the traditional imperialist (mostly Western European) powers and in the solution of which the USSR is unlikely to play even a marginal role. . . .

Why have we devoted so much space to the faltering role of the Soviet Union in world affairs? The answer is that unless this is understood and taken fully into account, it is impossible to uncover the real nature and meaning of U.S. foreign policy. This is not to discount the danger of a military confrontation between the United States and the Soviet Union. Both superpowers are equipped to blow up the world, and that situation will not change in the foreseeable future regardless of their relative positions of power and influence with respect to other countries. By the same token, neither can hope to improve its chances of winning an unwinnable nuclear war by gains in the international arena, nor will the security of either be significantly compromised by losses. If nevertheless both are intensely preoccupied by their power and influence in the world—as indeed they are—the explanation must be sought elsewhere than in the game of superpower rivalry.

Here we leave the Soviet Union and turn our attention to the United States. And what we find is that the United States is so thoroughly integrated into the global capitalist system as it has evolved under U.S. hegemony in the post-Second World War period that any changes, particularly if they are of a potentially cumulative character, threaten the viability of the U.S. economy in its present form and hence constitute a clear and present danger to the enormous wealth, power, and privileges of the business and financial elite which dominates the country's economic and political affairs. A full, up-to-date treatment of this theme would of course fill a book. Here we will focus on three key aspects: (1) direct foreign investment of U.S. multinational corporations; (2) the role of foreign investment in the country's balance of payments; and (3) the foreign involvement of U.S. banks.

Foreign Investment of Multinationals. In 1966 U.S. multinational corporations had $52 billion invested abroad, and this had grown to $168 billion by 1978 (the figures are for book value: market value would be much greater). This sizeable increase was to a large extent achieved by the reinvestment of the earnings of foreign branches. It is important to recognize that the multinational corporations sent only $50 billion out of the United States. The total direct investment abroad, however, produced $203 billion of income for the multinationals during this period. Part of the income was reinvested abroad. But $132 billion came back to the United States in the form of dividends, interest, royalties, fees, etc. In other words, while multinationals were *exporting* capital worth $50 billion, they were *importing* income to the tune of $132 billion, while at the same time more than tripling their foreign holdings. As the *Wall Street Journal* once remarked (November 1, 1973), "U.S. corporations have created real money-making machines by investing in operations abroad." What was true in 1973 is more so today. The significance of this phenomenon for the economy as a whole and for the formation of U.S. foreign policy is greatly enhanced by two further facts: first, almost all the multinationals are among the 500 or so giant corporations which dominate the economy; and second, by far the most lucrative area of foreign investment is in the underdeveloped countries (in the 1966-1978 period the outflow of capital to these countries was only $11 billion, while the return flow of income was a fabulous $56 billion.)*

Balance of Payments. Everyone who reads the financial pages of the newspapers these days knows that the U.S. balance of payments (i.e., the comparison of total inflows and outflows of funds on all accounts, private and public) is in plenty of trouble. Outflows consistently exceed inflows, and the dollars the United States ships out to make up the difference constitute in effect a debt owing to foreigners and at the same time swell the world's money supply, adding to already intolerable inflationary pressures. But how much worse the situation would be if it were not for the enormous inflows received from private foreign investments! Balance-of-payments statistics are notoriously tricky, and we will not attempt an accurate assessment of the overall importance of foreign investment income here. Suffice it to point out that for almost the entire period since the early 1950s, the persistent balance-of-

*All figures in this paragraph are from the annual surveys of foreign investment of the Department of Commerce's *Survey of Current Business,* the latest of which is in the issue of August 1979.

payments deficits of the United States were created by the fact that U.S. expenditures abroad for military operations, foreign aid, and foreign investment were larger than the gains made by an excess of exports over imports of goods and services. But even the latter positive balance would have been a whopping deficit if not for the large and growing income from investments abroad. (Investment income is counted as payment for the services of U.S.-owned capital, in accordance with accepted bourgeois theory.) Thus, we find that for the period 1966-1978 there was a cumulative surplus of $59.4 billion in the balance of goods and services. But if the flow of investment income were eliminated, this surplus would have turned into a *deficit* on goods and services of $152.7 billion.** It seems that not only the giant corporations but also the national economy as a whole has become crucially dependent on the income from foreign investment.

Foreign Involvement of Banks. During the last decade and a half a truly sensational explosion has taken place in the foreign operations of major U.S. banks. In 1960, eight U.S. banks had a total of 131 foreign branches with combined assets of $3.5 billion. By 1978 these figures had grown to 137 banks, 761 branches, and assets of $270 billion (increases respectively of 1,612 percent, 481 percent, and 7,614 percent). Furthermore, the share of foreign earnings in total earnings of the 13 largest U.S. banks grew from 18.8 percent in 1970 to 49.6 in 1976, an increase of 164 percent in six years.*** Nothing like this ever happened before in the history of banking in the United States or anywhere else. From being an essentially domestic institution the U.S. banking system almost overnight became international in the fullest sense of the term. In judging the significance of this international explosion of U.S. banking, one must keep in mind what has long been well known, that banks exercise great economic power; and what is only beginning to be well known, that their political power is commensurate with their economic power. . . .

The relevance of all this to U.S. foreign policy should be obvious. In the period since the Second World War during which the United States occupied a dominant position in the global capitalist system, the U.S. economy developed a whole network of relations with foreign countries which became increasingly crucial to the operation, stability, and profitability of American business and finance. Under these circumstances one does not need to be a crude economic determinist to understand that what is perceived to be the national interest, not only by those who are the chief beneficiaries of the system but also by those whose livelihood is threatened by an interruption or breakdown in its functioning, is the preservation of the international status quo and, where this is not possible, to hold change within the narrowest

---

**These figures were calculated from data presented in the *Survey of Current Business*, June 1979. They are not strictly comparable to the preceding figures on foreign investment: the inflow of income also includes, in addition to income on direct investment, income on other kinds of foreign investment.

***These percentages were calculated from data presented in the U.N. Commission on Transnational Corporations, *Transnational Corporations in World Development: A Re-Examination* (New York: United Nations Economic and Social Council, March 20, 1978), p. 218.

possible limits. And indeed this has been the main thrust of U.S. foreign policy during *every* postwar administration from Truman to Carter.

It follows that in order to understand U.S. foreign policy in the period ahead, we must first identify the forces which threaten the status quo in ways likely to upset the stability and profitability of the U.S. economy.

As we have already seen, the answer is *not* the Soviet Union, which in fact has become an increasingly valuable customer for U.S. goods and a borrower of U.S. funds in recent years. There have been many changes unfavorable to U.S. capitalism since the Second World War. None has been initiated by the USSR—from China in 1949 to Iran in 1979. It is true that the Soviet Union has helped some (though not all) of these initiatives, but attempting to deal with them by striking at the Soviet Union (which was the central idea of John Foster Dulles's ill-fated doctrine of "massive retaliation") was never feasible and would always have been self-defeating.

The *source* of these changes—aside from what may have originated in the growing strength of America's advanced capitalist allies, which is an entirely different story—was in every case national liberation movements in the Third World, usually combining nationalistic and social revolutionary elements and in all cases carrying threats to U.S. economic and political interests in the countries affected. All signs are that these movements are active in various parts of the world today (Southern Africa, Central America, the Caribbean) and are likely to become so in others (South America, the Middle East, Southern Asia) in the not distant future. Deteriorating economic conditions and mass living standards in all but a few Third World countries (OPEC, South Korea, Taiwan, Hong Kong, Singapore) virtually guarantee that what may be called the revolt of the Third World will steadily grow in intensity during the 1980s.

This, and not superpower rivalry, is the number one contradiction in the world today and in the foreseeable future, hence also the primary concern of U.S. foreign policy.* How can Washington seek to deal with the problem? Barring a fundamental change in internal U.S. politics, which is hardly a near-term prospect, the answer has to be that the U.S. course will continue along the lines followed during the whole post-war period—supporting reactionary and oppressive regimes where at all possible, CIA subversion, and as a last resort military intervention.

This is where the alleged threat from the USSR comes in handy. As we have seen, it isn't the real problem, but to the extent that it is believed to be, or that the public can be persuaded to believe it to be, the policies actually needed to combat the revolt of the Third World can be made politically palatable and

---

*This is not to say that somewhere along the road war with the Soviet Union may not break out. The U.S. budget for "defense" is geared to developing the capability of wiping out the Soviet Union in one blow. What we are arguing here is that underlying this rivalry and the accompanying arms race, from the standpoint of the United States and its allies, is the urgency to keep the status quo in what is left of the capitalist world, including, where possible, counter-revolutions in countries that have broken away from the imperialist system.

even popular. While the people of this country might balk at sending U.S. forces to fight against national liberation movements in, say, Southern Africa or Central America, they would obviously feel quite differently if they could be convinced that the purpose was to keep from being crushed by the other superpower. So a policy aimed at defeating the revolt of the Third World will in all probability continue to be pursued in the name of combatting the Soviet Union. The clearest possible proof of this intent is the much publicized plan of the Carter administration to build up a 100,000-man rapid strike force capable of instant intervention anywhere in the world. Ostensibly its mission would be to counter possible Soviet thrusts, supposedly most likely in the present conjuncture in the Persian Gulf area. But the truth is that its only rational use would be to intervene to put down revolts against oppressive Third World regimes no longer able to defend themselves against their own people.

Three final questions: Can such anti-popular and counter-revolutionary wars of intervention really be won in the world of today? Or will they prove to be new Vietnams? And if the latter, how long will the American people continue to support them? We don't know the answers, but we are pretty sure these are the right questions. **fOCus**

The neo-Marxist perspective suggested by Sweezy and Magdoff illustrates the fundamental role played by ideology in determining one's view of reality. It is important to emphasize the essential subjectivity of any consistent view of the world. In this respect, Robert Tucker's explicit emphasis on power politics and political realism—however reminiscent of Hans Morgenthau's "Six Principles of Political Realism"—is not without many of the assumptions characteristic of U.S. cold war internationalism. It is somewhat ironic that Hans Morgenthau reserved some of his most forceful criticisms of American foreign policy for those who analyzed Soviet foreign policy only from the perspectives of the cold war. Thus, both Robert Tucker's emphasis on the political dimensions of the economics of OPEC and Paul Sweezy and Harry Magdoff's emphasis on the economic (capitalist) dimensions of U.S. foreign policy should alert us to the more subtle, yet embracing, role that ideology plays in shaping our appreciation of world politics in the 1980s.

CHAPTER 4

Economic Interpretations of American Foreign Policy

Students of foreign policy have traditionally emphasized the fundamental importance of states and their access to power, as Hans Morgenthau's assessment illustrates in Chapter 3. Most analyses of power politics, however, see the economic capabilities of states as secondary to the more important instruments of state power—for example, diplomacy or war. Robert Tucker points this out in his analysis of OPEC and U.S. foreign policy. Since World War II, and especially after the worldwide instability of the U.S. dollar during the 1960s and 1970s, there have been clashing interpretations of the role played by the U.S. economy in American foreign policy, demonstrating the importance of both domestic and international politics in the policy-making process. These divergent ideological perspectives account for many of the conflicting assumptions of liberals (pluralists) and neo-Marxists (radicals). In the articles that follow—"New Challenges in International Investments" by Robert D. Hormats and "The U.S. Dollar, Petrodollars, and U.S. Imperialism" by Harry Magdoff—liberal and neo-Marxist assessments of the economic foundations of American foreign policy are explored. The third article, "Dollar Diplomacy" by Charles Krauthammer, underscores the significance of transnational agents (in this case, multinational corporations) as powerful and quite independent forces in the contemporary global environment.

The liberal, or pluralist, analysis of the economic aspects of U.S. foreign policy emphasizes the desirability of open and fluid global economic relations between states. The concept of unrestricted free trade is the cornerstone of this approach and was established by the United States following World War II in the Bretton Woods Agreement (1944), the International Monetary Fund (IMF) and the World Bank (the International Bank for Reconstruction and Development—IRBD), and the General Agreement on Tariffs and Trade (GATT) (1947). In each case the United States systematically sought to promote the unrestricted exchange of goods by reducing tariffs and other domestic measures involved in economic transactions among states. Liberals argued that the establishment of an unrestricted global market would benefit consumers everywhere in the world because the quality and cost of goods and services would be subject to the test of the free market. Toward this end, the United States revamped the chaotic and very restrictive system of international trade during the 1930s, which many argued helped to plunge the world into depression and thus foster the onslaught of World War II. It should be noted, in this context, that worldwide American military power and political influence reinforced America's predominance in global economic relations. The ideological assumptions of capitalism justified the U.S.'s emphasis on the necessity of free trade. The establishment of the Bretton Woods system tied the non-Communist world to the U.S. economy more closely than ever before. Moreover, the United States established itself in an undisputed position of predominance in global economic relations as it achieved political, military, and ideological hegemony. Thus, the United States first stabilized the price of gold, and then guaranteed that each dollar could be readily converted into gold. In so doing, the United States established the dollar as the world's currency, since a stable paper currency was essential for the conduct of global economic transactions. In addition, it based the value of the U.S. dollar on gold and backed it by the holdings of gold reserves at Fort Knox. The strength of the U.S. economy sprang from the productive capacity of American industry, which was untouched by the devastation of World War II, and which was at the zenith of its capabilities in 1946. The power of the U.S. military establishment quickly established a worldwide presence after the proclamation of the Truman Doctrine in 1947. This was achieved through a series of regional security organizations—for example, the Organization of American States (OAS) and the North Atlantic Treaty Organization (NATO)—as well as bilateral agreements (treaties) with countries everywhere in the world.

In order to maximize trade among countries with different economic systems, the Bretton Woods Agreement attempted to stabilize the value of all domestic currencies. The International Monetary Fund was established to provide short term loans to states encountering monetary problems that were caused by seasonal fluctuations in the production of goods (agricultural products, for example). The stated goal of the IMF was to prevent weaknesses in a state's monetary system which arise when an imbalance (deficit) occurs between money earned from the sale of domestic goods abroad (exports) and the cost of foreign goods purchased at home (imports). The stability of a country's balance of payments—the value of its exports compared to the costs of its imports—is an important indicator of the health of a state's economy. International trade is a crucial factor because it is the single most important way in which countries strike a balance between imports and exports and, thus, earn a living. International trade performs two functions. First, it helps to mobilize internal resources in a productive way. The logic of a global free market dictates the survival of the most competitive industries and products. Second, world trade makes external (foreign) resources available to countries. In the theory of liberal capitalism, all members of the world economy benefit from free trade. In other words, the fundamental value of goods which are exported and imported is determined by patterns of world trade. From this perspective, trade determines the *comparative advantage* of all the countries producing goods. Thus, international trade stimulates productivity by causing exporters to specialize in their most competitive products, while importers benefit from having a wide range of specialized goods from which to choose. The interdependence of the free market provides all its participants with the advantages of a global market without the prohibitively costly and unattainable goal of self-sufficiency.

The Bretton Woods system further fostered international trade because the value of the U.S. dollar was stabilized. This allowed the dollar to become the world's central currency (backed by gold). Consequently, it was easy for non-Communist countries to convert their domestic currencies into dollars for trading purposes. The IMF provided short term loans for countries facing temporary financial difficulties, further facilitating world trade. The General Agreement on Tariffs and Trade (GATT) was another attempt by the United States to reduce tariffs and other restrictive measures by promoting reciprocal agreements between the United States and its trading partners. GATT became a vehicle by which trade barriers were systematically reduced, often on an industry or product-wide basis. Through the granting of Most Favored Nation Status, the U.S. opened its vast markets in exchange for access to foreign markets. The GATT illustrates the belief that free trade benefits all producers and consumers by creating a climate in which the free enterprise system guarantees the best possible quality at the most affordable prices on a global scale. Moreover, the liberal approach argues that rigorous competition sharpens the productive capabilities of all sectors of the global economy. This includes the manufacture of highly technical goods, the exploitation of raw materials, and the production of foodstuffs (sugarcane, bananas, or coffee). All parties strengthen their particular skills, thus providing each producer with a comparative advantage. While liberals recognize that the distribution of income may not be entirely symmetrical for all sectors of the global economy (more profit may be derived from selling computers than sugarcane), it is argued that all parties benefit to some extent and that free trade reduces friction or conflict among states. The inherent benefits of global capitalism provide all parts of the world economy with the opportunity to prosper, argue its advocates. From this perspective, the free enterprise system must work to overcome the greedy self-interests of states which attempt to achieve short-term gains through tariffs and other obstacles to free trade instituted at the expense of all the other members of the world capitalist system. In order for capitalism to work most efficiently it must limit the interference of government.

The following article by Robert D. Hormats, Assistant Secretary of State for Economic and Business Affairs, illustrates the fundamental emphasis of Reagan's foreign policy on assumptions of free international trade. Unlike many of the economic policies of the Carter administration, the Reagan administration has insisted that developing countries, in particular, must rely on the workings of the world economy rather than on the United States for assistance. For example, President Reagan has called for a reduction in Federal economic assistance to Third World countries. Instead, the president has encouraged private sector economic aid. Moreover, the Reagan administration has supported a reduction in multilateral assistance through international organizations, favoring instead bilateral support that is more easily directed toward military-security purposes. The administration argues that it can better control U.S. economic assistance when it is provided on a bilateral basis. The emphasis on bilateralism and military-security assistance is a departure from the first three years of foreign policy under Carter.

Robert Hormats' analysis of the importance of private investments in the world economy underscores the U.S.'s refusal to accept now the Third World's explanations which blame the United States as a major cause of the systematic underdevelopment and exploitation of the world's poor countries. As Robert Tucker argues in Chapter 2, the Carter administration (at least on a rhetorical level) was more open to Third World demands for a restructuring of world capitalism. Assistant Secretary of State Hormats underscores the Reagan administration's new perspectives.

NEW CHALLENGES IN INTERNATIONAL INVESTMENT

Robert D. Hormats, Department of
State Bulletin, November 1981

Robert D. Hormats is Assistant Secretary of State for Economic and Business Affairs.

This evening I would like to discuss, in general, international investment issues and describe, in particular, two major challenges before us in the 1980s. The first challenge relates to the need to establish new international understandings to avoid short-term nationalistic approaches to investment. We risk today in the international investment area a deterioration in the climate similar to that experienced in the world trading arena in the 1930s. During that period, countries adopted nationalistic trading policies based on short-term economic perspectives. The economic and political costs have been well-documented in history. Following World War II, nations have made a major effort to avoid narrowly nationalistic trade policies. We have made considerable progress in developing an international framework for trade matters. Although we still have some distance to go, the direction and emphasis of our effort is correct.

In the investment area, however, no comparable framework has emerged, and there is a tendency on the part of developed and developing nations alike to move in the wrong direction—to increase intervention in the investment area to accomplish short-term objectives. This can only come at the expense of broader long-term interests. A major goal of the 1980s must be to reverse this trend through international understandings and rules leading to a more open and less interventionist investment climate.

The second challenge is to create, through cooperation among developed and developing nations, an international environment in which investment can make a greater contribution to the development process. Investment can be a powerful impetus to development and is particularly important at a time of tight aid budgets. The developing countries themselves have a major responsibility to improve their investment climates through respect for international laws and norms. And the international community can play a helpful role in facilitating investment to those countries which offer an attractive investment climate. The overall world economy can benefit as a result.

International Investment Climate

International investment capital was readily available until the mid-1970s, and foreign direct investment activities—except for several major expropriation cases early in the decade—proceeded at a healthy pace. Since the mid-1970s, there have been important changes in international trends and forms of investment. The pace of international direct investment flows has slowed, particularly to many developing countries, and the 1980s are likely to be a time of capital scarcity and competition for foreign investment. It also appears that what capital is available will be more expensive than we were accustomed to in the 1970s. Increasingly, many countries are turning to investment incentives to attract foreign investment in specific industries. A number are also utilizing performance requirements to boost exports or increase local content. In addition, the recent increase in foreign investment in the United States, coupled with instances of discrimination against U.S. investment abroad, is generating concerns which are increasing pressures for more restrictive U.S. policies on inward investment. We need to deal with these issues in ways which maintain and expand the fundamentally open international investment system so necessary for global economic efficiency.

Investment Flows

A brief review of international investment trends will help to put these issues in perspective. Although foreign investment has played an important role in the international economy since the last half of the 19th century, most was in fixed-interest portfolio investments until the 1920s. After World War II, the global economic climate improved dramatically and generated an upsurge in private direct investment. U.S. private investment in Europe increased markedly and was a key element in Europe's recovery. U.S. investment in some developing countries also expanded and played a significant role in the economic growth of many of those countries. The benefits of increased direct investment flows were and continue to be: additional employment, additional capital to expand plant capacity or create new facilities, transfers of new and improved technology and management skills, increased production, and greater competition.

The period from the early 1960s to the mid-1970s witnessed a rapid development of international direct investment both in absolute terms and relative to the growth of other economic aggregates such as trade, domestic investment, and gross national product (GNP). The United States remained the principal country of origin, although some European countries began to be more active as direct foreign investors.

International direct investment was heavily oriented toward developing natural resources at the outset of this period. However, direct investment in manufacturing sectors developed considerably as the period progressed. Over the 1960-73 period, the average annual growth rate of total outward international direct investment flows from the 13 largest OECD [Organization for Economic Cooperation and Development] countries was over 12% a year. This figure was approximately 1½ times the average growth of OECD gross domestic product and practically the same as the growth of international trade (14%).

This period also witnessed the rapid growth of multinational enterprises with extensive international operations. These enterprises have developed highly sophisticated production techniques and investor-supplier arrangements. Often, each subsidiary or subcontractor specializes in the production of a particular product or component. Product lines in the so-called world industries, such as the "world cars," often result from coordinated production activities in a number of countries. . . .

The period since the mid-1970s stands in quite sharp contrast with the period which preceded it in a number of important aspects. . . .

There recently has been a sharpening of differences in the ability of developing nations to attract investment. Taken together, the average annual growth rate of international direct investment flows from the 14 major members of the OECD's Development Assistance Committee to developing countries has increased over the last few years in current and real terms. Furthermore, the total share of developing countries as host countries for the foreign direct investment of almost all major investing countries has increased since 1974, thus reversing the generally declining trend of earlier periods. But this investment has been concentrated heavily in a few economies—in particular, in the Republic of Korea, Taiwan, Singapore, Hong Kong, and Brazil, which have emphasized exported growth. Such investment has played a major role in the rapid growth of manufacturing in these economies.

In contrast to the experience of these countries, international direct investment has tended to stagnate in other developing countries, with the exception of the oil-producing countries. It is of particular concern that U.S. and European direct investment in minerals has stagnated in recent years. The primary reasons for this are the slack demand for metals and minerals, due to the economic downturn in the developed countries, and increased investor perception of the political risk of investing in some mineral-rich developing countries. In view of the long lead times involved in developing new minerals resources, a global shortfall in exploration and new mine and smelter capacity could result in future shortages and/or sharply rising metals and minerals prices when the developed country economies turn upward again and world demand for these items increases. Such shortages and price increases could, in turn, constrain future global economic growth.

While there are sectoral reasons for low foreign investment in many developing countries (the temporary fall in demand for metals and minerals is a good example), there are other "investment climate" factors, such as questionable national economic policies, fear of political instability, and negative policies toward foreign investment. Increased perception of political risk among potential investors is a key factor. Unclear and restrictive investment laws and regulations, and the unpredictability of their application, are other important elements, as are the increased use of performance requirements and restrictions on equity holdings.

New Forms of Investment

There have also been important changes in the characteristics of international direct investment. Recent OECD studies indicate that borrowed funds—essentially local currency borrowing—now represent a key source of financing for many firms, especially U.S. enterprises. In addition, an increasing number of medium-sized and sometimes even small-sized firms have begun to invest abroad in recent years. The development and internationalization of firms engaged in providing services necessary to direct investment, such as banks, has grown at a rapid pace since the beginning of the 1970s.

Enterprises are also diversifying their forms of investment. European state-owned enterprises have become increasingly significant investors in the OECD countries and in many less developed countries (LDCs). In addition, the "traditional" wholly owned subsidiary form of operation is being increasingly replaced by nonequity forms of foreign direct investment, such as management contracts, licensing arrangements, etc.

The emerging trend seems to be a tendency toward flexible and pragmatic forms of ownership, management, and control. These increasingly complex arrangements often involve several forms of control, cross control, or joint activities. The emergence of new and more flexible forms of interfirm relations is particularly noticeable in developing countries that are now endowed with substantial financial resources of their own or which can borrow abroad on their own account. A country in this position may put less emphasis on attracting foreign capital than on attracting foreign technology and management capacities.

Private Sector Role in Developing Countries

Slower rates of global economic growth since the mid-1970s have hit most developing countries extremely hard. Adjustments to the soaring costs of energy and other resources, high interest rates, the decrease in the rate of growth of foreign investment in most developing countries, and sluggish world demand for many developing country exports have caused major problems for developing countries in addition to the traditional ones many already faced.

The United States has a strong interest in the economic development of developing countries. Taken together they are a larger market for U.S. exports than Europe and Japan combined. Foreign private direct investment flows can be a major—and increasingly important—supplement to other forms of resource transfers, principally official development assistance, in stimulating growth in developing nations.

There appears to be an increasing perception by many developing nations that increasing foreign direct investment will be vital to their prosperity in the 1980s, particularly as aid prospects appear less promising. Many developing nations are seeking actively to attract foreign investors. . . .

The U.S. Government is also seeking ways to facilitate U.S. private sector involvement in LDCs. Steps we have taken or proposed include improved treatment of foreign-sourced personal income; amendment of our Foreign Corrupt Practices Act so as to define better the proscribed conduct; support for export trading company legislation; and renewal of OPIC's [Overseas Private Investment Corporation] legislation with a broadening of the scope of its activities in developing nations. We are also considering proposals for the expansion of trade and development program grants for project feasibility studies and project design. . . .

We are also seeking to give new vitality to and broaden the international effort to enhance private sector investment in those developing countries where the environment is conducive to private sector growth. We believe the World Bank can play a highly effective role as a catalyst for increasing international flows of direct investment to developing countries through cofinancing with the private sector. Even if the Bank finances only a part of a project, its participation improves the climate of confidence between foreign investors and the country in which the investment is taking place. Within the Bank, the International Finance Corporation (IFC) has a particularly important role to play. For the last 25 years, the IFC has been working to encourage the growth of productive private investment in developing countries. Its equity participation in a small portion of an investment can attract private participation in the larger portion of that investment. The IFC should receive greater support from developed and developing nations alike.

Domestically, the new legislative authority for OPIC will permit it greater freedom to support private investment in middle-income developing countries. At the same time, we should consider the possibility of working with other developed and developing countries to establish a multilateral insurance agency. This could help to facilitate investment in developing countries and give greater confidence to new investors from countries which do not have their own national insurance agencies. Similar ideas have been considered before, but perhaps the timing now is more propitious because the desire among potential investors and potential recipients is greater. We also welcome the increased interest shown by private firms in issuing political risk insurance in developing countries and are exploring ways in which we can cooperate more closely with them in this field.

We have become increasingly concerned over the serious political, social, and economic problems faced by many countries in Central America and the Caribbean. We are currently seeking to cooperate with the Caribbean Basin states in a practical way to develop programs to stimulate more rapid economic growth in the region. The U.S. portion of this initiative will focus in large part on enhancing the role of the private sector in these economies. Growth of a modern efficient private sector is imperative to promote productive employment in the region and to generate exchange-earning exports. We have no preconceived blueprint for determining the actions, joint and separate, which should be taken to increase regional productive capacity and achieve needed economic revitalization. We are now engaged in a series of consultations with basin countries and other potential participants to determine those trade, aid, and investment measures which, when taken in combination with the efforts of the regional governments themselves to reduce internal constraints to economic growth, will help to reach our long-term goal of increased economic prosperity for the region. . . .

Treatment of Investment

The United Sates believes in two basic tenets for treatment of investment: the national treatment principle and the most-favored-nation treatment principle. The national treatment principle holds that foreign investors should be treated no less favorably than domestic investors in like situations. The most-favored-nation treatment principle holds that the investors of one foreign country should be treated no less favorably than the investors of other foreign countries. The two principles have the common characteristics of reducing instances of discrimination directed at foreign investment.

We have worked bilaterally and multilaterally to achieve the widest possible acceptance of these principles and to extend the application of such treatment to a wider range of enterprises. A particularly important step in this process took place in 1976 when the United States joined other OECD member governments in participating in the consensus adopting a declaration and related decision on national treatment. The declaration and decision were reviewed and reaffirmed in 1979 by a consensus of OECD countries in which the United States also participated. The declaration states, in part:

> . . . that member countries should, consistent with their needs to maintain public order, to protect their essential security interests, and to fulfill commitments relating to international peace and security, accord to enterprises operating in their territories and owned or controlled directly or indirectly by nationals of another member country . . . treatment under their laws, regulations and administrative practices consistent with international law and no less favorable than that accorded in like situations to domestic enterprises . . .

Since the declaration and related decision on national treatment were adopted in 1976, progress has been made toward refining the concept, including a listing of those exceptions which now exist and their rationales. Continuing work is in progress with a stated goal of extending the application of national treatment over time. We strongly support a more active OECD effort in this area. The very existence of the declaration and related decision on national treatment has probably had some effect in discouraging member countries from implementing measures which would constitute new derogations from the principle. Moreover, at the request of the United States, joined by several other OECD member countries, the consultation procedures of the OECD instruments were used for the first time in March 1981, to hold formal OECD consultations on the discriminatory policies of Canada's national energy program. National treatment is clearly in the interests of all concerned as it is a critical element in fostering an attractive climate for foreign investment.

In addition, we believe strongly that investors should be accorded treatment consistent with international law, including nondiscriminatory treatment and prompt, adequate, and effective compensation in the event of expropriation. Investor confidence that host countries would adhere to international law and norms would significantly facilitate investment flows.

It is, in my judgment, the responsibility of the U.S. Government to provide full support for American investors who desire it in order to insure that the principles of national and most-favored-nation treatment and their rights under international law are adhered to by host governments. American investments abroad make a positive contribution to our own economy and to that of host nations. The U.S. Government cannot remain neutral while its citizens, who invest in other countries relying on their good faith to adhere to international principles and laws, find their interests threatened by derogations from such principles and laws. We believe in the concept of fair play. We practice it, and our investors abroad should expect no less.

Codes of Conduct

Over the last half decade, the United States has been participating in the development of international codes of conduct relating to multinational enterprises. The OECD and the International Labor Organization have developed general codes for multinational enterprises. The U.N. Conference on Trade and Development (UNCTAD) has promulgated a more narrowly focused code on restrictive business practices. In addition, a U.N. working group has completed draft provisions on about two-thirds of an overall U.N. code relating to the activities and responsibilities of transnational corporations and governments. However, hard issues remain to be resolved, such as those on nationalization and compensation, and it is not certain whether the negotiations will be successful. Negotiations on a code of conduct relating to the transfer of technology are presently stalled and the matter has been referred to the U.N. General Assembly for further consideration.

In the U.S. view, guidelines which affirm standards of good practice for both enterprises and governments can contribute to improved relations between firms and governments and may limit the tendency for unilateral government intervention in investment matters. Through appropriate provisions on nationalization and compensation, jurisdiction, and dispute settlement they may also be able to reduce conflicts between governments over investment issues, thereby, facilitating the liberal climate for international investment which we seek. However, the United States can support only guidelines or codes that are voluntary; do not discriminate against multinational enterprises in favor of purely national enterprises; are balanced to include references to the responsibilities of governments as well as of multinational enterprises; and apply to all enterprises regardless of ownership—whether private, government, or mixed.

It appears that international interest in developing codes of conduct may well be diminishing as other investment issues, such as capital scarcity, have become more urgent. The principal investment issue is no longer controlling multinational enterprises but attracting investment by them.

Foreign Investment in the United States

The value of foreign direct investment in the United States has increased in recent years—28% in 1978 ($42.5 billion), 23% in 1979 ($54.5 billion), 20% in 1980 ($65.5 billion). (U.S. direct investment abroad, by contrast, is $213 billion.) Roughly one-third of the foreign direct investment in the United States is in manufacturing ($24 billion), wholesale and retail trade account for about 20%, and petroleum 19%. Real estate holdings by foreigners, while often publicized, amount to only about $2.5 billion. The largest single sources of foreign investment have been the Netherlands ($16 billion), the United Kingdom ($11 billion), and Canada ($9 billion). Less than $1 billion comes from the Middle East.

This investment has had a positive effect on many sections of our economy. It has helped to create jobs, added plant capacity and created new facilities, and brought in advanced technology and management skills. Moreover, additional inward investment flows will assist our economic revitalization efforts.

However, the recent rapid growth in this investment coupled with restrictions on and discrimination against U.S. investment in other countries are tending to generate pressures in the United States to control inward investment and/or regulate it on a more reciprocal basis. The reaction to Canada's restrictions against foreign investors, particularly in the energy sector, and the spate of new investments sought by Canadian firms in the U.S. minerals sector feed such pressures. There have been calls for prohibition on investment in specific sectors, greater screening of foreign investment, and the establishment of a reciprocity principle in U.S. treatment of investment.

Clearly, for the many reasons mentioned earlier, I believe that we should react strongly to unfair treatment of U.S. investment abroad. However, for a number of reasons, it is necessary to react in ways which genuinely serve our interests. Policies which would restrict inward investment, or retaliatory countermeasures, should be used only after all of their implications are weighed.

First, the ultimate results might adversely affect the United States as much as, or more than, other countries. We need to be cautious about limiting foreign investment because of the benefits from such investment. A secure and stable investment climate is one of the major strengths of our economy and a major source of our prosperity. Short-sighted or arbitrary actions which raise doubts among potential foreign investors would be harmful to our domestic economic interests. In the long run we might be the losers, not the country that we retaliated against.

Second, we must take into account the fact that the United States is also a large investor abroad and has been a major force in international trade. U.S. policies concerning foreign investment in the United States have a significant impact on the policies of other countries, and U.S. restrictions could invite retaliatory actions by others.

I, therefore, believe that while counterreactions of the type mentioned might in extreme cases be useful, we are clearly better served by policies that aim at the elimination of foreign practices that deviate from international norms than by policies of retaliation that could weaken these norms. With this principle in mind, we intend to take steps necessary to protect our rights and interests.

Conclusion

Many of the issues I have discussed today were nonexistent or only nascent just a decade ago. They have come to the fore over the last few years as a result of real economic forces, which are reflected in the investment trends I have outlined. The issues, such as investment incentives and performance requirements, must be addressed if we are to maintain and strengthen the open international investment system essential to global economic efficiency.

By their very nature, many of these problems will not lend themselves to easy solutions. In particular, urgent short-term national economic goals vary widely, thereby making more difficult the achievement of an international consensus on some of the issues. However, all countries have a stake in the long-term economic implications involved, and I believe that this common stake in the international economic system provides a good basis upon which to proceed in addressing these problems in earnest.

International fora, such as the OECD, the GATT, and specialized U.N. agencies will provide important arenas in which to tackle the problems involved. We must move soon from the discussion phase to a serious effort to develop and implement multilateral understandings and rules which reduce distortions of investment and move toward a more open global investment climate. This must be a major goal for the decade of the 1980s.   **focus**

In his emphasis on the benefits of free trade (through private investment, particularly) in developing countries and the need to eliminate "nationalistic" barriers to free trade, Hormats rejects any notion that the global economic system be restructured to provide greater benefits and accessibility to Third World countries—as epitomized in the demand to create a new international economic order. During the Seventh Special Session of the U.N. General Assembly in 1975, a unified Third World called for a more equitable restructuring of international trade which would raise the price of raw materials and allow developing countries more favorable access to the markets of developed countries. The call for the establishment of a new international economic order also would have provided for greater access to international capital, the policing of multinational corporations, technology transfers from wealthy countries to poor societies, and a reform of the lending policies of the IMF. These Third World demands called for a restructuring of global economic relations, rather than a complete transformation. However radical the Third World proposals may have appeared to the United States and other Western countries, they called overwhelmingly for reform rather than revolution. In the article by Harry Magdoff that follows, the neo-Marxist or radical approach is emphasized. Magdoff challenges the most fundamental assumptions of the liberal approach and contemporary American foreign policy.

First, Magdoff argues that global economic relations are an inseparable part of broader U.S. political, military, and ideological objectives. The establishment of a post-World War II American empire mandated the creation of the Bretton Woods Agreement, the IMF and the World Bank as well as the General Agreement on Tariffs and Trade. Thus, the control of world capitalism was the most basic objective of American imperialism.

Second, Magdoff maintains the post-World War II economic system is inherently asymmetrical, providing the United States and other Western countries with the vast majority of economic benefits. The military power of the United States has traditionally provided it with significant leverage to achieve its economic and political goals, whether dealing with its European allies or weak Third World states. In Magdoff's view, the extraordinary wealth generated by American imperialism is directly attributable to the exploitation of Third World countries. Moreover, he argues, because the U.S. continues to dominate the central institutions of world capitalism, any proposal to change the prevailing rules of the game are antithetical to the U.S. government and American multinational corporations.

Third, Magdoff contends U.S. dominance of world economic, political, and military relations insures conflict in three areas: 1) between the United States and the Soviet Union (because both compete for economic resources); 2) between the United States and Western Europe (over the economic spoils of capitalism); and 3) between the wealthy developed countries of the North (led by the United States) and the poor developing countries of the South that labor under the weight of continuous capitalist exploitation. Arms races, increasing political tensions, growing economic instability, and war are the logical consequences of such a system, says Magdoff.

Fourth, Magdoff argues that U.S. economic interests—particularly the goals of American-based multinational corporations—and the objectives of United States foreign policy are inextricably tied to each other. As the inherent weaknesses and destructiveness of global capitalism become evident (for example, the devaluations of the U.S. dollar in 1971 and 1973 and the end of the dollar's convertibility into gold, which destroyed the Bretton Woods system), the need for a radical alternative to capitalism has never been more imperative for the survival of humanity, maintains Magdoff.

THE U.S. DOLLAR, PETRODOLLARS, AND U.S. IMPERIALISM

Harry Magdoff, *Review of the Month,* January 1979
Harry Magdoff is an editor of the Monthly Review.

During the first week of November the U.S. government announced a package of strong measures designed to check the seemingly endless downward drift in the international value of the dollar. Washington was well aware that these steps might set off a recession, especially since one of the planned actions was to attract foreign capital by boosting the already high interest rates even higher. But the authorities, who were long held back from decisive action by fear of the consequences of a new recession, were finally confronted by an even greater danger—the likely onset of a world-wide financial panic. . . .

When all is said and done, however, the best that the new program can, or for that matter is intended to, accomplish is a temporary rescue operation. The reason for saying this is that, despite all the bold pronouncements, nothing substantial is being undertaken to tackle the underlying forces that in the first place have been propelling the dollar on its downward course. The speculators, including the multinational corporations and banks, have been behaving with normal capitalist rationality in response to a fundamental weakness of the dollar. They have been selling dollars in exchange for stronger currencies because they have been anticipating, and meanwhile contributing to, ever greater weakness of the dollar. There are two main proximate reasons for this weakness: first, a huge increase in the deficits in the U.S. balance of payments during the last two years; and second, the related and ever-growing surplus of dollars abroad, which represent a staggering mountain of U.S. liabilities.

It must be understood, however, that both of these reasons are only surface phenomena. At bottom, as will be explained later, the causes are to be found in current and past practices of U.S. imperialism. The U.S. ruling class has of course no intention of breaking with imperialism. In fact, its major aim is to hold on to as much as possible of its insecure hegemonic role in the world capitalist system. That being the case, the decision-makers are unable to cope in any significant way with either the pile-up of dollars abroad or the huge balance-of-payments deficits. Instead, the tendency in Washington, on Wall Street, and among bourgeois economists is to look for scapegoats. These substitute "explanations" for the dollar's troubles serve not only to cover up the root causes, they also help rationalize the shifting of the burdens of imperialism's crisis to the Third World and the domestic working class.

The scapegoats emerge mainly from two commonly accepted explanations of current difficulties. First is the claim that U.S. exports are lagging because its industries are becoming less competitive—an argument that rests in large measure on complaints about the laxity of the working class and a supposed resulting drag on productivity. Second is the blame put on the jump in oil prices, which happened to coincide with increasing dependence by the United States on oil imports.

Neither of these cover-ups, however, can stand up against either fact or reason. The talk about the relative loss of competitive ability by U.S. industry completely overlooks the overwhelming role of the multinational corporations in world trade. (The facts on this will be presented later on.) Apart from that, it should be recalled, the dollar's illness set in long before one could by the farthest stretch of the imagination complain about the efficiency of U.S. industry. The practice of living with perpetual balance-of-payments deficits, and therefore also with the piling-up of dollars abroad, began in the early 1950s. The official policy toward the potential danger of such behavior was typical of a hegemonic imperialist power: nothing serious would ensue because the rest of the world, including allies, could either like it or lump it.

But this attitude did not make the problem disappear. Disturbances in the international money markets began to crop up more and more frequently in the late 1960s. The crisis signals accelerated as the United States expanded its overseas expenditures for the seemingly endless invasion of Vietnam. By mid-1971 a critical boiling point was reached, resulting in the break-up of the post-Second World War international money system and the initiation of the first of two formal dollar devaluations. Neither of these rescue operations, however, served to get rid of the chronic balance-of-payments deficits and the dollar's weakness. All of this, remember, occurred well before the hike in oil prices at the end of 1973.

Against this background, the most that might reasonably be argued is that the increasing burden of larger and higher-priced oil imports worsened a long-standing bad situation. But there are still more telling reasons for rejecting the misconceptions about the presumed responsibility of higher oil prices. For example, consider the following: only 23 percent of the total energy requirements of the United States are met by oil imports, whereas this percentage is 92 percent for Japan and 67 percent for West Germany. (*The Economist,* July 8, 1978) If oil prices and heavy dependency on oil imports were the decisive influences on the international value of a country's currency, then one should expect the Japanese yen and the German mark, instead of the U.S. dollar, to have come tumbling down. What happened, obviously, was just the opposite.

But one need not rely on such indirect reasoning to expose the fallacy about the huge expenditure for oil imports being the cause of the more recent U.S. balance-of-payments deficits and of the dollar's downfall. For, as we shall see, the simple fact is that the oil-exporting nations have been returning more dollars to the United States than they have been receiving for their oil shipments to this country.

By now it should be clear that we have to dig deeper to understand the frailty, as well as the remaining strength of the dollar. Above all, we need to grasp and keep in mind a basic aspect of international money matters, one that is too often obscured by the maze of technical details that complicate such discussions. Fortunately, every once in a while the rockbottom truth shines through the technical intricacies, and this is more likely to happen at critical turning points. Thus, for example, when the IMF became embroiled in debate among the leading imperialist powers on how to cope with the mounting difficulties occasioned by U.S. arrogance in international monetary affairs, a senior economist at the Standard Oil Company (New Jersey)—now Exxon Corporation—pointed out:

> We may ask why, after a hundred years of international monetary conferences, men still have not resolved their differences. The answer lies in one word—*power*. That is what one hundred years of international monetary conferences have been about. The 22nd annual meeting of the International Monetary Fund held at Rio, where a new facility for creating international liquidity was recommended, is no exception to this general rule.*

A similar rule holds not just for the occasional conference but for the whole history of international money relations, because a country's dominance in this area is an enormously important source of additional power and wealth. Let us turn to a simple illustration to explain this. Suppose an individual has no savings, yet indulges in spending $15,000 a year while earning only $10,000. Clearly, this can be done only by someone who has access to credit. And unless he or she has a rich and magnanimous relative, such overspending cannot continue for too many years. Before long, the source of credit is bound to dry up and the accumulated debt must be repaid, with interest. If this individual's earnings do not increase, then the accumulated debt can only be paid off by a reduction in current spending below $10,000 a year—in other words, by belt-tightening.

This type of constraint to spending applies equally to most nations. In the normal course of events, a country can buy in international markets only an amount equal in value to what it can sell in those markets. In the absence of sufficient reserves from past savings, overbuying results in debt and, all other things being equal, in a reduction in living standards when the debt has to be repaid.

There are, however, exceptional nations that are able to live to a considerable extent outside the limits of this elementary "law" of economics. These are the countries whose *domestic paper currency* also functions as *international money*. In the economics trade, money that functions in this way is called a "key currency." Notably since the middle of the nineteenth century, the domestic money of some of the more powerful nations has served as key currencies. That is, throughout the capitalist world these currencies were accepted in addition to, and as a substitute for, gold and silver: (1) as a means of settling international transactions (e.g., in payment for imports and debt service), and (2) as a reserve to cope with trade-balance fluctuations.**

*Eugene A. Birnbaum, "Gold and the International Monetary System: An Orderly Reform" (International Finance Section, Princeton University: *Essays in International Finance*, No. 66 [April 1968]), p. 2. After making the above statement, the author proceeds to claim that there is one exception to the rule that the struggle for power is what it is all about: the United Nations Monetary and Financial Conference at Bretton Woods! This is a surprising opinion (perhaps not so surprising, coming as it does from a North American) about the conference that established the institutional framework for the long-lasting U.S. financial hegemony after the Second World War.

**For information on the extensive use of key currencies even in the heyday of the gold standard, see Peter H. Lindert, "Key Currencies and Gold, 1900-1913" (International Finance Section, Princeton University: Princeton Studies in International Finance, No. 24 [August 1969]).

It should be obvious that a key-currency country obtains clear-cut advantages. It can operate in the arena of international commerce and finance with a much greater degree of freedom than a run-of-the-mill nation, let alone a Third World country. If it overbuys from other countries, it can pay for these purchases by merely printing or otherwise creating more domestic money. It therefore can live for long periods quite comfortably with balance-of-payments deficits; instead of having to tighten its belt, it can become wealthier from an excess of imports over exports. Even more important, the ability to create unilaterally additional international money expands a country's ability to export capital, thereby enabling it to obtain assets yielding a steady return flow of interest and dividends.

Such power, to be sure, does not come out of the blue: not every country can elect to be a key-currency country. It arises from, and in turn helps maintain and enhance, a dominant world position in industrial production, in international trade and transportation, in empire, and in military power. At the same time, this type of dominance is never absolute and secure. Wars, the crises endemic to capitalism, and the continuing pressure of rivals—all these create the prerequisites for a shake-up in the hierarchical relations among the core countries of the imperialist system. The benefits attached to a top position in the hierarchy and the opportunities that arise from the changing fortunes of the capitalist nations set the stage for recurrent power struggles, and notably the struggle which arises from the determination of the top dog in the international money system to hold on to its privileges against the biting and snapping of hungry rivals.

In essence, what is happening in today's financial markets reflects a struggle of this last type. The top-dog position of the United States was unchallenged during the first two decades after the Second World War. The U.S. bid for leadership had already emerged early in the century, and the years between the two world wars were marked by increasing rivalry between New York and London for financial ascendancy. Building on the disorder of the Great Depression and the destruction of the Second World War, the United States reached by mid-century unparalleled supremacy in production, trade, military, and financial affairs. And the power that came with this supremacy was exercised without inhibitions and with unprecedented arrogance.

On the financial front this meant carrying on with an uninterrupted balance-of-payments deficit beginning in the early 1950s, and covering these deficits by flooding the banks of the rest of the capitalist world with U.S. dollars. The disturbances in world finance of recent years (and of today) are the inevitable consequences of this history, along with growing reluctance of rival powers to continue playing the game of follow the leader.

It is true that, looked at from an imperialist point of view, the United States has had unusually heavy international obligations. In the old days of colonialism, the mother country financed the costs of occupation and of additional colony-grabbing by taxing the natives. Furthermore, owning a colony automatically provided the metropole's capitalists with privileged market, finance, and investment preserves. Decolonization changed all that. Even though it opened up potentially vast new opportunities for U.S. business as against rivals from the old colonial powers, the exercise of control and influence in the Third World now called for large-scale spending for military and economic "aid." Also, along with the disruption of the Second World War and the spread of the national liberation movements came the real and, even more, the potential narrowing down of space for capitalist enterprise. Much money was therefore needed to operate military bases around the globe to contain the spread of socialism. Finally, the era of the multinational corporation had dawned, and giant U.S. corporations sought the wherewithal to move freely in foreign lands.

All of this heavy spending abroad became feasible for the United States as soon as the dollar blossomed after the Second World War into *the*, not just *a*, key currency of international finance. As a result, the United States could live year in and year out with balance-of-payments deficits. All that was needed was to create more dollars (either through the Federal Reserve Board or the expansion of domestic bank credit), which when shipped abroad had to be accepted, under the Bretton Woods system, by foreign banks as if they were as good as gold. The upshot of this method of financing U.S. imperialism, plus the foreign operations of U.S. multinational corporations and banks, is that by now the amount of dollars floating around Europe is almost as large as, if not larger than, the narrowly defined money supply within the United States itself. In the United States there are today about $360 billion in currency and checking accounts. In European banks, on the other hand, there were at the end of 1977, according to the very conservative estimates of the Bank for International Settlements, at least $270 billion of U.S. money (called Eurodollars). Others (e.g., the *Wall Street Journal* [November 20, 1978]) estimate that there are now over $500 billion on deposit outside the United States.

What needs to be understood is that it is precisely this fantastic and continuing accumulation of dollars abroad that underlies the instability of the dollar in foreign markets. For example, today about 80 percent of the reserves held by central banks around the capitalist world are in the form of U.S. dollars. Given the volume and endless growth of U.S. dollars abroad, central bankers are impelled by the simplest rules of financial prudence to diversify their holdings. In fact, the diversification process has already begun: only a few years ago as much as 90 percent of their reserves were in U.S. dollars. But this very process of diversification helps push the international value of the dollar down, and this drop in dollar value erodes the worth of the remaining dollars held by foreigners.

The capitalist world's central bankers are therefore on the horns of a dilemma. Too fast or too large a sale of the dollars they hold could disrupt foreign-exchange markets, lead to panic and crisis, and undermine the reserves they count on for their own stability. On the other hand, they are choked up with dollar reserves and they sit in fear that they will be caught with their pants down when other dollar holders or speculators sell off dollars. To a greater or lesser degree, the same dilemma faces all other big dollar holders overseas, who are caught between fear of further decline of the dollar and concern about protecting their dollar assets.

In sum, these are the contradictory forces that are at the heart of the dollar problem. For it is as a result of past and present practices of U.S. imperialism that (1) the dollar sinks in value as foreign holders seek to protect themselves against the inevitable impact of the unending dollar accumulation, and (2) the dollar nevertheless, and precisely because of the vast size of these dollar holdings, remains the key currency of international finance. Considering the overwhelming importance of these dollar-crisis-producing phenomena, it is indeed ironic for the onus of the problem to be placed on such factors as oil imports and labor productivity.

As for the question of the impact of oil imports, the facts are simple and clear. . . .

[T]he United States spent $106 billion in OPEC countries from 1974 to 1977. Almost all of this was for the import of oil. There were some relatively minor purchases of services, primarily about $1 billion to pay for labor and materials in Saudi Arabia in connection with the installation of U.S. armaments.

We see that during the same period the OPEC countries sent back $70 billion to the United States for goods and services. Almost three fifths (58 percent) of this was spent for merchandise such as capital goods, autos, consumer goods, and armaments from private manufacturers. These purchases were made primarily by Saudi Arabia, Venezuela, and Iran. A little over 27 percent of the return flow went to U.S. firms for dividends, interest, fees, and royalties. Another 13 percent was used to purchase armaments under U.S. government military-agency sales contracts, principally to Iran and Saudi Arabia. The remainder of the $70 billion was for miscellaneous services.

The net result of these back and forth sales was a U.S. deficit of $36 billion ($106 billion minus $70 billion). But this deficit was more than wiped out by the $38 billion of OPEC countries' investments in the United States. This was money placed in U.S. banks or used to purchase U.S. treasury bonds and corporate securities. Department of Commerce statisticians have been unable to obtain reliable estimates of other investments such as real estate in the United States by the oil exporters. But even disregarding this additional return flow of dollars, it should be evident enough that the large increase in U.S. spending for oil between 1974 and 1977 was definitely *not* the cause of the overall balance-of-payments deficits.

It is probable that OPEC member countries, like central bankers and multinational firms, began to shift out of dollars towards the end of 1977. But this was clearly a defensive move in reaction to the decline in the international value of the dollar that had begun much earlier in the year. The overriding fact is that the OPEC countries are necessarily integrated in the dollar system. For example, some 60 percent of the $160 billion of foreign assets held by OPEC countries is in dollar accounts, either in the United States or in Europe. (*Euromoney* [May 1978], p. 36) Equally significant is the flat statement made by Sheik Ali Khalifa Al-Sabah, president of OPEC's Committee of Experts: "There is no probability of abandoning the dollar as a means of payment. It is the only currency in which such huge transactions can take place." (*Business Week* [July 24, 1978], p. 138)

The other scapegoat—the alleged declining competitiveness of U.S. industry—also falls to the gound when exposed to a few basic facts. This argument clearly concerns exports of manufactures, since it would have little meaning if applied to exports of agricultural products or materials. Before we get to the substance of our case, it would be useful to point out that over half of U.S. manufacturing exports generally consist of capital goods. It should come as no surprise that exports of such goods have been sluggish in recent years. The reason for this has nothing to do with the alleged lack of competitiveness of U.S. industry and everything to do with the existence of industrial overcapacity in all the advanced capitalist countries. The onset of stagnation and the sluggish recovery from the recent recession have dampened the demand for capital goods, and this naturally shows up as lagging exports of U.S. capital goods.*

But an even more important aspect of this question has been almost completely ignored. And that is the large extent to which U.S. manufacturers are not competing for export business against foreign firms but against their own branches and affiliates located abroad. *U.S. manufacturing firms located abroad are selling almost three times as much as is being exported from the United States.* Note also that this ratio has moved up from 1.9 in 1960 to 2.8 in 1976, the last date for which statistics are currently available.

What has been happening, quite clearly, is that U.S. capital has been shifting from export activity to capturing markets abroad, or taking advantage of cheaper labor, by establishing factories in foreign lands. This is not because of any lack of competitiveness of U.S. industry, but because of the profit-making strategy of giant oligopolistic corporations. As part of this strategy, U.S. multinationals have indeed been exporting—from their overseas subsidiaries. Look, for example, how the $212.8 billion sales by U.S. foreign affiliates in 1976 were distributed: $161 billion worth of manufactured goods were sold in the countries in which the affiliates were located; $14.1 billion exported to the United States; and $37.7 billion exported to other countries. (*Survey of Current Business* [March 1978])

---

*This is also the judgment of the Bank for International Settlements. According to its most recent annual report (June 12, 1978), "U.S. export sales have been held back by the low level of fixed investment in the rest of the industrialized world." (p. 68).

Looked at purely as a game of numbers, the U.S. balance-of-payments deficits would soon disappear if the $37.7 billion of the export activity of the multinationals abroad, let alone a portion of the $161 billion they sell in the countries where they are located, were replaced by exports from the United States. But of course capitalist firms, and especially monopolistic corporations, do not work that way.

We cannot in the present context explore further all the complexities of the U.S. balance-of-payments problem. But the foregoing example of the manufacturing export situation puts the case in a nutshell. The way growth of multinationals has been financed is but one of many imperialist practices that have contributed to the problems of the dollar. The ruling class of an advanced capitalist society such as the United States cannot, nor does it want to, overcome its imperialist nature. The fundamental ills of the international money system therefore cannot be cured; the most that can be done is some tinkering in the hope of averting a major crisis. Meanwhile, confronted with the contradictions of its behavior as a hegemonic power, the U.S. ruling class seeks to divert attention from root causes to false issues from which some side benefits might be obtained. In particular, the hue and cry about the alleged declining competitiveness of domestic industry can serve to pave the way for increased exploitation of the working class and for tax relief for business ostensibly needed to modernize industry.   focus

The final essay, "Dollar Diplomacy" by Charles Krauthammer, illustrates the increasing independence of multinational corporations (MNCs) as significant forces in world politics. As the articles by Hormats and Magdoff rather ironically point out, liberals and radicals often tend to see the interests of MNCs as either supportive of principles of free international trade (as proposed by the Reagan administration) or as the primary agents of U.S. imperialism throughout the world. In other words, whether one supports U.S. economic relations or condemns the excesses of American economic exploitation, multinational corporations are viewed as primary vehicles of American foreign policy. Charles Krauthammer reminds us that the goals of MNCs frequently conflict with the political and ideological objectives of U.S. foreign policy—as the case of Poland illustrates. Moreover, Krauthammer argues that MNCs frequently find the foreign policy objectives of the United States to be fundamentally opposed to the full realization of a global capitalist system. Former Undersecretary of State George Ball has advocated the benefits of a new world order, premised not on the parochial interests of states but on the truly global cosmopolitan aspirations of multinational corporations, or as Ball has described them—cosmocorps.

DOLLAR DIPLOMACY

Charles Krauthammer, *New Republic,* October 28, 1981
Charles Krauthammer is executive editor of the New Republic.

> Merchants have no country of their own. Wherever they may be they have no ties with the soil. All they are interested in is the source of their profits.
>
> —Thomas Jefferson

If you thought that all Americans support the Solidarity movement in Poland in its struggle for political freedom, economic decentralization, and worker self-management, you are wrong. There are some who are quite agitated by these demands, and not because they fear for the safety of Lech Walesa and his followers. They are concerned about the dramatic decline in Poland's G.N.P. and productivity since last year's democratic revolution. These people tend to work for banks—Western banks. Together with Western governments, they have about $23 billion in outstanding loans to Poland. Paul McCarthy, a spokesman for Chemical Bank of New York, gave this view of Poland on the "McNeil-Lehrer Report":

> . . . worker self-management . . . would be counterproductive. In my opinion, what is needed for the immediate term . . . is for greater centralization. And therefore in my view, Solidarity has to . . . be willing to work with the government and it has to allow the government to retain centralized control over the economy. . . . Over the short run [meaning 'the next several months or perhaps the next couple of years'] . . . I am disturbed that Solidarity is taking some of the positions that it appears to be taking—a movement towards a decentralized decision process at all managerial levels of the economy.

One of the panelists, economist Howard Wachtel, was taken aback. He said of McCarthy, "He sounds to me like he is representing the Soviet position here."

Well, not exactly. He represents the banks' position, and in this particular case, the banks and the Soviets have much in common. They are both scared to death of Solidarity and what freedom for Poland could mean. Western banks have lent Poland about $12 billion. As the saying goes, if you owe the bank a dollar and can't pay, you're in trouble; if you owe the bank a billion dollars and can't pay, the bank's in trouble. The banks are in deep trouble. How they got into that position with Poland is interesting. They believed, as they kept throwing good money after bad, that in a command economy the party could always impose austerity on the society and force it to produce the surplus needed to pay off the loans. As a last resort, there was always the Soviet umbrella—the belief, based apparently on a feeling rather than on a firm commitment, that the Soviet Union would never allow one of its satellites to default and that ultimately it would act as guarantor of any loans. Solidarity has threatened both of these assumptions. In one year it has turned Poland from a command into a pluralistic economy. Without Solidarity the government cannot force the people into the sacrifices necessary to make up for the inefficiency of the last 30 years. And a 10 million-strong Polish opposition makes the Soviet Union reluctant to bail out what it sees as a free-spending, ungrateful, and unreliable satellite. It also makes an invasion prohibitively (so far) costly to the Soviets.

But admitting default on Poland's loans would be prohibitively costly to the banks. German banks are the most heavily involved. Some have credits to Poland larger than their net worth. Even the huge Dresdner Bank of Frankfurt, which has taken the lead in most Polish loan syndications, could go under. That would send shock waves through the entire banking system.

What are the banks to do? When private companies find themselves in a jam abroad they usually turn to government at home. Traditionally they lobby and try to persuade government that to act in their interest is to act in the national interest. Failing that, they try sharing the risk. When International Telegraph & Telephone faced expropriation in Chile under Allende, it was insured by a government agency, the Overseas Private Investment Corporation, for losses resulting from any seizure. This coverage, for example, would have given OPIC majority ownership in the I.T.T.-Chilean telephone company if it were seized. As Senator Frank Church pointed out at the time, "This [arrangement] blends the company interests and the American government's interests. The American government, having assumed . . . a contractual obligation to pay the company for the expropriated property, has a financial stake by virtue of the insurance policy." The banks in Poland have no such insurance policy. After all, they are faced with bankruptcy and not expropriation. But their very vulnerability has bought them a kind of insurance policy: if one bank collapses, that is a problem for the banks; if the whole banking system collapses, that is a problem for government. Of course, the banks have gotten themselves into this position by the reckless pursuit of profit. Nevertheless, the only way they can be rescued is for someone to force the Poles back to work.

Who will do it? There are only two candidates. The banks would not be sorry to see the Soviets march into Poland and restore party rule. That's a quick way to achieve what McCarthy calls "greater centralization." The Soviets, apparently, are unwilling to oblige the banks. That leaves only one other candidate: Western governments. The banks want the International Monetary Fund to readmit Poland, lend it the money to pay off the banks, and thus leave the I.M.F. holding worthless Polish paper. That would transfer the risk from the banks to government. It would bail out the banks and leave the West (operating through the I.M.F.) to enforce austerity on the Polish people. So, to restore an economy ruined by 30 years of inefficient Communist rule, the West would bear the responsibility for forcing a drastic reduction in Polish living standards. If Western governments were forced into this political disaster in order to avoid economic disaster, it would constitute one of the most spectacular examples on record of corporate shaping—and distorting—of Western foreign policy.

But not the first. After all, the business of business is profits, and business has long tried to make Western governments define their interests that way, too. "It is time the United States developed an economic foreign policy instead of a political foreign policy," says Fred Borch, former head of General Electric. That is not a new idea. At the outbreak of the World War II, the great oil and chemical companies that had cartel arrangements with German firms tried to keep the U.S. out of war with Germany. In 1973 the Philippine subsidiary of Exxon refused to send oil to the U.S. Navy at Subic Bay in compliance with the Arab boycott of the United States. In banana republics like Guatemala in the 1950s, corporations like United Fruit succeeded in making U.S. policy an instrument of their economic interest. The threat of nationalization was enough to bring out the Marines to restore "normality." And when Washington was not quite militant enough for the corporations, as in Chile at the time of Allende, companies like I.T.T. practically created their own foreign policy. (The president of I.T.T. even offered the C.I.A. a million dollars to help prevent Allende's election. The C.I.A. politely refused.)

Widely publicized examples of multinationals in pursuit of their own "economic foreign policy," like I.T.T.'s meddling in Chile, have given rise to two myths. First, that business has a preference for right wing dictatorships. In fact, business has a preference for stability. It abhors revolution, war, and, when it produces instability, democracy. From Lenin's New Economic Policy to postcolonial Africa, business has made an art of ideological neutrality. The other myth is that the multinationals, although they have no loyalty to the third world countries that host their branch plants, have a special solicitude for the interests of the United States where they are more often than not headquartered. Carl Gerstacker, former chairman of Dow Chemical and corporate globalist, would disagree. He speaks almost mystically of a new kind of "one worldism" in which business is freed from the shackles of national loyalty. "I have long dreamed of buying an island owned by no nation and establishing a world headquarters of the Dow Company on the truly neutral ground of such an island, beholden to no nation or society." (And he adds thoughtfully, "We could even pay any natives handsomely to move elsewhere.") Or, as a spokesman for Union Carbide put it: "It is not proper for an international corporation to put the welfare of any country in which it does business above that of any other."

Union Carbide ought to know. When Ian Smith was in control of Rhodesia, Union Carbide supported American mineral imports from Rhodesia in violation of international sanctions. That made Union Carbide the target of boycotts and protests in the U.S. Now, reports the *Washington Post,* Union Carbide has "quickly settled into a comfortable relationship with former guerrilla leader Robert Mugabe's government." When company chairman William Sneath recently attended a dedication ceremony in Zimbabwe, he declared to Mugabe: "Union Carbide supports your goals." Meanwhile in

Angola Gulf Oil was happy to support the Portuguese colonial government as long as it was allowed to pump its oil. I can remember a planning meeting for a Vietnam War protest that bogged down over the demands of one student faction that the demonstration be a joint protest against Vietnam and against Havard's refusal to divest itself of Gulf stock. The slogan then was "Gulf out of Angola." That was 1972. Well, instead Portugal got out of Angola. Gulf stayed.

Today Gulf almost singlehandedly props up the economy of Angola's Marxist regime. Gulf has poured more than $500 million in investments into Angola, pays more than $320 million a year in taxes and royalties, and gives half its oil to the Angolan government which then exports it to the West (accounting for most of Angola's one billion dollars a year in exports). The government, in turn, protects Gulf from various untamed liberation fronts. As one Gulf spokesman said of the Cuban troops in Angola: "Ipso facto, they are guarding the oil wells." In return, Gulf does what it can, not only to protect but to promote the Angolan regime.

The president of Gulf Oil Exploration and Production Company, Melvin Hill, regularly takes to Capitol Hill to extol the pragmatic, nonideological, business-like ways of the Angolan regime. On April 1, Hill and Gulf Oil president James Lee lobbied Vice President Bush on behalf of Angola. Gulf isn't the only company with a big stake in Angola. There are 17 Western oil companies, mostly from the U.S., who have agreements, or are "in line" for agreements, with the Angolan government. And Boeing, General Electric, Bechtel, Lockheed, General Tire, I.B.M., and other American companies are also doing a brisk business there. So are the banks. Chase Manhattan Bank's letter for corporate customers has been promoting Angola, not only for its oil and diamonds, but also for its "sound economic management and policies." Chairman of the Board David Rockefeller is reported to have sent a letter to the White House before his retirement which expressed his displeasure with the Administration's Angolan policy. The position of the U.S. government from the Ford through the Carter and Reagan Administrations has been that as long as the Soviets retain control over Angola by means of a 20,000-man Cuban army, not only is Angola a geopolitical threat to the West, but it has forfeited its independence. Therefore, the U.S. will refuse to recognize the current regime.

Business is most upset now about the Reagan Administration's desire to repeal the Clark Amendment, which prohibits the U.S. from giving aid to Jonas Savimbi, leader of a defeated faction of the Angolan revolution who continues to wage guerrilla war from the southeastern part of Angola against the current regime. Now, there are reasonable arguments that can be made against the repeal. Some are ideological—for example, that Savimbi gets aid from South Africa. Some are pragmatic—that repeal would anger black African nations like Nigeria. But business opposition stems from the central fact that Savimbi is a threat to the stability of a regime with which these companies have a cozy and profitable commercial relationship. That is not quite how the banks put it. According to Brian Henderson, Chase Manhattan's manager for west African affairs, our economic relations with Angola have "effectively limited Soviet influence and strengthened the government's commitment to nonalignment." For the untrained, noncorporate eye these benefits are hard to discern. The Russians still have 20,000 Cuban troops propping up a pliant regime and preventing any real test of its popularity vis-à-vis Savimbi. (According to *African Index*, a respected, nonpartisan observer of African affairs, Savimbi was favored to win the election scheduled for October 1975.)

As for nonalignment, business has an idiosyncratic understanding of the term. "They are pragmatic people," says Gene Bates, a Texaco vice president, of the Angolans. "Although they lean toward a Marxist style of government, their Marxist friends cannot give them what they need, so they turn to the West." And, indeed, they do. Allowing Western companies to pump your oil, export it overseas, pay you royalties, and transfer technology may make for good business; but it is not nonalignment. It is typical of the willful confusion of "economic foreign policy" with "political foreign policy" that the word nonalignment can be used in conjunction with Angola. After all, by any political measure, Angola is solidly committed to the Soviet bloc. Not only is it occupied by an army of Cuban proxies, but on international issues it can be counted on to follow slavishly Moscow's line. When an overwhelming majority of nonaligned countries at the United Nations condemned the Soviet invasion of Afghanistan, Angola stood with only a handful of Soviet satellites in voting no.

But isn't there something to the argument that corporate ties encourage moderation and promote friendship between nations? Not much. One never hears it argued that heavy private investment in, say, Chile is to be encouraged because political liberalization will follow in its wake. The extraordinary interdependence of European states early in this century did not prevent them from engaging each other in the two most destructive wars in history. And in the third world, corporate investment and trade tend to *follow*, not cause, political liberalization (as in Sadat's Egypt). Our experience with the Soviets is also instructive. Here again expanded trade followed a policy of detente; it did not produce it. Nor is there any evidence that our complex web of relationships with the Soviets has served to moderate Soviet adventurism. The Soviets appeared quite uninhibited by the threat of losing their Western ties when they decided to invade Afghanistan and inject themselves militarily into Angola, Ethiopia, South Yemen, and Libya. Indeed, commercial ties have had their effect on the other party. The threat of losing the Soviet connection or abdicating the competition to another, more unscrupulous, Western competitor has induced one Western government after another to avoid too stiff a response to Soviet misconduct. That was the case with the rather sorry U.S. attempt to isolate the Soviets economically after the Afghan invasion. Now the West Europeans are about to build a multibillion-dollar natural gas pipeline from the U.S.S.R. to Western Europe. Is there any doubt whom that tie will bind?

No one disputes the right of private enterprise to pursue its own economic interest or even to lobby to get government to conform its foreign policy to corporate interests. But it is grating to see business wrap itself in the national interest—to see Mobil, for example, in yet another ad, urge support for yet another act of obeisance to the Saudis as a reward for their moderation on oil prices. Most people are not taken in by such pronouncements from a company that made billions as a result of a Saudi policy of price moderation that raised the price of oil from $2 to $32 in ten years. But some are taken in when the message is issued in the dulcet tones of detente. Mary McGrory of the *Washington Post* recently applauded the improvement in corporate international behavior from its Chile days (bad) to its Angola days (good). The fact is, however, that there has been no change. Corporate motives, like death and taxes, have a certain inevitability to them. Business is business. If Allende had guaranteed I.T.T.'s property as Angola did Gulf's, I.T.T. would have hailed his pragmatism and lobbied against any moves to subvert him. And if Savimbi should succeed in producing a serious enough conflict in Angola to disrupt oil production, you can be sure that Gulf will take to Capitol Hill to call for moderation, a coalition government, and, if worst comes to worst, free elections. And if God forbid, Savimbi wins, one can already hear Union Carbide reassuring him, "We support your goals."

Liberals have long taken an unsentimental view of these sudden corporate conversions. In *Global Reach*, an extensive study of the power of multinational corporations, Richard Barnet and Ronald Müller come to this succinct conclusion:

> The goal of corporate diplomacy is nothing less than the replacement of national loyalty with corporate loyalty. If they are to succeed in integrating the planet, loyalty to the global enterprise must take precedence over all other political loyalties. Wherever possible, business diplomats will try to persuade governments, local businessmen, or anyone who will listen, that there is no conflict between corporate goals and national goals.

If we are to avoid another banker's Poland, it would be wise to keep that in mind. **fOCUs**

An appreciation of liberal and radical assessments of U.S. economic relations are absolutely fundamental for an understanding of U.S. foreign policy during the 1980s and for the increasing conflict that has characterized North-South relations. While many Third

World demands for the reform of global economic relations fall between liberal and radical analyses, Third World critiques of U.S. economic objectives and North-South relations have given strength to the criticisms of the radicals through the force of Third World political and moral demands. It should be noted, however, as Chapter 1 (Neo-Marxist and Liberal Explanations of American Foreign Policy, p. 16) illustrates, the persuasiveness of liberal or neo-Marxist arguments are rooted in a distinctive philosophical or ideological view of human nature. No assessment of the unpopularity of American foreign policy in the Third World can fail to appreciate the primary arguments of the neo-Marxists and radicals. Finally, the increasing power of transnational actors in a world of heightening levels of global interdependence, as epitomized by multinational corporations, needs to be underscored. Perhaps the economic influence of MNCs will be one of the most significant agents of global change.

CHAPTER 5

The Role of Secrecy in a Democratic Society

The Central Intelligence Agency (CIA) is a significant member of the American foreign-policy-making establishment. Throughout the 1970s, revelations about CIA involvement in secret (covert) operations since World War II sparked a storm of controversy about Central Intelligence Agency practices. The debate over the appropriate role of the CIA and effective executive and congressional control of the organization continues in the 1980s. On June 23, 1982, President Ronald Reagan signed the Intelligence Identities Protection Act of 1982, which made it a crime to disclose the name of a U.S. secret agent—even if the agent's name was learned from a public source. The Intelligence Identities Protection Act has been hailed by supporters of the CIA as an important means of protecting American intelligence personnel throughout the world. The act is also seen as an attempt by the president and Congress to end the restrictions placed on CIA activities by Congress and the Ford and Carter administrations in 1974, 1976, and 1978. Controversy over the appropriate role of the CIA continues, however. The argument rests on two distinct perspectives. Those favoring an active CIA presence in the world argue that United States' national security depends on effective intelligence-gathering activities and the ability of the CIA to undertake secret or covert operations. President Reagan and others see the Central Intelligence Agency as a crucial means of conducting American foreign policy in the face of ruthless ideological opponents. These advocates maintain that United States' national security and the day-to-day goals of American foreign policy depend on an effective Central Intelligence Agency. Supporters of the CIA further argue that Congress and the American public overreacted to allegations of illegal CIA intrusions into the domestic political process during the 1960s and 1970s. They claim the recent restrictions placed on CIA activities were based on the good intentions of the American public but fail to understand the fundamental threat to U.S. national security posed by enemies of the U.S.; thus, the Soviet Union and other adversaries of the United States were the beneficiaries of attempts to control CIA activities.

Critics of the CIA argue that the organization has evolved into a powerful bureaucracy that escaped adequate executive and legislative control. They claim the CIA wrapped its activities in a cloak of secrecy, and justified its role by arguing that U.S. national security depended on an organization capable of carrying-out operations that could not be acknowledged by the United States government. In this atmosphere of excessive secrecy, the Central Intelligence Agency became a quasi-independent force—at times actually making American foreign policy, say critics. In other situations, the Central Intelligence Agency became the private tool of successive U.S. presidents to carry out illegal, or at least questionable, activities at home and abroad without the knowledge or accountability of the American people. These critics argue that the absence of adequate control which result from the CIA's unnecessary secrecy does not serve the interests of American foreign policy. Furthermore, it is argued that a secret CIA underground network in the United

States (the burglars who broke into Democratic National Headquarters in the Watergate Building in 1972 had previous ties to the CIA, while the CIA provided equipment for the break-in of Dr. Daniel Ellberg's psychiatrist's office in 1971) threatens the democratic process.

In order to explore the controversy over CIA activities further a brief history of the agency follows. The Central Intelligence Agency was established in 1947 by the National Security Act, which attempted to coordinate U.S. intelligence activities in several bureaucracies under the control of the recently established National Security Council. These agencies included the Department of Defense, the State Department, the Federal Bureau of Investigation (FBI) and the newly created CIA. The Central Intelligence Agency was the outgrowth of the Office of Strategic Services (OSS), a branch of the Department of War created after the Japanese bombing of Pearl Harbor on December 7, 1941. The OSS analyzed data and conducted commando-type missions behind enemy lines during World War II. With the creation of the CIA in 1947, many former member of the OSS (which was disbanded in 1945) joined the new agency. The CIA was strengthened in 1949 through the passage of the Central Intelligence Agency Act which made secret "the functions, names, official titles, salaries, or numbers of personnel employed by the Agency."[a] As the cold war began to intensify, the U.S. government's reliance on the CIA increased when a series of secret National Security Council directives provided the agency with additional latitude.[b] Because it was believed that the United States was under constant and relentless pressure from worldwide Soviet expansionism, the secrecy of the CIA was viewed as a necessity. The majority of CIA resources (some estimates are as high as two-thirds) were allocated for covert operations, rather than for the analysis of data.[c] The evolution of the CIA during the 1950s and 1960s complemented U.S. cold war internationalism. Indeed, the CIA was an organization into which constructive feelings of patriotism could be channeled. While global political conditions favored the development of the CIA, so too did the bureaucratic needs of the organization.

The United States intelligence community is comprised of about 12 major organizations, including the CIA. Defense Department agencies dominate the field including the National Security Agency, the Defense Intelligence Agency, the National Reconnaissance Office, and Army, Air Force, and Navy Intelligence. In addition, intelligence agencies are located in the State Department's Bureau of Intelligence and Research, the FBI's Internal Security Division, and offices of the Atomic Energy Commission, the Treasury, and other bureaucracies.[d] The Pentagon (Department of Defense) dominates the field in terms of manpower and the size of its budget. The Pentagon commands the most sophisticated technology, including satellites, telecommunications systems, and listening posts around the world. In addition to its technological superiority, the Department of Defense also maintains covert operations units in Army, Navy, and Air Force Intelligence. The survival of the CIA from a bureaucratic perspective demanded that the organization establish a secure niche for itself in the competitive and decentralized U.S. intelligence community. Since the CIA could not compete with the Pentagon's ability to do research, the secrecy of the agency provided it with the wherewithal to launch covert operations throughout the world. The Foreign Intelligence Advisory Board was established in 1956 to oversee covert operations. In addition, the CIA reported to a very small number of senior congressmen. Presidential control was exercised at a policy-making level through the National Security Council and economically through the Office of Management and Budget, which controlled the CIA's budget. During the cold war years, especially 1947-1962, when strong bipartisan agreement characterized congressional support for U.S. foreign policy, the Central Intelligence Agency flourished. As popular support for the goals of U.S. foreign policy began to erode in the late 1960s and early 1970s, CIA activities were examined in a more critical light. CIA activities in Southeast Asia and throughout the world were revealed in the Pentagon Papers. The Watergate scandal in 1972, raised disturbing questions about CIA activities in the United States. Further revelations about CIA involvement in American politics revealed the opening of mail to and from the U.S.S.R., the infiltration of domestic organizations, and the testing of drugs on unknowing Americans.[e] A storm of criticism followed. In 1976, President Gerald Ford issued an executive order that severely limited CIA intrusion into U.S. politics. In 1978 President Jimmy Carter created new procedures requiring the director of the CIA to clear "sensitive" intelligence gathering operations in advance with the National Security Council. In addition, the U.S. Congress took a more active role in its review of CIA activities and set up two permanent committees to review intelligence activities.[f] By 1980, however, a new mood emerged supporting the removal of many of the restrictions placed on the CIA by Congress and the executive branch. With the Soviet invasion of Afghanistan and the capture of American hostages by Iranian militants in 1979 and the decreasing significance of both the Vietnam War and Watergate for the American public in the late 1970s, pressure mounted to loosen controls placed on the Central Intelligence Agency. Ronald Reagan charged during the 1980 campaign that the intelligence capabilities of the United States had been seriously weakened—thereby threatening American national security. The debate between those supporting the CIA and those calling for tight restrictions of its activities continues.

In the following article by Washington Post staff member, George Lardner, Jr., published in 1981, the author argues that any attempt to "revitalize" the CIA is a threat to the democratic process in the United States. Lardner suggests that without extensive congressional control, the power of the CIA will grow in an atmosphere of secrecy and national security. Lardner's criticism of the Intelligence Reform Act of 1980 illustrates the intensity of those who fear the absence of adequate control in a democratic society.

Footnotes

a   David Wise, "Covert Operations Abroad, An Overview," in *The CIA File,* edited by Robert L. Borosage and John Marks (New York: Grossman Publishers, 1976), p. 9.
b   *Ibid.*
c   Victor Marchetti, "An Introductory Overview," in *The CIA File* edited by Borosage and Marks, p. xii.
d   *Ibid.,* p. xi.
e   *Ibid.*
f   Stansfield Turner and George Thibault, "Intelligence: The Right Rules," *Foreign Policy,* Number 48, (Fall 1982) p. 123.
g   *Ibid.*

MOYNIHAN UNLEASHES THE C.I.A.

George Lardner, Jr., *Nation,* February 16, 1980

George Lardner is a member of the national staff of the Washington Post.

The C.I.A. has spied on our own people. The F.B.I. has committed burglaries. . . . This is a time for change in our country. I don't want the people to change. I want the Government to change.
                                    —Jimmy Carter, Dallas, September 24, 1976

Television crews and Congressional aides squeezed up against one another in a Senate hearing room last month for a bizarre lesson in semantics. The drive for "reform" of the Central Intelligence Agency and the rest of the nation's intelligence community had taken a new turning, as Senator Daniel Patrick Moynihan proceeded to demonstrate at a crowded press conference.

It was the day after President Carter's State of the Union Message with its alarums over the Persian Gulf and what Carter called "unwarranted restraints" on our intelligence-gathering activities. Moynihan and six colleagues—four Republicans and two Democrats—seized on the occasion to introduce what they christened the Intelligence Reform Act of 1980. Simply put, the proposal amounts to an official secrets act. It would enable the C.I.A. to close the door on most of its misdeeds, past, present or anticipated. It would repeal the law governing covert operations and lift Congressional restraints in effect for the past six years. It would provide for the prosecution of citizens who disclose certain information, even if it is in the public domain.

Moynihan, of course, characterized the measure differently. It was simply a modest beginning, he said—a three-part proposal that "should be seen as but the first blocks in the reconstruction of our intelligence community, not the final edifice." "For too long," Moynihan continued, "we have seen in our own nation a threat to our liberties which, more properly, ought to be seen in places outside our country. Simply stated, we have enemies in the world. It is the K.G.B., not the C.I.A., which threatens democracy."

The speech was vintage Moynihan. But the bill, known as S. 2216, could have been written by the C.I.A.—as indeed much of it was. Moynihan seemed chagrined by a reporter's question to that effect, until an aide informed the Senator that not a few of the provisions had come from C.I.A. headquarters in Langley, Virginia. Whereupon Moynihan harrumphed that he saw nothing wrong with that. "We have made no effort to exclude them," he said of the C.I.A.'s draftsmen. Senator Malcolm Wallop, a co-sponsor of the measure, called it "normal procedure" for a bill affecting a Government agency. Neither dwelt on what that did to the word "reform."

With all the war talk bubbling around Washington, however, it is comforting to dream that the C.I.A. can magically pull us back from the brink. The Moynihan bill has an ominous head of steam behind it. Similar legislation is already pending in the House. The Carter Administration seem[ed] especially keen on giving the Agency a freer hand for covert actions, in a harking back to "the good old days" of the 1950s and 1960s when it restored the Shah of Iran to his throne, engineered the overthrow of President Jácobo Arbenz Guzmán in Guatemala and finally plunged us into the Bay of Pigs. The new drive has raised speculation about the possibility of covert aid to the Moslem rebels in Afghanistan—as though covert aid were somehow unthinkable. Secrecy is more beguiling. It avoids hard questions, such as whether we really want to go to war—and where—and when.

Although the crisis in Iran and the Soviet invasion of Afghanistan have solidified the new mood, it has been building for some time, beginning, in fact, with the final days of the Senate and House investigations of 1975-76 into the C.I.A.'s and the Federal Bureau of Investigation's excesses in the name of national security. A new rule of law was promised. The only result was the creation of the permanent Senate and House intelligence committees, which were assigned the task of supervising America's spies and counterspies. They quickly fell prey to the Washington rule that the regulators shall lie down with the regulated and became even more secretive. The two committees have produced only one law of any significance: a statute setting up a special court that issues secret warrants permitting electronic surveillance of American citizens in national security cases. The chairman of the Senate Select Committee on Intelligence, Birch Bayh, hailed its passage in 1978 as "a landmark in the development of effective legal safeguards for constitutional rights." He predicted that it would pave the way for enactment of compre-hensive legislative charter to govern the U.S. intelligence community.

The President who said he wanted "the Government to change" promised a charter, too. He assigned Vice President Mondale as his point man, charged with the task of producing controls that the intelligence agencies could digest. They digested Mondale instead. The Vice President turned out to be so ineffectual—and so inattentive—that he launched the Carter-Mondale re-election effort last year unaware that the charter legislation had yet to be sent to Capitol Hill. This lapse caused some embarrassment when Mondale opened the campaign last September in Florida and listed reform of the intelligence agencies as one of the Administration's accomplishments. He professed surprise on being told by a reporter, after the speech, that the C.I.A. charter had not yet been introduced. He promised the reporter an interview on the subject. Then he went on to California to tell a crowd there that, "we have proposed legislation for charters for the F.B.I. and the C.I.A." Mondale subsequently declined to be interviewed about the matter. "He just feels he has had no time to focus on it," a spokesman said.

Then came Iran and Afghanistan. The Administration began pressing hard for one of the C.I.A.'s long-stated objectives: repeal of the Hughes-Ryan amendment governing covert operations. Suddenly, the new vogue word was "revitalization" of the C.I.A.

An irony of the alleged dismantling of the Agency as a result of the 1975-76 investigations is that the two most significant reforms were enacted before the exposés took place. One was the Hughes-Ryan amendment, which Congress tacked onto the 1974 Foreign Assistance Act following a furor over C.I.A. activities in Chile. The amendment provided that covert action—"other than activities intended solely for obtaining necessary intelligence"—could be undertaken only if the President finds each such operation "important to the national security" and reports it "in a timely fashion . . . to the appropriate committee of the Congress." . . .

The C.I.A. has been railing against the rule ever since, denouncing it as an invitation to leaks since it requires reports to eight Congressional committees—the Foreign Affairs, Armed Services, Appropriations and Intelligence committees of both House and Senate. By Moynihan's arithmetic, that means disclosure to "some 180 legislators and almost as many staff" whenever the C.I.A. undertakes a mission outside the realm of intelligence collection.

Actually, the circle of lawmakers privy to such secrets is much more limited. On some of the committees, only the ranking members are informed. On the intelligence committees, which would continue to receive reports of "substantial" undertakings under the Moynihan bill, only the members plus a few top aides are apprised. What seems to bother the C.I.A. most about Hughes-Ryan is the restraint it imposes. According to Senator Walter Huddleston, the Agency has decided against some projects—and modified others—out of fear of disclosure.

With characteristic understatement, Huddleston, a ranking member of the Senate intelligence committee, allows that such restraint may have been "a good thing." He also told a reporter that he knows of no leaks that could definitely be blamed on Hughes-Ryan. The risks of disclosure by Congress have, in any case, always been exaggerated. A 1971 C.I.A. study found that only one of every twenty serious leaks of information come from Capitol Hill. Most of them can be traced to high-level Administration officials, to the Pentagon and to the intelligence and diplomatic communities. In the early 1970s, there were an estimated 400,000 to 500,000 people within the executive branch alone who were cleared for top secret information.

Moynihan's proposed Intelligence Reform Act of 1980 would do much more than restrict the reporting of what used to be called "dirty tricks" to the House and Senate intelligence committees. It would also restore, at least to a limited extent, the doctrine of Presidential "deniability," whereby the Chief Executive could disclaim any knowledge of such undertakings. The President would have to approve only those covert operations involving "substantial resources or risks." The National Security Council would pass on the rest, and these would not have to be reported to any Congressional committee at all. "You can defeat the purpose of reporting by reporting too much," Moynihan declared in justification of this provision. "We are requiring the reporting of events we will really pay attention to."

The other key reform proposed by Moynihan and company involves the Freedom of Information Act (F.O.I.A.), which has had the C.I.A. grumbling ever since it was forced to comply with it under a series of amendments Congress enacted in 1974. Until then, C.I.A. documents could be automatically withheld from public scrutiny simply by invocation of the "national security" exemption, but Congress changed the rule by providing that the reasons for such secrecy could be challenged in court. It also set down deadlines for compliance.

To hear the C.I.A. tell it, the information released has been thoroughly inconsequential. "[T]he information furnished is almost always fragmentary and is often misleading," C.I.A. Deputy Director Frank C. Carlucci argued last August in a letter to the White House Office of Management and Budget. "Therefore the information is more often than not of little use to the recipient." Never mind that the law has produced volume after volume about the assassination of President Kennedy, the C.I.A.'s controversial drug-testing programs and its illegal domestic spying operations. Never mind that the documents released under the F.O.I.A. show far more extensive surveillance than even the Rockefeller Commission was told about. . . .

The C.I.A.'s proposal—drafted by Langley and introduced by Moynihan word for word as part of his bill—would permit general freedom of information requests only for what Carlucci called "finished intelligence products." For the rest of its files, only American citizens could apply and they could ask, Carlucci said, only for "what, if any, information we have on them personally."

That may touch off a stiff fight. "All properly classified information is protected under the law now," says the American Civil Liberties Union's legislative representative, Jerry Berman. "None of it has leaked out under F.O.I.A. Vital secrets have been lost to spies, but not under the Freedom of Information Act."

The last of the "modest measures" (Wallop's phrase) in the joint Moynihan-C.I.A. package could prove even more controversial. It was actually drafted by C.I.A. lawyers and staffers of the House Select Committee on Intelligence and introduced in the House last year as a separate measure by all fourteen members of the committee. It would make it a crime to disclose the names of C.I.A. operatives stationed abroad—even if the disclosure came after the agent had returned home.

The stiffest penalties in the bill—ten years in prison and a $50,000 fine—would be imposed on offenders who have had authorized access to classified information—former C.I.A. employees, for example. Others, such as journalists, would face a year in prison and a $5,000 fine if the Government could show they intended "to impair or impede the foreign intelligence activities of the United States." The proposal even contains a little fillip designed to overcome a World War II-era court decision that barred an espionage prosecution for sending material already published in U.S. newspapers and magazines to Germany. Under the new bill, it would still be a crime to "disclose" a name taken from public sources—for instance, an old State Department biographical register—so long as the Government was still "taking affirmative measures to conceal such individual's intelligence relationship to the United States."

The C.I.A. has depicted this proposal as being aimed solely at Agee* and an anti-C.I.A. "coterie dedicated to exposing the names of agents," but it would

*Phillip Agee is a former C.I.A. agent who has been accused of exposing the names of intelligence officers—Ed.

clearly have a much broader impact. "There's a lot of intelligent people who think the bill is unconstitutional," said one House lawyer. "I said intelligent people, not intelligence people. Sometimes there's a difference."

The Carter Administration has already given its blessings to the three-part package as part of the long-promised charter for the C.I.A., but there are few officials who think that so comprehensive a measure stands a chance of enactment. The charter, moreover, has been evolving from a strict code of conduct for the intelligence community into a license for wide-ranging secret activities with few blanket prohibitions. Still to be introduced at this writing, it would, for instance, ban assassinations but impose no penalties on those who ignore the injunction. It would also sanction everything from burglaries to wiretapping of law-abiding Americans abroad, so long as the Government thinks some important information might be acquired.

Huddleston still hopes to get a charter through the Senate, rather than just the Moynihan bill, but he agrees that in its present mood the House will give the C.I.A. only the cold-war rearmament of S. 2216. The charter might get bogged down in election-year rhetoric and besides, the C.I.A. can burgle abroad right now, without having to meet statutory standards for breaking and entering.

As a result, Huddleston isn't even sure he can get a charter reported out of his own Senate intelligence committee. Moynihan, Wallop and two other sponsors of S. 2216, Senators Henry M. Jackson and John H. Chafee, all sit on the same panel. As chairman of the subcommittee on charters and guidelines, Huddleston could bottle up S. 2216 and insist on taking it from there only as part of an overall charter. But he says he doesn't intend to try that gambit. He plans to report out both S. 2216 and a comprehensive charter, and then let the full committee make up its mind.

Administration insiders say the Carter White House isn't going to push hard for "a full charter" either. Who ever said the C.I.A. did anything really wrong anyway? Jimmy Who?   **focus**

The Intelligence Reform Act of 1980 did not receive the approval of the 96th Congress. An almost identical version of the bill, entitled The Intelligence Identities Protection Act of 1982, however, was passed by the 97th Congress. Its passage and a new executive order by President Ronald Reagan have attempted to revitalize the role of the Central Intelligence Agency. The Reagan administration, in particular, views those controls restricting CIA activities as a threat to U.S. national security. The administration has given the director of the CIA greater discretion in what intelligence-collecting operations are submitted to the National Security Council for approval. Moreover, Reagan's executive order allows greater CIA activities in the United States, as long as those activities are not intended to influence U.S. public opinion. As the following remarks by Ronald Reagan, delivered at the signing of the Intelligence Identities Protection Act, suggest, the president sees the CIA as a front line in the defense of the United States. He also sees the Central Intelligence Agency as a crucial instrument in the development of American foreign policy.

REMARKS ON SIGNING THE INTELLIGENCE IDENTITIES PROTECTION ACT OF 1982

Ronald Reagan, June 23, 1982
Ronald Reagan is the 40th president of the United States.

. . . When President Dwight Eisenhower came here almost 23 years ago to dedicate the cornerstone of this building here, he spoke of heroes—"heroes," he said, "who are undecorated and unsung, whose only reward was the knowledge that their service to their country was unique and indispensible."

Well, today I speak again of those heros, the men and women who are locked in a dangerous, sometimes deadly conflict with the forces of totalitarianism, the men and women whose best accomplishments, whose greatest deeds can never be known to their countrymen, but only to a few of their superiors and ultimately only to history. These men and women, these heroes of a grim twilight struggle are those of you who serve here in the Central Intelligence Agency.

Whether you work in Langley or a faraway nation, whether your tasks are in operations or analysis sections, it is upon your intellect and integrity, your wit and intuition that the fate of freedom rests for millions of your countrymen and for many millions more all around the globe. You are the trip-wire across which the forces of repression and tyranny must stumble in their quest for global domination. You, the men and women of the CIA, are the eyes and ears of the free world.

Like those who are part of any silent service, your sacrifices are sometimes unappreciated; your work is sometimes misunderstood. Because you're professionals, you understand and accept this. But because you're human and because you deal daily in the dangers that confront this nation, you must sometimes question whether some of your countrymen appreciate the value of your accomplishments, the sacrifices you make, the dangers you confront, the importance of the warnings that you issue.

And that's why I have come here today; first, to sign an important piece of legislation that bears directly on your work, an act of Congress whose overwhelming passage by the representatives of the American people is a symbol of their support for the job that you do every day. But even more than this, I've come here today to say to you what the vast majority of Americans would say if they had this opportunity to stand here before you. We're grateful to you. We thank you. We're proud of you. . . .

As I've said, the enactment of the Intelligence Identities Protection Act is clear evidence of the value this nation places on its intelligence agencies and their personnel. It's a vote of confidence in you by the American people through their elected representatives. It's also a tribute to the strength of our democracy.

The Congress has carefully drafted this bill so that it focuses only on those who would transgress the bounds of decency; not those who would exercise their legitimate right of dissent. This carefully drawn act recognizes that the revelation of the names of secret agents adds nothing to legitimate public debate over intelligence policy. It is also a signal to the world that while we in this democratic nation remain tolerant and flexible, we also retain our good sense and our resolve to protect our own security and that of the brave men and women who serve us in difficult and dangerous intelligence assignments.

During the debate over this bill, some have suggested that our focus should be not on protecting our own intelligence agencies, but on the real or imagined abuses of the past. Well, I'm glad that counsel was rejected, for the days of such abuses are behind us. The Congress now shares the responsibility of guarding against any transgression, and I have named a new Intelligence Oversight Board and Foreign Intelligence Advisory Board to assist me in ensuring that the rule of law is maintained in areas which must remain secret and out of the normal realm of public scrutiny.

Beyond this, I have full confidence that you'll do your job vigorously and imaginatively while making sure that your activity is lawful, constitutional, and in keeping with the traditions of our way of life. And while you're at your job and while I'm President and while these Congressmen stand at watch, we'll work together to see to it that this powerful tool of government is used to advance, not abuse, the rights of free people.

Today, after nearly a decade of neglect and sometimes overzealous criticism, our intelligence agencies are being rebuilt. This is altogether in keeping with the American tradition. Such activities have been crucial to our survival as a nation. The sacrifice of Nathan Hale, whose statue stands near here, is a national legend. And in our own time, the valiant performance of our intelligence agencies at crucial battles like Midway and Normandy is a matter of historical record. It is out of this valiant service during World War II that your agency was born.

As some of you perhaps know, it was in 1943 that General Bill Donovan decided to penetrate the Third Reich with secret agents. He did so against the advice of our more experienced allies, who said it was an impossible task. It was only 35 years later that the story of those efforts were fully brought to light in a book called "The Piercing of the Reich," by Joseph Persico.

I thought you'd be interested to know that the young New York lawyer who was given the job of penetrating Nazi Germany was described in this book as "a man with boundless energy and confidence, a man with an analytical mind, tenacious will, and a capacity to generate high morale among his staff. He delegated authority easily to trusted subordinates and set a simple standard: results."

As some of you know by now, the name of that young lawyer who performed the impossible task of putting 103 missions into Germany is William Casey, and he is now your DCI. He's a close friend to whom I owe a great personal debt, and I know that debt grows greater every day with the job that you and he are doing together.

I'm familiar with the important changes that have been made in CIA analysis and operations under Bill's leadership, and I know that together you're writing another important and inspiring chapter in the history of those who've worked in America's intelligence agencies. We'll need this kind of excellence from you, for the challenges in the months and years ahead will be great ones.

As some of you may know, I've spoken recently about the fading appeal of totalitarianism and about the internal decay of the Soviet experiment. And some have asked in response why I place such an emphasis on the strength of our military and of intelligence agencies if indeed it is our adversaries who are approaching the point of exhaustion. Well, the answer to that is not difficult. History shows that it is precisely when totalitarian regimes begin to decay from within, it is precisely when they feel the first real stirrings of domestic unrest, that they seek to reassure their own people of their vast and unchallengeable power through imperialistic expansion or foreign adventure.

So, the era ahead of us is one that will see grave challenges and be fraught with danger, yet it's one that I firmly believe will end in the triumph of the civilized world and the supremacy of its beliefs in individual liberty, representative government, and the rule of law under God.

And that's why we must now summon all the nations of the world to a crusade for freedom and a global campaign for the rights of the individual, and you are in the forefront of this campaign. You must be the cutting edge of freedom in peace and war, and in the shadowy world in between, you must serve in silence and carry your special burden. But let me assure you, you're on the winning side, and your service is one which free men will thank you and future generations honor you.   **focus**

When analyzing the role played by the Central Intelligence Agency in developing foreign policy, three assumptions need to be emphasized. First, most students of foreign policy acknowledge the importance of the collection and analysis of intelligence by states. Clearly, U.S. foreign policy in military, economic, and political arenas depends on reliable intelligence estimates. The Central Intelligence Agency, however, is only one of a dozen organizations comprising the U.S. intelligence community. The decentralization of the intelligence bureaucracies and the sheer size of the Pentagon makes the CIA's central function ambiguous. Second, whether one supports or opposes the CIA's covert operations as an instrument of American foreign policy depends on how one conceives prevailing patterns of international politics. If world politics is placed in a rigid cold war framework which emphasizes the danger of the implacable enemies of the United States, then the importance of the CIA tends to increase. If world politics is viewed as an arena emphasizing conflict and cooperation among states over different issues, then an emphasis on the covert operations of the CIA seems less vital, given the size of the U.S. intelligence community. Third, perceptions of the CIA's role in domestic politics are rooted in questions of political theory. Opponents of the CIA's covert operations argue that there is a contradiction between a democratic process based on accountability—the idea of separation of powers and checks and balances—and the existence of a secret bureaucracy accountable only to the executive branch of government. Supporters of the CIA see it as essential to the preservation of a democratic system of government in a world of hostile political, economic, and military interests.

CHAPTER 6

The Continuing Legacies
of the Cold War

With the advent of détente between 1971 and 1975, American foreign policy changed course. The hard-line ideological rhetoric of the cold war years lessened. The Soviet Union was considered more of a traditional rival; coexistence and cooperation, as well as conflict, with the Soviets were believed possible. This changing outlook was manifested in arms limitations agreements between the United States and the Soviet Union, increased economic trade, cultural exchanges, and unprecedented levels of Jewish emigration from the Soviet Union. American foreign policy's traditional emphasis on anti-communism and internationalism also seem to be transformed. President Richard M. Nixon and Secretary of State Henry Kissinger were guiding forces behind détente. The agonizing end of the Vietnam War had forced a reevaluation of the basic cold war assumptions of post-World War II American foreign policy.

By 1982 many of the assumptions characteristic of the brief years of détente had disappeared. They had been replaced by a re-emphasis on cold war policies and assumptions, as epitomized in the final years of the Carter administration and Ronald Reagan's foreign policy. The menace of a Soviet-dominated Communist insurgency throughout the world had become the principal focus of American foreign policy since 1979. Accompanying this outlook was an emphasis on American internationalism similar to the Manifest Destiny of the late 1940s and 1950s. In order to appreciate the dramatic transformation of American foreign policy during the 1970s—from détente to renewed anti-communism—the impact of the Vietnam War must be discussed.

Debate still continues on the causes and consequences of American involvement in Vietnam. Many see American military participation in Vietnam as the logical consequence of the "domino theory" and the post-World War II strategy emphasizing the containment of communism. There remains significant disagreement as to the validity of the containment doctrine in the wake of the fall of Vietnam and Cambodia and perceptions of Communist inroads in Central America. A second perspective points to the importance of U.S. economic interests in helping to explain American involvement. This approach points to the alliance between the U.S. Defense Department and the American military-industrial complex. Thus, big business, especially weapons-producing industries, benefited from the massive American military presence in Vietnam. A related argument suggests that the military-industrial complex sought abundant natural resources, oil for example, in Southeast Asia. A third explanation sees the Vietnam debacle as the result of poor decision-making in the Kennedy administration, which was intensified during the Johnson presidency—especially after LBJ's 1964 landslide electoral victory. Not only were governmental decision-makers incorrect in their political and military strategies, but the "acceptable" policy options were limited by bureaucratic goals. In other words, the U.S. Defense Department was committed to a military victory. With each escalation of U.S. troops to Vietnam it became more difficult for the Johnson administration to reverse its stated goal—the defeat of North Vietnam. Thus, the administration found itself being pulled deeper and deeper into a political, military, and bureaucratic quagmire. From this perspective, it was easier to increase the American commitment to Vietnam than to confront the more difficult question of finding a resolution to the war.

The U.S. experience in Vietnam raises a number of important issues about American foreign policy, including the nature of U.S. anti-communism, internationalism, and Manifest Destiny. Moreover, the bitter heritage of Vietnam raises a number of issues directly affecting U.S. domestic and international politics: the role of national security bureaucracies (the Defense Department, the CIA, and the FBI) in policy-making; the appropriateness of a U.S. policy on human rights; U.S. involvement in Third World conflicts; and the omnipresence of superpower conflict, even in the more remote reaches of the developing world. Perceptions of these and related issues comprise many of the "lessons learned in Vietnam" by the American people. As Reagan's foreign policy toward the Soviet Union in 1983 illustrates, however, the Vietnam experience is subject to reinterpretation in light of domestic and international politics.

The thirteen-year history of the Vietnam War (1960-1973) is one of the most important chapters of American foreign policy since World War II. With the fall of Saigon on April 30, 1975, America's political, military, and economic commitments to Vietnam ended. Yet debate over the "lessons" of American involvement in Vietnam continues to exert a powerful influence over the formulation of American foreign policy. For many Americans, the war in Vietnam was the logical conclusion of the misguided and dangerous policy of trying to contain Soviet-dominated communism. From this perspective, the excesses of a cold war ideology so distorted American foreign policy that U.S. involvement in Vietnam was inevitable. The "arrogance of American power" and the creation of a post-World War II American empire (in political, military, and economic terms, see Chapter 1, p. 10) created the domestic and international climate necessary for American involvement in Vietnam. The atmosphere immediately following the Vietnam debacle, therefore, resulted in three policy prescriptions: first, the rejection of America's role as world policeman; second, legislative restrictions on the ability of the president to send U.S. troops abroad (The War Powers Act of 1973); and third, restrictions on the U.S. national security establishment service and restrictions on the covert operations of the national security establishment in two areas: 1) the end of the draft and the creation of an all-volunteer military service; and 2) restrictions on the covert operations of the C.I.A. at home and abroad.[a] Thus some of the most important consequences of the Vietnam War were psychological. Americans questioned the wisdom of established policies, rejected the foundations of cold war internationalism, and raised doubts about the morality of American foreign policy.

A second faction argued that guilt over the Vietnam War endangered the future of the United States and the West. The threat of Soviet expansionism still had to be confronted. As the 1970s came to a close, a chorus of voices argued that American non-involvement in world affairs encouraged Soviet aggression. In other words, American reluctance to challenge the Soviet Union in the Third World (even in Central America) created a void into which the U.S.S.R. moved. By 1979 the United States was faced with a Soviet threat on every continent: the invasion of Afghanistan in 1979; Soviet and Cuban troops in Ethiopia and Angola; the Vietnamese invasion of Cambodia; and Soviet-sponsored subversion in the Caribbean and Central America—Grenada, Nicaragua, and El Salvador. From this perspective, the containment of Soviet expansion throughout the world should be the single most important aspect of American foreign policy in the 1980s.

The arguments of either side suggest the importance of competing visions of domestic and international politics—and of human nature itself. Those who reject U.S. interventionism argue that the "lessons of the Vietnam War" cannot be forgotten. They point to the political and strategic bankruptcy of the containment doctrine and the domino theory. The American experience in Vietnam would suggest that communism is no longer exclusively dominated by the Soviet Union. The rift between the U.S.S.R. and the People's Republic of China, dating from the late 1950s, and the nationalistic aspect of communism in Third World states illustrates the limits of the Soviet Union's power. The Truman Doctrine of 1947 maintained that all communism was directed by Moscow and that without the active opposition of the United States (containment), non-Communist states would fall under the onslaught of Soviet-dominated expansion (the domino theory). The containment doctrine and the domino theory were the principal justifications for American involvement in Vietnam during the administrations of Harry S. Truman, Dwight D. Eisenhower, John F. Kennedy, and Lyndon B. Johnson. By 1966, however, the United States found itself in the midst of a major war without an acceptable political solution. Winning the war became secondary to ending the fighting and bringing American troops home. Thus, the underlying assumptions of American foreign policy were challenged in three areas as a result of Vietnam. First, the Vietnam War revealed the fragmentation of world communism between the Soviet Union and China. The image of monolithic Soviet communism was reversed. The ensuing normalization of relations between the U.S. and China from 1971 onward documents the U.S.'s changing perspective. Second, as the process of détente grew, U.S. perceptions of the Soviet Union changed to emphasize their mutual interests, especially in the area of nuclear weapons. The first strategic arms limitation agreement (SALT I) and the Vladivostok Accords indicated a new more complex appreciation of the Soviet Union. Third, as U.S.–U.S.S.R. détente moved forward, the Soviet Union was viewed less as an aggressor and more as a significant power with a range of interests. The goal of the containment of communism broke down as American reluctance to engage in future Vietnams intensified. The Vietnam experience became synonymous with failure. By 1975, however, the Ford administration banished any reference to détente, although negotiations on a new SALT Treaty proceeded. The election of Jimmy Carter in 1976 presented an opportunity for new departures in American foreign policy. Carter's emphasis on unofficial détente through the negotiation of SALT II, the Panama Canal Treaty of 1978, and human rights policies were further attempts to move beyond the legacy of Vietnam. The Carter administration hoped to create a new era of global cooperation and development through American foreign policy. However, by 1978-79, Carter's foreign policy was in shambles. Only the Panama Canal Treaty was secured. Human rights policies were attacked as naive and inconsistent in the face of Soviet aggression. The SALT II agreement was withdrawn by the Carter administration in the wake of the Soviet invasion of Afghanistan. Defense expenditures increased dramatically (best symbolized by the decision to produce an MX missile system). A grain embargo against the Soviet Union and U.S. withdrawal from the 1980 Olympics (held in Moscow) were attempts by the Carter administration to punish the U.S.S.R. With the election of Ronald Reagan in 1980, hostility toward the Soviet Union and cold war policies intensified. The "lessons" of the Vietnam War were reversed. Fear of Soviet motivations throughout the world became the dominant theme of American foreign policy. It would seem that the Vietnam experience had been put aside.

In the following article by Michael T. Klare, "Assault on the 'Vietnam Syndrome,' " the transformation of American foreign policy during the late 1970s is analyzed. Klare defines the "Vietnam Syndrome" as the American reluctance to "engage in further military interventions in internal Third World conflicts" (p. 122). Klare points to the crucial role played by business, political, and national security elites in calling for a return to the containment policies of the cold war years.

Reference

[a]Michael T. Klare, "Beyond the Vietnam Syndrome" U.S. Intervention in the 1980s (Washington, D.C.: Institute for Policy Studies, 1981), p. 2.

THE ASSAULT ON THE VIETNAM SYNDROME

Michael Klare, *Beyond the Vietnam Syndrome,* the Institute for Policy Studies, 1981

Michael Klare is a fellow at the Institute for Policy Studies in Washington, DC.

For seven years, the United States fought a costly and ultimately futile war in Southeast Asia. When the war in Vietnam ended, a new war began. Not a war with guns and bullets, but a war with words—the war to reverse the "Vietnam Syndrome." Although this propaganda war is still underway, it has already had a decisive impact on American politics and may, when the last battle is finally decided, affect the course of history even more profoundly than the Vietnam conflict itself.[1]

Stated simply, the "Vietnam Syndrome" is the American public's disinclination to engage in further military interventions in internal Third World conflicts. For many Americans, this "Syndrome" is a prudent and beneficial alternative to the interventionist policies which led us into Vietnam in the first place. Not only is it sparing of the lives of our young men and women, but it also facilitates the search for creative, non-military solutions to the problems facing all nations in an increasingly interdependent world. For other Americans, however, the Vietnam Syndrome is an unacceptable restraint on Washington's capability to protect critical U.S. interests abroad. These individuals believe that any reluctance on our part to engage in military action invites attack by hostile forces and thus endangers America's privileged world position. And because they are determined to revive intervention as a legitimate instrument of U.S. foreign policy, they have launched a vigorous and unceasing campaign to "cure" America of the Vietnam Syndrome.

Although, for most of the past ten years, U.S. leaders attempted to steer a middle course between these two conflicting outlooks—eschewing involvement in "peripheral" contests like those in Angola (1976) and Nicaragua (1978) while sanctioning intervention if needed to protect "vital" interests such as Middle Eastern oil—it is now apparent that the anti-Syndrome forces will not rest until they have secured the total victory of their position. When and if that moment arrives—and it could arrive soon—America may find itself embroiled in a new round of conflicts that will make Vietnam look like a minor skirmish. Until then, however, the Syndrome will continue to act as a brake on aggressive U.S. military behavior abroad, and thus advocates of interventionism will continue to make war on all surviving expressions of this deeply-rooted stance.

When first developed, the Vietnam Syndrome had both institutional and subjective manifestations. Institutionally, the Syndrome assumed a number of specific forms: (1) the War Powers Act, and other legislative restrictions on presidential war-making abroad; (2) the abolition of conscription and the establishment of an all-volunteer service; (3) restrictions on covert operations by the CIA and other intelligence agencies; and (4) military alliances with "surrogate gendarmes" like Iran (under the Shah) and Egypt (under Sadat).

These developments had profound consequences for the entire national security establishment. The Armed Services lost nearly half of their uniformed personnel, thus eliminating future openings for thousands of generals, admirals and other top career officers. The Pentagon budget was reduced (in non-inflated, "real" dollars), causing a significant drop in business for the nation's bloated arms industry. The CIA was forced to undergo an unprecedented public probe of its secret operations, and lost many veteran "spooks" through a massive layoff of senior personnel. All told, it was the greatest institutional setback for the warfare state since the demobilization ordered by President Eisenhower after the Korean War.

More serious than these institutional reverses, however, was the subjective response. Once all U.S. troops had been withdrawn from Indochina, the nation breathed a collective sigh of relief and adopted a "never again" stance on the use of U.S. troops to control political changes in the Third World. Summarizing this perspective in 1975, Senator Edward Kennedy declared that "the lesson [of Vietnam] is that we must throw off the cumbersome mantle of world policeman." In the same spirit, Senator Alan Cranston observed, "The United States should be a peaceful world neighbor instead of a militant world meddler."[2] This view prevailed in 1976, when Congress voted to prohibit U.S. military involvement in Angola (under the so-called "Clark Amendment"), and again a year later, when Washington elected to remain on the sidelines during the Ethiopian-Somalia conflict.

President Carter, who was elected when the Vietnam Syndrome was at its peak, generally adhered to the noninterventionist outlook expressed by Senators Kennedy and Cranston in 1975. Although some of his advisers—particularly Zbigniew Brzezinski—advocated a military response to particular crises, Carter vetoed direct U.S. involvement in such conflicts as the Zaire upheavals of 1976 and 1978, the Iranian Revolution, and the Nicaraguan civil war. And, in the one instance where Carter did sanction the use of force—the abortive hostage rescue mission of April 1980—he confined such action to a small-scale commando raid.

As the 1970s drew to a close, however, more and more policymakers viewed this non-interventionist stance as an intolerable constraint on U.S. power at a time of growing challenges to American interests abroad. These leaders—representing powerful segments of the military, intelligence and business communities—argued that America's unwillingness to use force in responding to minor threats abroad would only invite more serious and intractable challenges later. The Vietnam Syndrome, in their view, actually fosters instability because it encourages hostile powers to exploit the emerging gaps in the West's global security system. "Worldwide stability is being eroded through the retrenchment of American policy and power," James R. Schlesinger wrote in *Fortune* after his dismissal as Secretary of Defense in 1976. "This growing instability reflects visible factors such as the deterioration in the military balance, but also, perhaps more immediately, such invisible factors as the *altered psychological stance* of the United States, a nation apparently withdrawing from the burdens of leadership and power."[3] (Emphasis added.)

For these critics, U.S. non-involvement in Angola, Ethiopia, and Iran constituted a sign of American *weakness*, rather than a calculated policy of restraint. "Vietnam caused a loss of confidence in the ability of the U.S. to defend non-Communist regimes in Third World countries against subversion and military takeovers by Moscow's allies," *Business Week* observed in 1979. "This perception of paralysis was confirmed when the U.S. stood by helplessly as Russian-backed insurgents, aided by Cuban troops, took over Angola. And it was enhanced when the Soviet-aligned Ethiopian government crushed separatist movements in Eritrea and the Ogaden."[4]

For advocates of a renewed interventionist posture, the Vietnam Syndrome is not merely a misguided policy approach, but evidence of a far more profound psychological disorder. "Our internal preoccupations and our political divisions of recent years," Schlesinger avowed, underlie the "growing *infirmity* of American policy." Frequently, these critics used words with psycho-sexual overtones: America's allies have lost confidence in "the *firmness* of American policy;" Europeans deplore "the *faltering* of American purpose;" American restraint has "created an image of U.S. *impotence*."[5] (Emphasis added.)

Because Jimmy Carter generally pursued a non-interventionist approach to overseas conflicts, he became the principal target for such charges. As the 1980 election drew closer, he was often castigated for his timidity and vacillation in dealing with foreign crises. "The Administration's response to the multiplying challenges and disorders abroad," conservative columnist George F. Will charged in *Newsweek*, "has been a litany of things it will not do: interventions it will not contemplate, bases it will not seek, weapons it will not build."[6] When Carter declined to defend the Shah of Iran against a popular upheaval in 1978, Senator Howard Baker spoke for many proponents of intervention when he avowed that White House inaction "invite[s] the interpretation that we do not have the will or the resolve to act under any circumstances." And, in an extraordinary 1979 address to the Coalition for a Democratic Majority, Senator Henry Jackson charged that the Administration's placidity in the face of growing Soviet belligerence has "the mark of appeasement."[7]

These attacks culminated in March 1979 with a special issue of *Business Week* on "The Decline of U.S. Power," featuring a dramatic picture of the Statue of Liberty in tears. Arguing that, since Vietnam, the United States "has been buffeted by an unnerving series of shocks that signal an accelerating erosion of power and influence," the magazine's editors called for a revitalized military capacity to protect U.S. interests abroad. Without a more activist foreign policy, they argued, America's favored economic standing may soon vanish. "The policies set in motion during the Vietnam War are now threatening the way of life built since World War II."[8]

The *Business Week* issue was particularly significant because it constitutes a rare public airing of the intense policy debate which has gripped the U.S. power structure ever since Vietnam. This debate actually originated in the elite struggle over the war itself: after Tet and the appearance of a broad-based antiwar movement at home, the elite world split into factions favoring the continuation of the war and others calling for an American withdrawal. After the war, this debate was transformed into a deeper conflict over America's role in the "post-Vietnam" world. Although U.S. leaders were unanimous in their belief that America had to act decisively to shore up its dominion over the non-Communist world, they were divided both in their perceptions of the principal obstacles to this goal, and also in their strategies for attaining it. This division, which lasted until 1979, underlay the rancorous foreign policy debates which buffeted Washington throughout the 1970s.

The "Traders" and the "Prussians"

One side in this debate, composed largely of corporate managers and international bankers, argued that the greatest threats to U.S. hegemony were divisions within the capitalist world and growing economic nationalism on the part of the Third World. To overcome these difficulties, this group—which I have dubbed the "Traders"—called for greater economic collaboration between the major capitalist powers (and especially between the "trilateral" bloc of America, Japan, and Western Europe) along with the co-optation of Third World elites through token concessions on North-South trade issues. The Soviet Union, while meddlesome, was viewed as a secondary threat because of its economic backwardness and preoccupation with unruly clients and satellites (not to mention former satellites like China). To assure stability in turbulent Third World areas, meanwhile, the Traders sponsored the rise of "surrogate gendarmes" like Iran to assume regional peacekeeping responsibilities.

This approach was challenged, however, by another bloc composed of military officers, intelligence operatives, Cold War intellectuals, arms producers, and some domestic capitalists. This group, which I call the "Prussians," argued that the principal threat to U.S. hegemony was uncontrolled political and social "turbulence" in the Third World, coupled with the growing military assertiveness of the Soviet Union. To guarantee continued U.S. access to the mineral and agricultural wealth of the Third World while ensuring the quiescence of Moscow, this bloc called for a more vigorous U.S. "police" presence abroad plus a massive expansion of America's nuclear arsenal.* . . .

The most common expression of this struggle, of course, is the dispute over the "Soviet threat." Because data on Soviet military strength is subject to the wide range of interpretations, debate over the size and character of Soviet capabilities is often used as a surrogate for the more profound contest over foreign policy. While the Traders argue that Moscow is far too pre-occupied with domestic problems and growing restiveness in Eastern Europe to embark upon any major confrontations with the West, the Prussians insist that Moscow will use its awesome military muscle to dominate key Third World areas— particularly the Middle East—and thus to undermine the Western economies. And while both sides recognize that it is unlikely that Moscow would ever be foolhardy enough to threaten any *really* vital American interests, like Persian Gulf oil (despite all the talk of Soviet intervention in the Middle East, Moscow has been very, very careful to avoid any action that could be interpreted as a threat to Western oil supplies) the Prussians argue that the mere *existence* of large Soviet forces might encourage maverick Third World governments to be more obstinate in their dealings with the West than they would be otherwise.[10]

The debate over military policy has also arisen in discussions of the Vietnam War itself. While most Americans still believe that we were right to pull U.S. troops out of Indochina, many "realist" intellectuals now argue that we would be better off today in the Middle East and elsewhere if we'd stuck it out in Vietnam and demonstrated our "resolve" to protect vital U.S. interests. (Indeed, Ronald Reagan went so far as to call the Vietnam War "a noble cause" during the 1980 presidential campaign.[11])

As these debates proceeded, both sides demonstrated assorted strengths and weaknesses. By choosing early to support Jimmy Carter in 1976, the Traders succeeded in placing some of their leading representatives in high Administration posts. Cyrus Vance became Secretary of State, Paul Warnke was named director of the Arms Control & Disarmament Agency, and Andrew Young was made U.S. Ambassador to the United Nations. The Prussians, on the other hand, proved adept at manipulating public opinion and at using the "Soviet threat" anxiety to mobilize opposition to Administration policies. For a

---

*The concept of the "Traders and Prussians" should be viewed as an analytical tool rather than as precise sociological classifications. While we can distinguish two poles in this often acrimonious debate, and we can associate a few prominent individuals with one or another of these poles, most U.S. leaders normally hovered somewhere in between until international events or career imperatives forced a more conscious shift to one side.

time, Paul Nitze's "Committee on the Present Danger" and other Prussian organizations were being quoted as regularly as the White House itself.

While the two sides in this debate once appeared evenly matched, by the late 1970s the Trader position began to exhibit major weaknesses. To begin with, detente never provided the benefits—in terms of increased Soviet cooperation in curbing Third World upheavals—originally promised by its architects. Secondly, the Traders never provided an adequate explanation for the continued expansion of Soviet military power; while both camps recognized that Moscow's overall capabilities remained inferior to those of the West, the Traders—betrayed by their own anti-Communist outlook—declined to challenge the exaggerated claims of the Prussians and thus accorded tacit endorsement to their alarmist conclusions. Finally, by relying so heavily on "surrogate gendarmes" like the Shah of Iran, the Traders inevitably invited revolt against the very "pillars" of their strategic design. With the fall of the Shah in January 1979, the Trader position appeared fundamentally indefensible and large numbers of policymakers defected to the Prussian camp.

What ultimately destroyed the Trader position, however, was not so much any particular crisis but rather a growing sense among policymakers that the postwar global order they helped create was breaking down, and that military force alone could assure the survival of this order, and with it, America's continued economic prosperity. This view, widely propagated by dissident policymakers during the late 1970s became the dominant outlook in the months succeeding the flight of the Shah. Thus, when *Business Week* argued in March 1979 that America had to adopt an assertive military policy to protect "the way of life built since World War II," it was reflecting a consensus that had already taken root in elite circles. This consensus was reflected in statements by Secretary of Defense Brown and Secretary of Energy Schlesinger to the effect that the United States was now prepared to consider "the use of military force" to protect Persian Gulf oil, and in a secret White House decision to alert U.S. forces for possible intervention in the Yemen border war of March 1979.[12]

The Brown-Schlesinger statements over oil, coupled with Carter's muscle-flexing over Yemen, were cited by observers both inside and outside the Administration as proof that official Washington had now recovered from the Vietnam Syndrome. "This country went through a very deep philosophical-cultural crisis as a result of the war in Vietnam," national security adviser Zbigniew Brzezinski acknowledged in April, but "it is now emerging from that crisis." The Administration's response to Yemen, he noted, "signalled to others that we will use force when necessary to protect our important interests."[13]

The events in Iran and Yemen also had a big impact in Congress. "The tide that swept back U.S. intervention in Vietnam, Cambodia, and Angola could now be turning the other way," *The Washington Post* reported in June. "Strong pressures are beginning to build up that could pave the way for a return to a more interventionist policy, based on military presence, to guarantee U.S. access to foreign energy supplies."[14] And in a comment that captured the mood of many in Congress, Senator Sam Nunn noted that "I'd rather flex our muscles a little bit on a weekly basis than have to resort to a great display of force at some very high level of danger."[15]

With official Washington now "recovered" from the Vietnam Syndrome, the Administration began the reconstitution of America's interventionary apparatus. In June 1979, Army Chief of Staff Gen. Bernard W. Rogers revealed plans for a "Unilateral Force"—later to be renamed the Rapid Deployment Force (RDF)—for use in combatting armed insurgencies abroad. At about the same time, the National Security Council (NSC) adopted a new strategic plan for the Persian Gulf calling for an expanded U.S. naval presence and the acquisition of additional basing facilities.[16] Because the public still generally adhered to a non-interventionist stance, however, these plans were mostly kept secret until, several months later, the Iranian hostage crisis transformed public attitudes and thus permitted disclosure of the Administration's moves. But while the hostage situation—and the public outcry it produced—was used by government officials to justify formation of the RDF and implementation of the NSC strategy, the fact is that those moves had already been initiated *prior to the Iranian crisis,* and in response to *elite* rather than public pressure.

Nevertheless, the Iranian hostage crisis did produce a major shift in public attitudes. In a characteristic expression of the new mood, Democratic Party chairman John White noted that "We may have reached a turning point in our attitudes towards ourselves, and that is a feeling that we have a right to protect legitimate interests anywhere in the world."[17] This shift became even more pronounced several weeks later, when powerful Soviet forces moved into Afghanistan. In the aftermath of the invasion, President Carter publicly endorsed the Prussian position when, on January 23, 1980, he announced that the United States was now fully prepared to use military force in defense of Persian Gulf oil supplies, and that, to lend credibility to the Administration's new stance, he would ask Congress to authorize registration for the draft. "In terms of domestic politics," one White House staffer noted at the time, "this has put an end to the Vietnam Syndrome."[18]

The Triumph of Interventionism—
And the Persistence of the Syndrome

Although Jimmy Carter finally embraced an interventionist position in the closing months of his Administration, his "conversion" came too late to satisfy his opponents—most of whom (including many former Democrats) rallied to the banner of Ronald Reagan. Throughout the campaign, Reagan denounced Carter's "vacillation" in the face of overseas crises. In a major address to the Chicago Council on Foreign Relations on March 17, he asserted that by following a policy of "vacillation, appeasement, and aimlessness," Mr. Carter was bringing dishonor and humiliation to the United States "all over the world." Similarly, in his nomination speech of July 17, Reagan charged that "the Carter Administration gives us weakness when we need strength; vacillation when the times demand firmness." In place of such defeatism, Reagan promised to make the restoration of American power his "No. 1 priority."[19]

Upon entering the White House, Mr. Reagan moved swiftly to implement his hard-lined military program. His choices for Secretary of State and Defense, Alexander Haig and Caspar Weinberger, are both ideologically committed to an expanded military and an assertive posture abroad. With evident White House approval, Mr. Haig has initiated an intensive counterinsurgency campaign in El Salvador—the first of its type involving U.S. advisers since Vietnam—and Mr. Weinberger has introduced a new five-year military budget calling for an increase of $185 billion over Carter's proposed defense budget. Top Administration officials have also argued that we must expand our capacity to use force in the defense of U.S. interests abroad. Thus, in an address to the American Newspaper Publishers Association on May 5, 1981, Weinberger affirmed that we must be prepared to engage "in wars of any size and shape and in any region where we have vital interests."[20]

So far, the Administration has placed all its emphasis on expanding our *capability* for intervention abroad. This means, Secretary Weinberger explained on May 5, "developing urgently a better ability to respond to crises far from our shores, and to stay there as long as necessary" to protect key U.S. interests.[21] But anyone exposed to official thinking on these matters cannot help but conclude that Washington is equally concerned with demonstrating a will to *use* force. Thus, in defending his decision to establish a permanent U.S. military presence in the Middle East, President Reagan argued that American forces must be sufficiently visible so that potential adversaries will know "that if they made a reckless move, they would be risking a confrontation with the United States."[22] And, as history has shown only all too often, this sort of preoccupation with "showing resolve" and "restoring credibility" can easily evolve into a decision to use force solely to demonstrate a *willingness* to do so.

For many observers, the Administration has already taken this step by moving into El Salvador in order to show, as Reagan put it on March 3, 1981, that we will "not just sit passively by and allow this hemisphere to be invaded by outside [*sic*] forces."[23] But while the Administration clearly remains committed to a major counterinsurgency effort in El Salvador, it has not deployed U.S. combat forces there in any sort of strength. Such a show-of-force may yet occur in Central America, or could occur in some other Third World area—Libya, perhaps, or Angola or Yemen—where "vital" U.S. interests are supposedly threatened by hostile forces. Military intervention, should it occur, could take several forms:

—An *"Energy War"* to protect Persian Gulf oil imports as dictated by the "Carter Doctrine," which has been fully endorsed by the Reagan Administration.

—A *"Resource War"* to protect U.S. imports of critical minerals, as dictated by the "Haig Doctrine."

—A *Counterinsurgency War* designed to crush a national liberation movement or urban uprising in some strategic Third World country.

—An *Overseas "Police Action"* designed to combat "terrorism" or other forms of "international turbulence" sponsored or facilitated by the Soviet Union.

But while the Reagan Administration is clearly prepared to adopt any of these scenarios, it is also fearful of another defeat like Vietnam ("never again," President Reagan declared on March 3, 1981, will we "send an active fighting force to a country to fight unless it is for a cause that we intend to win"[24]) and thus will have to choose carefully in selecting a site for U.S. intervention. For, as many recent events have demonstrated, today's world is a far different place than the world of the 1950s and early 1960s, when American power seemed essentially limitless and Third World conflicts were viewed as "brush-fire wars" easily doused by American troops. Because many Third World armies are now equipped with modern aircraft, missiles, and tanks—acquired, in many cases, from the United States or its allies through the international arms market—and because the Soviet Union can now provide its allies and clients with considerable military backing, any U.S. intervention could result in conflict on a much larger scale and at a much higher *level of violence* than that experienced in Vietnam. Such an encounter will be inherently dangerous—risking, as it does, confrontation with the U.S.S.R. and escalation to thermonuclear war—and thus will not be lightly countenanced by Washington no matter how eagerly U.S. officials seek a dramatic show-of-force in the Third World. . . .

Because many U.S. leaders, including top Administration officials, are determined to fully erase the Vietnam Syndrome from the public consciousness, we can expect renewed attacks on this stance in the months and years ahead. Such attacks will assume all of the forms already encountered—warnings of the overpowering "Soviet threat" to U.S. friends and allies, of the upsurge of "terrorism" and "turbulence" in the Third World, and of the growing threat to U.S. energy supplies and other strategic raw materials—and may assume still new forms—e.g., discovery of an *internal* threat to U.S. security posed by opponents of military preparedness (as suggested by selected witnesses in testimony to the newly-created Senate Subcommittee on Security and Terrorism). Nevertheless, the memories of U.S. paralysis and despair in Vietnam remain potent and, thanks to the efforts of many Vietnam War veterans and former antiwar activists, very much in the public eye. So long as these memories remain alive, and the public remains skeptical about official explanations for government conduct, the Vietnam Syndrome will continue to discourage indiscriminate military intervention abroad. . . .

Footnotes

1   The concept of a concerted campaign to erase the Vietnam Syndrome was first explored by the author in: "Curing the Vietnam Syndrome," *The Nation* (Oct. 13, 1979), pp. 321, 337-40.
2   Quoted in *The Defense Monitor*, Vol. IV, No. 7 (September, 1975), p. 5.
3   James Schlesinger, "A Testing Time for America," *Fortune* (February, 1976), p. 76.
4   "The Decline of U.S. Power," *Business Week* (March 12, 1979), p. 88.
5   Extracts from Schlesinger, "A Testing Time for America," pp. 74-77; and "The Decline of U.S. Power," pp. 36-96.
6   George Will, "No More 'No More Vietnams,' " *Newsweek* (March 19, 1979), p. 104.
7   The Baker quote is from "The Decline of U.S. Power," p. 88; the Jackson quote from *The Washington Post*, June 13, 1979.
8   "The Decline of U.S. Power," pp. 36-41.
9   The concept of the Traders and the Prussians was first introduced by the author in "The Traders and the Prussians," *Seven Days* (March 28, 1977), pp. 32-3.
10 For discussion, see: *The Wall Street Journal*, January 21, 1980.
11 Quoted in *The New York Times*, July 19, 1980.
12 The Brown and Schlesinger statements were cited in *The New York Times*, February 26, 1979; the secret Yemen moves were disclosed in *The Washington Post*, June 3, 1979.
13 Interview, *U.S. News and World Report* (April 16, 1979), pp. 49-50.
14 Jim Hoagland in the *Washington Post*, June 3, 1979.
15 Quoted in "The Decline of U.S. Power," p. 88.
16 See: *The Washington Post*, June 22, 1979; and *The New York Times*, June 28, 1979.
17 Quoted in *The New York Times*, December 2, 1979.
18 *Ibid.*
19 Quoted in *The New York Times*, March 18 and July 18, 1980.
20 Quoted in *The New York Times*, May 6, 1981.
21 *Ibid.*
22 Quoted in *The New York Times*, February 4, 1981.
23 Quoted in the *San Francisco Chronicle*, March 4, 1981.
24 *Ibid.*

fdCus

Klare's analysis of deteriorating U.S.–U.S.S.R. relations provides an overview of contemporary American foreign policy. It may also illustrate the need to transcend the guilt associated with the Vietnam experience. In redefining American-Soviet relations in the 1980s, Reagan's foreign policy may attempt to recapture the political, economic, and military power characteristic of the United States in the 1950s. For Michael Klare and others, the Vietnam War illustrates the limitations of American power to transform Third World societies through military means. Klare's perspective is disputed in the following article, "U.S. Security and Latin America" by Jeane Kirkpatrick, written in 1981 before her appointment as U.S. Ambassador to the United Nations. Kirkpatrick attacks the post-Vietnam assumptions of the Carter presidency. She argues that American retrenchment encourages Soviet aggression throughout the world, particularly in the western hemisphere. Kirkpatrick warns against viewing all Third World upheavals as new "Vietnams" pointing to the geographical, cultural, economic, and political differences between the countries of Central America and Vietnam. For Kirkpatrick, the political stability of Latin America must be the central goal of American foreign policy. To compromise American national security because of a reluctance to engage in internal Third World politics is dangerous and misguided, she says. Kirkpatrick attacks the Carter administration's emphasis on democratic social change in Latin America because, she points out, there is a Soviet network that supplies resources to Communist insurgents in Central America. According to Kirkpatrick, the Soviet Union has made the subversion of Latin America a central foreign policy goal.

U.S. SECURITY AND LATIN AMERICA

Jeane Kirkpatrick, *Commentary*, January 1981

Jeane Kirkpatrick is the U.S. Ambassador to the United Nations.

While American attention in the past year has been focused on other matters, developments of great potential importance in Central America and the Caribbean have passed almost unnoticed. The deterioration of the U.S. position in the hemisphere has already created serious vulnerabilities where none previously existed, and threatens now to confront this country with the unprecedented need to defend itself against a ring of Soviet bases on and around our southern and eastern borders. . . .

The first fruits of these efforts are the new governments of Grenada and Nicaragua, whose commitment to Marxist-Leninist principles and solidarity with Soviet/Cuban policies led Castro to brag on returning from Managua, "Now there are three of us." There may soon be four. El Salvador, having arrived now at the edge of anarchy, is threatened by progressively well-armed guerrillas whose fanaticism and violence remind some observers of Pol Pot. Meanwhile, the terrorism relied on by contemporary Leninists (and Castroites) to create a "revolutionary situation" has reappeared in Guatemala. . . .

American policies have not only proved incapable of dealing with the problems of Soviet/Cuban expansion in the area, they have positively contributed to them and to the alienation of major nations, the growth of neutralism, the destabilization of friendly governments, the spread of Cuban influence, and the decline of U.S. power in the region. Hence one of the first and most urgent tasks of the Reagan administration will be to review and revise the U.S. approach to Latin America, and the Caribbean.

Such a review should begin not just with the previous administration's policy in the hemisphere, but with the quiet process by which new theories of hemispheric relations came to preempt discussion within that somewhat amorphous but very real group known as the foreign-policy establishment. For to an extent unusual in government, Carter administration policies toward Latin America and the Caribbean (as in the world more broadly) were derived from an ideology rather than from tradition, habit, or improvisation.

Indeed, nothing is as important as understanding the relationship between the recent failures of American policy—in Latin America and elsewhere—and the philosophy of foreign affairs that inspired and informed that policy. Such an effort of understanding requires, first, that we disregard the notion that the failure of the Carter policy was the personal failure of a man unskilled in the ways of diplomacy; and, second, that we look beyond superficial day-to-day policy changes to the stable orientations that reasserted themselves after each discrete crisis in world affairs.

Those orientations had their roots in the Vietnam experience, less as it was fought in Southeast Asia than as it was interpreted in Washington and New York. President Carter, after all, was not the only political leader in America to have lost his "inordinate" fear of Communism, lost his appetite for East-West competition, grown embarrassed by the uses of American power, become ashamed of past U.S. policies, and grown determined to make a fresh start. By the time Richard Nixon had left office, a large portion of the political elite in America, including a majority of the Congress, had drawn away not only from Vietnam but from what was more and more frequently called the cold war—the revisionists' preferred term for U.S. determination to resist the expansion of Soviet power. . . .

The new approach was to be free of paternalism, "respectful of sovereignty," tolerant of political and economic diversity. Above all, it was to be set in a consistent global framework.

Most of the specific recommendations of the two Linowitz reports—negotiating the Panama Canal treaties, "normalizing" relations with Cuba, "liberalizing" trade and "internationalizing" aid, promoting human rights, and never, ever, intervening militarily—flowed from these new assumptions. Given détente, the U.S. could and should "keep local and regional conflicts outside the context of the superpower relationships" and no longer "automatically" see "revolutions in other countries and intraregional conflicts . . . as battlefields of the cold war." And given interdependence (manifested in global phenomena like inflation and multinational corporations), the U.S. should no longer hope for or seek "complete economic and political security . . ." but instead participate in the new international agenda.

Despite the commission's determined globalism, it recognized that Cuba constituted a special case. Both reports recommended U.S. initiatives toward "normalization" of relations with Cuba and some acts (removing restrictions on travel, increasing scientific and cultural exchanges) regardless of overall progress on normalization. But the second report also noted Cuba's military involvement in Africa and its support for "militant" and violence-prone Puerto Rican *independistas,* and concluded that full normalization of relations, however desirable, could take place only as Cuba gave assurances that its troops were being withdrawn from Angola and that it had no intention of intervening elsewhere.

The most striking characteristic of the Linowitz recommendations was their disinterested internationalist spirit. U.S. policy, it was assumed, should be based on an understanding of "changed realities" and guided by an enlightened confidence that what was good for the world was good for the United States. Power was to be used to advance moral goals, not strategic or economic ones. Thus sanctions could be employed to punish human-rights violations, but not to aid American business; power could be used "to the full extent permitted by law" to prevent terrorist actions against Cuba, but not to protect U.S. corporations against expropriation. Nor was power to be a factor in designing or implementing economic aid or trade programs *except* where these were intended to promote human rights, disarmament, and nuclear non-proliferation.

The Linowitz reports were, in the most fundamental sense, utopian. They assumed that technological change had so transformed human consciousness and behavior that it was no longer necessary for the United States to screen policies for their impact on national security. To be sure, neither argued that self-interest, conflict, or aggression had been entirely purged from the world. But Brzezinski asserted (and the Linowitz commission apparently believed) that only the Soviet Union was still engaged in truly "anachronistic" political behavior against which it was necessary to defend ourselves. Since no Latin American nation directly threatened the position of the United States, relations with them could be safely conducted without regard for national security.

Adopting the Linowitz commission's recommendations thus required abandoning the strategic perspective which had shaped U.S. policy from the Monroe Doctrine down to the eve of the Carter administration, and at the center of which was a conception of the national interest and a belief in the moral legitimacy of its defense. In the Brzezinski-Linowitz approach, morality was decoupled from the national interest, much as the future was divorced from the past. The goals recommended for U.S. policy were all abstract and supranational—"human rights," "development," "fairness.". . .

This whole cluster of ideas—of facing painful truths, making a fresh start, forswearing force, and pursuing universal moral goals—was enormously attractive to Jimmy Carter. No sooner was he elected than he set out to translate them into a new policy for dealing with the nations of the hemisphere.

The repudiation of our hegemonic past was symbolized by the Panama Canal Treaties, to which the Carter administration—from the President on down—attached great importance and of which it was inordinately proud. As Vice President Mondale put it in Panama City, the treaties symbolized "the commitment of the U.S. to the belief that fairness and not force should lie at the heart of our dealings with the nations of the world."

Anastasio Somoza's Nicaragua had the bad luck to become the second demonstration area for the "fresh start" in Latin America. Just because the regime had been so close and so loyal to the U.S., its elimination would, in exactly the same fashion as the Panama Canal Treaties, dramatize the passing of the old era of "hegemony" in Central America and the arrival of a new era of equity and justice. As the editor of *Foreign Affairs*, William Bundy, noted, "Somoza [was] as good a symbol as could have been found of past U.S. policies in Latin America." . . .

Incorporating the nations of Latin America into a "global framework" meant deemphasizing U.S. relations with them. Especially, it meant reducing U.S. assistance to the area, since from the perspective of North-South relations, Latin America's claim to assistance was not nearly as impressive as that of most other nations of the so-called Third World. And, once the strategic perspective was abandoned, there was no reason at all for military assistance. . . .

The global approach involved deemphasizing Latin American relations, not destabilizing governments. But other aspects of the Carter doctrine committed the administration to promoting "change." "Change," indeed, was the favorite word of administration policy-makers. In speeches with titles like "Currents of Change in Latin America," Carter, Vance, and their associates reiterated their conviction that the world was in the grip of an extraordinary process of transformation which was deep, irresistible, systematic, and desirable. Administration spokesmen reiterated in the fashion of a credo that "our national interests align us naturally and inescapably with the forces of change, of democracy, of human rights, and of equitable development" (Philip Habib). And the belief that the whole world was caught up in a process of modernization moving it toward greater democracy and equality subtly transformed itself into an imperative: the U.S. should throw its power behind the "progressive" forces seeking change, even if they "seemed" anti-American or pro-Soviet.

If commitment to "change" was the rock on which Carter's Latin American policy was built, his human-rights policy was the lever to get change started. Two aspects of the Carter approach to human rights are noteworthy. First, concern was limited to violations of human rights by governments. By definition, activities of terrorists and guerrillas could not qualify as violations of human rights, whereas a government's efforts to repress terrorism would quickly run afoul of Carter human-rights standards.

Secondly, human rights were defined not in terms of personal and legal rights—freedom from torture, arbitrary imprisonment, and arrest, as in the usage of Amnesty International and the U.S. Foreign Assistance Acts of 1961 and 1975—but in accordance with a much broader conception which included the political "rights" available only in democracies and the economic "rights" promised by socialism (shelter, food, health, education). It may be that no country in the world meets these standards; certainly no country in the Third World does. The very broadness of the definition invited an arbitrary and capricious policy of implementation. Panama, for instance, was rather mysteriously exempt from meeting the expansive criteria of the State Department's human-rights office, while at the same time the other major nations of Central America were being censored (and undermined) for violations. . . .

Ignoring the role of ideology had powerful effects on the administration's perception of conflicts and on its ability to make accurate predictions. Although Fidel Castro has loudly and repeatedly proclaimed his revolutionary mission, and backed his stated intentions by training insurgents and providing weapons and advisers, Carter's Assistant Secretary for Inter-American Affairs, William Bowdler, described Cuba as "an inefficient and shabby dictatorship"—a description more appropriate to, say, Paraguay, than to an expansionist Soviet client state with troops scattered throughout the world. The refusal to take seriously, or even to take into account, the commitment of Fidel Castro or Nicaragua's Sandinista leadership to Marxist-Leninist goals and expansionist policies made it impossible to distinguish them either from traditional authoritarians or from democratic reformers, impossible to predict their likely attitudes toward the United States and the Soviet Union, impossible to understand why in their view Costa Rica and Mexico as well as Guatemala and Honduras constituted inviting targets. Ignoring the force of ideology—and its powerful contemporary embodiments—fatally distorted the Carter administration's view of politics in Central America and elsewhere.

The policies which grew out of these expectations have had a large impact on U.S. relations with most nations of South America. In Central America in particular, the direction of administration policy interacted with the presence there of weak regimes and Cuban-supported insurgents to transform the region into a battleground in an ideological war that the administration did not understand and could not acknowledge. . . .

A democratic façade—elections, political parties, and fairly broad participation—is a feature of these systems. But the impact of democratic forms is modified by varying degrees of fraud, intimidation, and restrictions on who may participate. Corruption (the appropriation of public resources for private use) is endemic. Political institutions are not strong enough to channel and contain the claims of various groups to use public power to enforce preferred policies. No procedure is recognized as *the* legitimate route to power. Competition for influence proceeds by whatever means are at hand: the Church manipulates symbols of rectitude; workers resort to strikes; businessmen use bribery; political parties use campaigns and votes; politicians employ persuasion, organization, and demagoguery; military officers use force. Lack of consensus permits political competition of various kinds in various arenas, and gives the last word to those who dispose of the greatest force. That usually turns out to be the leaders of the armed forces; most rulers in the area are generals.

Violence or the threat of violence is an integral, regular, predictable part of these political systems—a fact which is obscured by our way of describing military "interventions" in Latin political systems as if the system were normally peaceable. Coups, demonstrations, political strikes, plots, and counterplots are, in fact, the norm.

Traditionally, however, actual violence has been limited by the need to draw support from diverse sectors of the society and by the fact that politics has not been viewed as involving ultimate stakes. The various competitors for power have sought control of government to increase their wealth and prestige, not for the "higher" and more dangerous purpose of restructuring society. In traditional Latin politics, competitors do not normally destroy each other. They suffer limited defeats and win limited victories. The habit of permitting opponents to survive to fight another day is reflected in the tendency of Latin regimes to instability. In such a system a government normally lasts as long as it is able to prevent a coalition from forming among its opponents. Because there is no consensus on what makes government itself legitimate, successive regimes remain vulnerable to attacks on their legitimacy. They are also especially vulnerable to attacks on public order, which tends to be tenuous and to lack a firm base in tradition, habit, and affection.

To these patterns of political interaction there has been added in recent years the unfamiliar guerrilla violence of revolutionaries linked to Cuba by ideology, training, and the need for support, and through Cuba to the Soviet Union. Such groups rely on terrorism to destroy public order, to disrupt the economy and make normal life impossible, to demoralize the police, and mortally wound the government by demonstrating its inability to protect personal security and maintain public authority. As Robert Chapman has emphasized, with the advent of terrorism as a *form* of revolution, a revolutionary situation can be created in any country whose government is weak or whose economy is vulnerable or dependent, with or without the participation of the masses.

The nations of Central America (including Mexico) and the Caribbean suffer from some form of institutional weakness—because significant portions of the population have not been incorporated into the political system, and/or because political action is not fully institutionalized, and/or because the legitimacy of the government is in doubt, and/or because there is no consensus concerning legitimacy within the political elite, and/or because the economy is vulnerable to shifts in the international market, and/or because regular infusions of aid are required, and/or because rising expectations have outstripped capacities. All are vulnerable to disruption, and must rely on force to put down challenges to authority.

It is at this point that the roles of Cuba on the one hand, and the U.S. on the other hand, become crucial. Cuba stands ready to succor, bolster, train, equip, and advise revolutionaries produced within these societies and to supply weapons for a general insurgency when that is created. The U.S. is important as a source of economic aid and moral and military support. Traditionally it has also exercised a veto power over governments in the area and reinforced acceptable governments with its tacit approval. Thus, to the objective economic and political dependency of nations in the area has been added a widespread sense of psychological dependency. When aid and comfort from the U.S. in the form of money, arms, logistical support, and the services of counterinsurgency experts are no longer available, governments like those of Nicaragua, El Salvador, and Guatemala are weakened. And when it finally sinks in that the U.S. desires their elimination and prefers insurgents to incumbents, the blow to the morale and confidence of such weak traditional regimes is devastating. . . .

At the time the Carter administration was inaugurated in January 1977, three groups of unequal strength competed for power in Nicaragua: the

President [Anastasio Somoza Debayle] and his loyal lieutenants—who enjoyed the advantages of incumbency, a degree of legitimacy, a nationwide organization, and the unwavering support of the National Guard; the legal opposition parties which had been gathered into a loose coalition headed by Joaquin Chamorro, editor of *La Prensa*; and several small revolutionary groups whose Cuban-trained leaders had finally forged a loose alliance, the FSLN (Sandinist National Liberation Front).

From the moment the FSLN adopted the tactics of a broad alliance, the offensive against Somoza was carried out on a variety of fronts. There was violence in the form of assassinations and assaults on army barracks. When the government reacted, the U.S. condemned it for violations of human rights. The legal opposition put forward demands for greater democracy which had the endorsement of the FSLN, thus making it appear that democracy was the goal of the insurgency.

Violence and counterviolence weakened the regime by demonstrating that it could not maintain order. The combination of impotence and repression in turn emboldened opponents in and out of the country, provoking more reprisals and more hostility in a vicious circle that culminated finally in the departure of Somoza and the collapse of the National Guard.

What did the Carter administration do in Nicaragua? *It brought down the Somoza regime.* The Carter administration did not "lose" Nicaragua in the sense in which it was once charged Harry Truman had "lost" China, or Eisenhower Cuba, by failing to prevent a given outcome. In the case of Nicaragua, the State Department *acted* repeatedly and at critical junctures to weaken the government of Anastasio Somoza and to strengthen his opponents.

First, it declared "open season" on the Somoza regime. When in the spring of 1977 the State Department announced that shipments of U.S. arms would be halted for human-rights violations, and followed this with announcements in June and October that economic aid would be withheld, it not only deprived the Somoza regime of needed economic and military support but served notice that the regime no longer enjoyed the approval of the United States and could no longer count on its protection. This impression was strongly reinforced when after February 1978 Jimmy Carter treated the two sides in the conflict as more or less equally legitimate contenders—offering repeatedly to help "both sides" find a "peaceful solution."

Second, the Carter administration's policies inhibited the Somoza regime in dealing with its opponents while they were weak enough to be dealt with. Fearful of U.S. reproaches and reprisals, Somoza fluctuated between repression and indulgence in his response to FSLN violence. The rules of the Carter human-rights policy made it impossible for Somoza to resist his opponents effectively. As Viron Vaky remarked about the breakdown in negotiations between Somoza and the armed opposition: ". . . when the mediation was suspended we announced that the failure of the mediation had created a situation in which it was clear violence was going to continue, that it would result in repressive measures and therefore our relationships could not continue on the same basis as in the past." When the National Palace was attacked and hostages were taken, Somoza's capitulation to FSLN demands enhanced the impression that he could not control the situation and almost certainly stimulated the spread of resistance.

Third, by its "mediation" efforts and its initiatives in the Organization of American States (OAS), the Carter administration encouraged the internationalization of the opposition. Further, it demoralized Somoza and his supporters by insisting that Somoza's continuation in power was the principal obstacle to a viable, centrist, democratic government. Finally, the State Department deprived the Somoza regime of legitimacy not only by repeated condemnations for human-rights violations but also by publishing a demand for Somoza's resignation and by negotiating with the opposition. . . .

Why did the Carter administration do these things? Because it thought the fall of Somoza would bring progress to Nicaragua. . . .

History was against Somoza. He was an obstacle to progress. He should relinquish power to make room for "change." When he declined to do so, the Carter administration accused him of "polarizing" the situation. When the National Guard responded to FSLN violence with violence, the State Department said that the National Guard had "radicalized the opposition."

On the other hand, the fact that Cubans were supplying arms to the FSLN was not regarded as being of much importance. Brandon Grove, Jr., Deputy Assistant Secretary for Inter-American Affairs, explained to the Committee of the House (June 7, 1979):

> The flow of such supplies is a symptom of the deeper problem in Nicaragua: polarization and its attendant violence that day by day are contributing to the growing alienation of the Nicaraguan government from its people. . . .
> The real cause for concern today should be the breakdown . . . of trust between government and people essential for the democratic process to function.

Since the "real" problem was not Cuban arms but Somoza, obviously the U.S. should not act to reinforce the regime that had proved its political and moral failure by becoming the object of attack. Because the State Department desired not to "add to the partisan factionalism," it declined to supply arms to the regime. "The supplying of arms in a war situation we feel only adds to the suffering. We have urged others not to do that."

In the event, the Carter administration did a good deal more than "urge." In June 1979, after the U.S. and the OAS had called for Somoza's resignation, and U.S. representatives William Bowdler and Lawrence Pezzulo had met with the FSLN, the State Department undertook to apply the final squeeze to the Somoza regime—putting pressure on Israel to end arms sales, and working out an oil embargo to speed the capitulation of Somoza's forces. They were so successful that for the second time in a decade an American ally ran out of gas and ammunition while confronting an opponent well armed by the Soviet bloc. . . .

The Carter administration expected that democracy would emerge in Nicaragua. Their scenario prescribed that the winds of change should blow the outmoded dictator out of office and replace him with a popular government. Even after it had become clear that the FSLN, which was known to harbor powerful anti-democratic tendencies, was the dominant force in the new regime, U.S. spokesmen continued to speak of the events in Nicaragua as a democratic revolution. In December 1979, for example, Warren Christopher attempted to reassure doubting members of the Senate Foreign Relations Committee that "the driving consensus among Nicaraguans" was "to build a new Nicaragua through popular participation that is capable of meeting basic human needs."

The expectation that change would produce progress and that socialism equaled social justice made it difficult for Carter policy-makers to assess Nicaragua's new rulers realistically, even though grounds for concern about their intentions, already numerous before the triumph, continued to multiply in its aftermath.

Revolution begins with destruction. The first fruit of the destabilization of Somoza and the reinforcement of his opponents was a civil war in which some 40,000 Nicaraguans lost their most basic human right (life), another 100,000 were left homeless, and some $2-billion worth of destruction was wrought. Nicaragua was left in a shambles.

Where did the expectations, the hopes, the intentions of the Carter administration then lead us, and the Nicaraguans who took the consequences? Although the FSLN had solemnly committed itself to hold free elections, its leaders have shown no disposition to share the power they seized in July 1979. To the contrary, the consolidation and centralization of power have moved steadily forward. Despite the strenuous opposition of the two non-FSLN junta members, the Sandinista directorate which has effectively ruled Nicaragua since the fall of Somoza moved in the spring of 1980 to institutionalize its control of Nicaragua's Council of State by expanding and "restructuring" it to insure the Sandinistas a permanent majority. (Under the reform they would be assured of 24 of 47 seats where previously they had been entitled to only 13 of 33.)

Meanwhile, the election to which the FSLN had committed itself has been pushed further and further into a receding future, even though the new rulers, who need all the help they can get, have been under heavy pressure from the governments of Venezuela, Costa Rica, and the United States to set a date. . . .

In the last days of August 1980, the restructured Council of State announced that elections will not be held before 1985. And those elections, declared Humberto Ortega Saavedra (Minister of Defense), "will serve to reinforce and improve the revolution and not to give just anyone more power, which belongs to the people." Meanwhile, no "proselytizing activities" on behalf of any candidate will be permitted before candidates are officially designated by an electoral agency which itself will be created in 1984 (and violations will be punished by terms of three months to three years in jail).

Decrees accompanying these decisions have underscored the junta's distaste for criticism. Henceforth, dissemination of news concerning scarcities of food and other consumer goods is prohibited on pain of imprisonment (from two months to two years), as is "unconfirmed" information concerning armed encounters or attacks on government personnel.

These restrictions constitute one more significant step in the Sandinistas' gradual campaign to control the climate of opinion. The television and radios had already been brought under control. Among opposition newspapers, only *La Prensa* remains; it has already come under pressures more harsh than those applied to the media during the Somoza era, and its continuation as an independent critical voice is at best uncertain. The requirement that all professional journalists join a new government-sponsored union as a condition of employment represents yet another move to bring the press under control. The literacy campaign has extended the junta's reach further into the minds of Nicaragua's people as well as into the countryside. Every lesson in the literacy textbooks instructs students (and teachers) in the prescribed interpretation of Nicaragua's past, present, and future.

Parallel efforts to organize and coordinate other traditionally non-governmental associations reflect the characteristic totalitarian desire to absorb the society into the state, to transform social groups into agencies and instruments of government. This has required taking over some existing institutions (banking, industries, television and radio, trade unions), coopting and/or intimidating others (the private sector, trade unions, the educational establishment, portions of the press), and forcibly eliminating still others—such as the National Guard, whose members have either fled into exile or remain in prison with little prospect of ever being tried, much less released. . . .

Among the traditional pillars of Nicaraguan society only the Church remains relatively intact. While the presence of priests in prominent roles in the Sandinista directorate has facilitated communications between the two groups, this has not been translated into political domination of the Church hierarchy.

But the Sandinistas do not rely on control of these agencies or rules to preserve their power. To accomplish that task new institutions have been forged, the most important of which are an enormous, all-new revolutionary army whose training (military and political) and equipment have been provided by Cubans, and a new internal police force which is already more extensive and effective than Somoza's. . . .

The most telling indicator of Sandinista intentions and commitments is their unambiguous identification of Nicaragua with the foreign policy and perspectives of the Soviet Union. The first step was somewhat tentative: Nicaragua only "abstained" on the UN resolution condemning the Soviet invasion of Afghanistan. Subsequent moves have left less room for doubt. At the Havana conference for the nonaligned nations, Nicaragua became one of the few countries in the world to recognize Kampuchea (the regime imposed by North Vietnam on Cambodia), an act which Foreign Minister Miguel d'Escoto explained as "a consequence of our revolutionary responsibility as Sandinistas to recognize the right of the peoples of Kampuchea to be free." In Pyongyang, another Sandinista leader, Tomás Borge, assured the North Koreans of Nicaraguan solidarity, and promised, "The Nicaraguan Revolution will not be content until the imperialists have been overthrown in all parts of the world."

In March 1980 the Sandinista directorate offered a public demonstration that its ties extended beyond Cuba to the Socialist Fatherland itself when four top leaders—Moises Morales Hassan, Tomás Borge, Henry Hernandez Ruiz, and Humberto Ortega Saavedra—paid an official visit to the Soviet Union. A joint communique formalized the attachment of Nicaragua to Soviet global policy. In addition to signing multiple agreements concerning trade and cooperation, condemning South Africa and Chile, applauding Zimbabwe, Khomeini's Iran, and the "legitimate national rights of the Arab people of Palestine," the "two sides" strongly attacked the NATO decision to deploy medium-range nuclear missile weapons and condemned the "mounting international tension in connection with the events in Afghanistan, which has been launched by the imperialist and reactionary forces aimed at subverting the inalienable rights of the people of the Democratic Republic of Afghanistan and of other peoples . . . to follow a path of progressive transformation." . . .

Nothing that happened in Nicaragua seemed able to dampen the Carter people's enthusiasm for "change" in Central America. In El Salvador, Guatemala, Bolivia, and wherever else the opportunity presented itself, the administration aligned the United States with the "forces of change." . . .

To meet the challenge the administration welcomed with enthusiasm a military coup in El Salvador which, in October 1979, overthrew President Carlos Humberto Romero, an event the State Department described as a "watershed date" on which "young officers broke with the old repressive order" and along with "progressive civilians" formed a government committed to "profound social and economic reforms, respect for human rights and democracy."

Until the violent events of November-December 1980, which also saw the suspension of U.S. aid, the Carter administration backed the new Salvadoran junta in the only way it knew how: by helping it to bring about "profound social and economic reforms." In the effort to preempt the revolution and expedite the achievements of "social justice," the administration supplied experts who have planned the most thorough-going land reform in the Western hemisphere. To encourage and finance these and related reforms, the U.S. embassy provided nearly $20 million in long-term loans at very low interest. Under the direction of the American Institute for Free Labor Development, an AFL-CIO-sponsored group, a plan was drafted to transfer to some 250,000 of El Salvador's 300,000 peasants ownership of the land they work.

So far, not all the land has been transferred, and titles have not been delivered for much of what has been transferred. Few of the former owners have yet received any significant compensation. In theory, the reforms will vaccinate the masses against Communism by giving them a stake in the society. In practice, as was made dramatically clear by the murder of three American nuns and a social worker in early December, continuing violence from Communists, anti-Communists, and simple criminals has brought death and destruction to El Salvador. Under the pressure of that violence, the society has begun to come apart. "There is no name for what exists in my country," commented a Salvadoran, describing the almost random murder, intimidation, and looting. But there is a name; it is anarchy.

The U.S. under Carter was more eager to impose land reform than elections in El Salvador. Although claims and counterclaims have been exchanged, there is no way of knowing whether the junta (in any of its manifestations) has enjoyed much popular support. It combines Christian Democrats, committed to finding a middle way of "true democracy" between capitalism and Communism, with representatives of various tendencies within the armed forces. It is chronically threatened with schism from within and coup from without. Though its civilian members and their State Department supporters have consistently emphasized the danger from the Right—that is, from authoritarian, intensely anti-Communist defenders of the status quo—El Salvador is more likely in the long run to fall to a coalition of revolutionaries trained, armed, and advised by Cuba and others. The cycle of escalating terror and repression is already far advanced. By failing to offer the junta the arms and advice required to turn back the well-equipped insurgency, the Carter administration undermined the junta's ability to survive and encouraged the insurgents in their conviction of ultimate victory. . . .

Because it failed to take account of basic characteristics of Latin political systems, the Carter administration underestimated the fragility of order in these societies and overestimated the ease with which authority, once undermined, can be restored. Because it regarded revolutionaries as beneficent agents of change, it mistook their goals and motives and could not grasp the problem of governments which become the object of revolutionary violence. Because it misunderstood the relations between economics and politics, it wrongly assumed (as in El Salvador) that economic reforms would necessarily and promptly produce positive political results. Because it misunderstood the relations between "social justice" and authority, it assumed that only "just" governments can survive. Finally, because it misunderstood the relations between justice and violence, the Carter administration fell (and pushed its allies) into an effort to fight howitzers with land reform and urban guerrillas with improved fertilizers.

Above all, the Carter administration failed to understand *politics*. Politics is conducted by persons who by various means, including propaganda and violence, seek to realize some vision of the public good. Those visions may be beneficent or diabolic. But they constitute the real motives of real political actors. When men are treated like "forces" (or the agents of forces), their intentions, values, and world view tend to be ignored. But in Nicaragua the intentions and ideology of the Sandinistas have *already* shaped the outcome of the revolution, as in El Salvador the intentions and ideology of the leading revolutionaries create intransigence where there might have been willingness to cooperate and compromise, nihilism where there might have been reform.

The first step in the reconstruction of U.S. policy for Latin America is intellectual. It requires thinking more realistically about the politics of Latin America, about the alternatives to existing governments, and about the amounts and kinds of aid and time that would be required to improve the lives and expand the liberties of the people of the area. The choices are frequently unattractive.

The second step toward a more adequate policy is to assess realistically the impact of various alternatives on the security of the United States and on the safety and autonomy of the other nations of the hemisphere.

The third step is to abandon the globalist approach which denies the realities of culture, character, geography, economics, and history in favor of a vague, abstract, universalism "stripped," in Edmund Burke's words, "of every relation," standing "in all the nakedness and solitude of metaphysical abstraction." What must replace it is a foreign policy that builds (again Burke) on the "concrete circumstances" which "give . . . to every political principle its distinguishing color and discriminating effect."

Once the intellectual debris has been cleared away, it should become possible to construct a Latin American policy that will protect U.S. security interests and make the actual lives of actual people in Latin America somewhat better and somewhat freer. **focus**

The legacies of the cold war are important because they help to frame current American foreign policies. U.S. perceptions of the Soviet Union are a central dimension of Reagan's foreign policy. The rapid changes in American attitudes toward the U.S.S.R. suggest there is no secure foundation defining U.S. policies. For those like Michael Klare, who reject the prevailing anti-Communist and anti-Soviet perspectives of the Reagan administration, U.S. foreign policy must come to terms with its national security elite, the military-industrial complex, and the realities of an interdependent global setting which greatly limits American power. Because the political power of American foreign policy has declined significantly since the 1950s, Klare argues that the subjective perspectives of American power must also change. He predicts that as long as the legacies of the Vietnam War continue, American military involvement in the Third World will remain limited. Reagan's foreign policy in Central America illustrates a reluctance to introduce American troops.

For Jeane Kirkpatrick, American foreign policy is handicapped by misguided and historically incorrect lessons learned from Vietnam. She believes Soviet foreign policy has remained consistent during the entire history of the cold war, and American misperceptions, grounded in liberal democratic values, have imposed harmful constraints on U.S. foreign policy. The intentions of the Soviet Union will become increasingly apparent in the Third World, however, maintains Kirkpatrick, adding that American foreign policy toward Latin America must reflect a realistic and sober appreciation of Soviet objectives. As the articles by Klare and Kirkpatrick document, the legacies of the cold war continue to define contemporary American foreign policy.

CHAPTER 7

American Foreign Policy and Human Rights

The human rights policies of the Carter administration continue to generate vigorous debate. For many Americans, human rights seemed to be a means to revitalize American foreign policy in the post-Vietnam era. It was hoped that emphasis on human rights would restore credibility to U.S. foreign policy after the revelations of CIA involvement in Chile, the fall of Vietnam, and the political upheaval of Watergate. For the Carter administration, human rights became a way to distance itself from the domestic and foreign policies of Richard Nixon, Henry Kissinger, and Gerald Ford. Supporters of human rights predicted the creation of a new era in the domestic and international politics of both right-wing and left-wing dictatorships. In other words, they hoped that the United States had launched a new crusade capable of creating a better world. Moreover, it was hoped the human rights campaign would rebuild the domestic and foreign policy consensus destroyed during the upheavals of Vietnam and Watergate.

Opponents of the Carter administration's human rights stand argued that these policies were naive at best. First, they maintained human rights could not be applied consistently in a complex global environment because fundamental American political and economic interests would ultimately take precedence over human rights concerns. The result, they claimed, would be a foreign policy that was hypocritical. Second, the human rights philosophy came at a time of declining American power in world politics. The "Vietnam Syndrome" called for less military and political involvement in Third World countries. The critics questioned how United States foreign policy could promote human rights if its ability to exert influence in international politics was declining. Third, opponents argued that human rights policies were attempts to implement a moral imperative which was unsuited to the existing levels of political and economic development in most countries. Fourth, the human rights emphasis of American foreign policy embraced a liberal democratic ideology that obscured the basic political, military, and economic motivations of states, said critics. From this perspective, the power politics (See Chapter 3) approach of the Nixon-Kissinger years and the cold war politics of the Reagan administration offered a more realistic framework for American foreign policy, they maintained. The evolution of the Carter administration's human rights policies illustrates the significance of conflicting assumptions of American foreign policy in the 1980s.

The development of human rights policies originated in the U.S. Congress during Richard M. Nixon's second term. Rising dissatisfaction over the issue of executive-congressional authority to determine foreign policy making spurred several attempts by the Congress to limit the power of the presidency. The Wars Powers Act of 1973, congressional hearings on the role of the CIA in domestic and international politics (See p. 109), and the embargo on arms to Turkey in 1974 were Congress' attempt to assert more control over the policy-making power of the presidency. It was in this context that

Congress began to emphasize the importance of human rights as an objective of American foreign policy. Thus, Congress established the position of Assistant Secretary of State for Human Rights and Humanitarian Affairs; the State Department was required by law to report to Congress on its human rights activities and on the status of human rights throughout the world; and Henry Kissinger's emphasis on power politics became a target of human rights legislation. There was growing opposition to Kissinger's personal status, and the centralization of foreign policy making in his hands alienated increasing numbers of congressmen. During the days of Watergate and Gerald Ford's succession to the presidency, American foreign policy appeared to many to be Henry Kissinger's personal foreign policy. Kissinger's emphasis on balance-of-power diplomacy and power politics underscored the Secretary of State's European perspective. Thus, Kissinger's policies were increasingly attacked for their lack of moral principle. His pragmatism seemed to symbolize the moral bankruptcy of American life, as epitomized in the tragedies of Vietnam and Watergate. Moreover, Kissinger's diplomatic style seemed to represent a distinctly European approach to American foreign policy making. For those most critical of Henry Kissinger's foreign policy preeminence, he came to symbolize the triumph of pragmatism over idealism. From this perspective, the achievements of the Nixon-Kissinger years represented the loss of principles and, thus, the betrayal of America's mission. Detente, nuclear arms limitation agreements, the opening of relations with China, shuttle diplomacy in the Middle East, and the end of the war in Vietnam were attacked for their amorality. The United States needed a new crusade.

The election of Jimmy Carter in 1976 reflected the self-doubt and pessimism of many Americans. President Carter launched his administration by calling for a return to the democratic principles which had made the United States great. A human rights focus provided Jimmy Carter with an opportunity to create a new bipartisan foreign policy consensus. The after-shocks of Vietnam and Watergate called for new creative directions. The Carter administration hoped that human rights would serve as the basis for a redirection of American foreign policy. Jimmy Carter's outlook supported a moral interpretation of both domestic and international politics.

The impact of changing international conditions also seemed to underscore the need for new departures in American foreign policy. The Arab oil embargo in the winter of 1973-74 called attention to the United States and the West's vulnerability to the demands of resource-rich Third World states. United States dependence on oil, and the economic effects of the embargo—a reduced growth rate, inflation, and a deepening economic recession—dramatically heightened America's awareness of Third World demands. A sense of the limitations of American power, rooted in these economic and political vulnerabilities, emphasized the need for a new approach to global problems. The post-World War II era of U.S. global dominance gave way to a recognition of the interdependence of all countries. Third World demands for a redistribution of Western economic resources in order to alleviate declining economic growth rates, malnutrition, and other social conditions associated with poverty in the underdeveloped countries, underscored the need for a change in American foreign policy. The Carter administration hoped that sincere efforts in the area of human rights would help to create a more favorable global climate for American foreign policies. Thus, it was asserted there was a need for U.S. leadership, based on moral issues, in world politics.

The overwhelming thrust of U.S. human rights policies emphasized those civil and political rights, which illustrated the evolution of American civil liberties throughout the U.S. history. American foreign policy called for the rights of freedom of thought, religion, assembly, speech, and press, as well as the right to be free from governmental interference through torture; to be spared from cruel, inhumane, and/or degrading punishment; to be protected from arbitrary arrest or imprisonment; and to be allowed a fair trial. A third area of human rights—basic human or socio-economic needs for food, shelter, health care, and education—were not emphasized nearly as much as civil and political rights. American human rights policies did not satisfy the central concerns of most Third World states for economic and social assistance. Many Third World countries argued that the U.S. push for civil liberties was a deliberate attempt to side-step the need for the redistribution of economic and social resources. The Third World charged that rather than illustrating a sincere American desire to create a more equitable global environment, human rights were a means of fostering continued American dominance. U.S. attempts to force repressive Third World governments to stop abuses of civil liberties resulted in a storm of criticism. American military and economic assistance to many repressive countries (Argentina, Brazil, Nicaragua, El Salvador, and Guatemala) was greatly diminished or ended altogether. However, the U.S. goal of greater leadership in the Third World backfired, resulting in increased hostility. U.S. human rights policies were criticized for their inconsistency and incoherence. American attempts to procure greater civil liberties for Soviet Jews and dissidents were quickly ended when the U.S.S.R. threatened to withdraw from the SALT negotiations. Critics argued that human rights created a double standard favoring those countries that were politically important to the United States. Therefore, civil liberties abuses were ignored in the Soviet Union, China, Iran (under the Shah), and South Korea. The U.S., however, vigorously pursued its human rights policies against less important countries—for example, Uganda, Nicaragua, Haiti, and Cuba. Opponents of the U.S. human rights policies argued that important historic allies of American foreign policy were jeopardized by a moralistic vision that could not be realistically acheived under contemporary global conditions.

In the following remarks delivered by Patricia Derian, Assistant Secretary of State for Human Rights during the Carter administration, the benefits of U.S. human rights policies are outlined. Derian argues that all members of the world community benefit from human rights, especially the victims of repression and their families. Second, she argues that if the goals of U.S. foreign policy and American values are to be taken seriously, then the United States must demonstrate its good faith—however uncomfortable it may be for America's allies and adversaries. Third, because she believes the real world imposes limits on human achievements, Derian recognizes the limitations of American foreign policies and, by extention, its inconsistencies. However, she argues that the U.S. must begin to make inroads against the forces of repression. In so doing, Derian maintains, the United States helps to create the forces necessary for global change.

U.S. COMMITMENT TO HUMAN RIGHTS

Patricia Derian, *Current Policy*, Number 198, June 13, 1980

Patricia Derian was Assistant Secretary of State for Human Rights and Humanitarian Affairs for the Carter Administration.

. . . The only way we—as individuals and Americans and citizens of the world—can survive and prosper is if everyone does. The rewards and the responsibilities are joint. Our concerns are common concerns; our problems are shared problems. Even those who do so regretfully, acknowledge that isolationism is no longer possible or useful in our shrinking world. No abuse of human rights can truly remain within the borders of a nation. Each abuse affects its neighbors and the world. No war today can truly be internal or bilateral as nations become increasingly interdependent and nuclear weapons continue to proliferate.

Most of us can describe the way we want the world to be for ourselves and for our children. We want peace, we want prosperity, and we want the freedom to enjoy the rewards of a peaceful and prosperous world.

Most of us are willing to sacrifice a little prosperity for peace. And, if history is any guide, most of us will sacrifice them both to achieve the basic human right of freedom—freedom to and freedom from:

- Freedom to fulfill such vital needs as food, shelter, health care, and education; freedom to enjoy civil and political liberties; freedom of thought, religion, assembly, speech, and the press; freedom of movement and freedom to take part in government.

- Freedom from governmental violation of the integrity of the person: summary execution; torture and cruel, inhuman, or degrading treatment or punishment; arbitrary arrest or imprisonment; denial of fair, public trial and invasion of the home.

The Universal Declaration of Human Rights, whose values I have just listed, is now more than 30 years old. It is not universally implemented, but, with few exceptions, even its worst violators at least pay lip service to its principles. Lip service seems to come easily with abstract concepts, and most of the words I have used so far—peace, prosperity, freedom—are relative, abstract terms. Prosperity for a Cuban refugee is not necessarily prosperity for a native-born citizen of the United States. Freedom for a Russian writer is not necessarily freedom for an American journalist. And peace in northern Ireland or the West Bank may merely be a temporary halt in an undeclared war. . . .

President Carter didn't invent human rights for the United States or for the world, but he did raise some fallen banners and illuminate some values that had grown dim while we were busy containing communism, arms racing, selling America abroad, and devastating our nation's morale with war. In his inaugural address, the President said, "Our commitment to human rights must be absolute. . . . Because we are free, we can never be indifferent to the fate of freedom elsewhere."

Now in the 20 or so years immediately preceding that statement our free nation was too often identified with repressive regimes. There were revelations of Central Intelligence Agency abuse in an attempt to overthrow a democratically elected government in Chile and of interference in Angola, which then brought Cuban troops to the African Continent. We fought a bitter battle in Vietnam to support an authoritarian regime with little popular support. We were so concerned with detente that at times it seemed as if we condoned the brutal, authoritarian Soviet rule. . . .

Policy Criticisms

In the process of implementing this policy, we have acquired our critics. Some have accused us of losing sight of the distinction between totalitarian countries, where there are virtually no human rights and no hope for their emergence, and authoritarian countries, which have some hope for or measure of freedom. We put too much pressure on our authoritarian friends, the critics say, and we will lose them as allies if we concern ourselves with their human rights problems. My reply is that suffering and oppression can take place in any society—totalitarian, authoritarian, democratic, or other—and that it is our obligation to work to obliterate human rights abuses wherever they occur. When we have found it convenient for "practical" purposes of military alliance or economic advantage to ignore our authoritarian allies' human rights violations, in the long run the United States and the world have paid a terrible price.

Six years ago our friendship with the colonels who ran Greece and our very warm relations with the junta had given people of that country every reason to believe that the United States stood firmly behind that government and endorsed its policies. When it changed, it wasn't surprising that the new government was somewhat dubious about us and our intentions and denied us access to the very bases our original policy had been designed to secure.

In South Korea at this very moment we have a vivid illustration of how quickly things can change and how difficult it often is, particularly in times of stress, to harmonize our most important foreign policy objectives. What had appeared to be a gradual improvement in the human rights situation in that country, has suffered a dramatic reversal. Our human rights policy—indeed, our long-term national security interests—require that we do everything we reasonably can to encourage a return to the path of evolutionary political liberalization. Yet, we must safeguard our regional security interests in the process.

Some say that if we distance ourselves from the new regime significantly in the military field, regional security would be at risk (meaning North Korea might invade). To withhold military assistance would be taking a risk. But the dilemma is that if we continue to supply this aid in spite of warning signals, we risk perhaps equally drastic and damaging consequences in the long run. If we so support a military government that has jailed its opposition, imposed full martial law, and heavily censored its nation's press, we appear not just to condone but to reward these violations of basic human rights. If some of South Korea's generals are determined to establish a dictatorship, economic and moral pressure may not be sufficient to dissuade them from this goal. They have presumably appraised the situation and may have decided that we are exclusively concerned with regional security. If we do not remain true to our ideals, we risk a strong anti-American backlash.

What we have done to date is talk seriously with the present government.

We have explained our position and emphasized we view the situation as extremely grave. We hope it has the desired effect.

We recognize that supporting a military dictatorship is no guarantee of stability nor of a profitable or useful long-term bilateral relationship. By now we should have learned some other lessons. As a nation, we tried taking the line of least resistance on the human rights issue in the past, and it doesn't work. Greece, Soviet repression of Eastern Europe, Batista's Cuba, the Shah's Iran, Park's Korea, Somosa's Nicaragua, and the list goes on. We have paid a long-term price wherever we have ignored human rights violations in the interests of short-term expediency. And our world has perhaps come a little closer to stopping each time. For those who are "counters"—and I am not—the price in human lives cannot be measured but economic costs can, and they must total a staggering sum in equipment lost, trade stopped, buildings burned, and companies nationalized. And how do you count the loss in world influence and prestige?

For every critic who says that human rights policies run counter to our national interests, there is another who says, "In countries where there are oppressive regimes but liberal elements working to bring about gradual change, doesn't your calling for immediate reforms frustrate the liberals and bring about even harsher, more repressive controls?" Well, this is what the repressive regimes say. But I don't know why anyone should be surprised when a repressive government tries to blame its repressive measures on human rights advocates.

The oligarchs and tyrants of the world will always find an argument to justify repression. They say that economic development must be the first priority, that political repression is an unfortunate but acceptable precondition. . . .

Some say that aid is the process by which the poor of a rich country subsidize the rich of a poor country; that all aid really does is prop up the oligarchs. Others say that if the United States doesn't give aid to the oligarchs, there would be helpful revolutions and the world would therefore be a nicer place in which to live. Americans—right, left, and middle—have decided that they don't want their tax dollars financing repression or making a few people rich in a poor country. And we have made progress in this respect in the last few years, disassociating our government from repressive regimes even when other U.S. interests remain. Though in places like Iran and Cuba we are still paying the price for our former policies. . . .

Other critics say, why don't you straighten out your own affairs before calling attention to others' abuses? How can you implement a human rights policy in foreign affairs while your own domestic performance needs correcting? The answer is, of course, that human rights cannot wait. We cannot ask a victim in another country to wait while we redress our own injustices. Our domestic and foreign efforts must go forward together, as complementary parts of the whole. President Carter, in signing the international human rights covenants 2 years ago and submitting them to the

Senate for ratification, attested our commitment to work for human rights in both areas. We as a nation must now reaffirm our commitment by ratifying these documents. They are crucial to the continued international credibility of this country's policy, and their nonratification is an embarrassment. We need to work, we are working, for full public education on the importance of these documents. It is part of the reason I am here today.

These documents also respond to one last common criticism, that our human rights policy represents uniquely Western or American ideals. Not so. Nobody wants to be tortured. People everywhere want food, water to drink, an opportunity to express themselves, and some notion that they are protected, rather than threatened, by the might of the state. It is arrogant to assume that we have a right to a special set of values others are too backward to understand. It is also ignorant. The proof is in the covenants' list of ratifying states that covers the map from East Europe to South America, Africa, and the Mideast—hardly a Western bloc or a uniquely American idea.

For the last quarter of a century we have been on the ideological defensive. Our national pride and our credibility as a world power have suffered. But now, our willingness to press for human rights progress, even among our military allies, has helped to restore the world's belief in our commitment to freedom. It has also helped us, as a nation, to arrive at a new consensus, secure in the foundations of our own freedom and our resolve to help the rest of the world achieve the same.

Since President Carter assumed office, we have not been oblivious to torture, disappearances, political imprisonment, racism, or other violations of human rights. We have not identified ourselves with authoritarian dictatorships around the world. Instead we have tried to persuade governments with poor human rights records to make changes—through example, through quiet diplomacy, by withholding military or economic aid and performing the symbolic acts I mentioned earlier. We have made progress. It is hard to take credit for the release of political prisoners, the disappearance that didn't happen, or the would-be refugee who remained at home when freedom was increased. And there are many organizations—governmental and non-governmental from many countries—working in the field of human rights. None of us unlocks jails, rewrites laws, or changes practices and traditions anywhere but in our own country. The people on the spot take care of that. So we don't say, "Attention world, the United States has just achieved a marvelous human rights coup." It is not the intention of this effort to make us look good. It is not a publicity gimmick or a public relations trick. What it is is an honest humanitarian effort. We do it because we have international obligations that demand it, because it is in the interest of the United States, and because it is right. . . .   **focus**

Patricia Derian's argument illustrates the sense of hope and accomplishment that accompanied the early years of the Carter administration. As time progressed, the human rights policies were submerged in heightening fears of Soviet aggression throughout the world. The Reagan administration's emphasis on Communist insurgency in Central America illustrates the renewal of cold war hostilities. It should be pointed out that in its last years, the Carter administration moved increasingly in this direction. In the following essay by Professor Samuel Huntington, "Human Rights and American Power," U.S. support for human rights is examined in the context of heightening concerns of Soviet aggression. Huntington argues that American power is the key force in the attempt to restrict the repressive policies of right-wing dictatorships. Only when U.S. foreign policy is strong and credible in the Third World can the United States limit governmental abuses of civil liberties. Huntington points out that the Carter administration's emphasis on human rights was accompanied by a decline in American power in the Third World. Thus, he says, the effectiveness of American human rights policies was limited by the U.S.'s inability to exert influence on right-wing dictatorships. Huntington attributes U.S. non-involvement during the Carter years to a reaction to America's Vietnam experience.

HUMAN RIGHTS AND AMERICAN POWER

Samuel P. Huntington, *Commentary*, September 1981

Samuel P. Huntington is Clarence Dillon Professor of International Relations at Harvard.

During the 1960's and 1970's many intellectuals—foreign and American—expounded what can perhaps best be termed "the myth of American repression"—that is, the view that American involvement in the politics of other societies is almost invariably hostile to liberty and supportive of repression in those societies. The United States, as Hans J. Morgenthau put it in 1974, is "repression's friend": "With unfailing consistency we have since the end of World War II intervened on behalf of conservative and fascist repression against revolution and radical reform. In an age when societies are in a revolutionary or prerevolutionary stage, we have become the foremost counterrevolutionary status quo power on earth. Such a policy can only lead to moral and political disaster." His argument, like the multitudinous statements of other intellectuals supporting the myth of American repression, suffers from two basic deficiencies.

First, it confuses support for the Left with opposition to repression. In this respect, it represents another manifestation of the extent to which similarity in immediate objectives can blur the line between liberals and revolutionaries. Yet those who support "revolution and radical reform" in other countries seldom have any greater concern for liberty and human dignity than those who support "conservative and fascist repression." In fact, if it is a choice between right-wing and left-wing dictatorships, there are at least three good reasons in terms of liberty to prefer the former to the latter.

1. The suppression of liberty in right-wing authoritarian regimes is almost always less pervasive than it is in left-wing totalitarian ones. In the 1960's and

1970's, for instance, infringements of human rights in South Korea received extensive coverage in the American media, in part because there were in South Korea journalists, church groups, intellectuals, and opposition political leaders who could call attention to those infringements. The absence of comparable reports about the infringements of human rights in North Korea was evidence not of the absence of repression in that country but of its totality.

2. Right-wing dictatorships are, the record shows, less permanent than left-wing dictatorships; Portugal, Spain, and Greece are but three examples of right-wing dictatorships that were replaced by democratic regimes. Despite the hopeful movement toward pluralism in Poland, as of 1981 no Communist system had been replaced by a democratic regime.

3. As a result of the global competition between the United States and the Soviet Union, right-wing regimes are normally more susceptible to American and other Western influence than left-wing dictatorships, and such influence is overwhelmingly on the side of liberty. Soviet influence, on the other hand, is invariably and powerfully exerted—as happened twice in Czechoslovakia—on the side of repression.

This last point goes to the other central fallacy of the myth of American repression as elaborated by Morgenthau and others. Their picture of the world of the 1960's and 1970's was dominated by the image of an America that was overwhelmingly powerful and overwhelmingly repressive. In effect, they held an updated belief in the "illusion of American omnipotence" that attributed the evil in other societies to the machinations of the Pentagon, the CIA, and American business. Their image of America was, however, defective in both dimensions. During the 1960's and 1970's American power relative to that of other governments and societies declined significantly. By the mid-70's the ability of the United States to influence what was going on in other societies was but a pale shadow of what it had been a quarter-century earlier.

When American power had an effect on other societies, however, it generally was to further liberty, pluralism, and democracy. The United States is, in practice, the freest, most liberal, most democratic country in the world, with far better institutionalized protections for the rights of its citizens than any other society. As a consequence, any increase in the power or influence of the United States in world affairs generally results—not inevitably, but far more often than not—in the promotion of liberty and human rights in the world. The expansion of American power is not synonymous with the expansion of liberty, but a significant correlation exists between the rise and fall of American power in the world and the rise and fall of liberty and democracy in the world.

The single biggest extension of democratic liberties in the history of the world came at the end of World War II, when stable democratic regimes were inaugurated in the defeated Axis countries: Germany, Japan, Italy, and—as a former part of Germany—Austria. In the early 1980's these countries had a population of over 200 million, and included the third and fourth largest economies in the world. The imposition of democracy on these countries was almost entirely the work of the United States. In Germany and Japan, in particular, the United States government played a major role in designing democratic institutions. As a result of American determination and power, the former Axis countries were, as John D. Montgomery put it, "forced to be free."

Conversely, the modest steps taken toward democracy and liberty in Poland, Czechoslovakia, and Hungary were quickly reversed, and Stalinist repression instituted, once it became clear that the United States was not able to project its power into Eastern Europe. If World War II had ended in something less than total victory, or if the United States had played a less significant role in bringing about that victory (as was, indeed, the case east of the Elbe), these transitions to democracy in Central Europe and Eastern Asia would not have occurred. But—with the partial exception of South Korea— where American armies marched, democracy followed in their train.

The stability of democracy in these countries during the quarter-century after World War II reflected, in large part, the extent to which the institutions and practices imposed by the United States found a favorable social and political climate in which to take root. The continued American political, economic, and military presence in Western Europe and Eastern Asia was, however, also indispensable to this democratic success. At any time after World War II the withdrawal of American military guarantees and military forces from these areas would have had a most unsettling and perhaps devastating effect on the future of democracy in Central Europe and Japan.

In the early years of the cold war, American influence was employed to insure the continuation of democratic government in Italy and to promote free elections in Greece. In both cases, the United States had twin interests in the domestic politics of these countries: to create a system of stable democratic government and to insure the exclusion of Communist parties from power. Since in both cases the Communist parties did not have the support of a majority of the population, the problem of what to do if a party committed to abolishing democracy were to gain power through democratic means was happily avoided. With American support, democracy survived in Italy and was sustained for a time in Greece. In addition, the American victory of World War II provided the stimulus in Turkey for one of the rarest events in political history: the peaceful self-transformation of an authoritarian, one-party system into a democratic, competitive party system.

In Latin America, the rise and fall of democratic regimes also coincided with the rise and fall of American influence. In the second and third decades of this century, American intervention in Nicaragua, Haiti, and the Dominican Republic produced the freest elections and the most open political competition in the history of those countries. There, as in other countries in Central America and the Caribbean, American influence in support of free elections was usually exerted in response to the protests of opposition groups against the repressive actions of their own governments, and as a result of American fears that revolution or civil war would occur if significant political and social forces were denied equal opportunity to participate in the political process. . . .

Thus in its interventions in eight Caribbean and Central American countries between 1900 and 1933, the United States acted on the assumption that "the only way both to prevent revolutions and to determine whether they are justified if they do break out, is to guarantee free elections." In Cuba, the effect of the Platt Amendment and American interventions was, in the words of Jorge I. Dominguez, "to pluralize the Cuban political system" by fostering "the rise and entrenchment of opposition groups" and by multiplying "the sources of political power so that no single group, not even the government, could impose its will on society or the economy for very long. . . . The spirit and practice of liberalism—competitive and unregulated political, economic, religious, and social life—overwhelmed a pluralized Cuba." The interventions by United States Marines in Haiti, Nicaragua, the Dominican Republic, and elsewhere in these years often bore striking resemblances to the interventions by federal marshals in the conduct of elections in the American South in the 1960's: registering voters, protecting against electoral violence, insuring a free vote and an honest count.

Direct intervention by the American government in Central America and the Caribbean came to at least a temporary end in the early 1930's. Without exception, the result was a shift in the direction of more dictatorial regimes. It had taken American power to impose even the most modest aspects of democracy in these societies. When American intervention ended, democracy ended. For the Caribbean and Central America, the era of the Good Neighbor was also the era of the bad tyrant. The efforts of the United States to be the former gave a variety of unsavory local characters—Trujillo, Somoza, Batista—the opportunity to be the latter.

American attention was primarily directed toward Europe and Asia in the years immediately after World War II. Latin America was, by and large, neglected. This situation began to change toward the late 1950's, and it dramatically shifted after Castro's seizure of power in Cuba. In the early 1960's Latin America became the focus of large-scale economic-aid programs, military training and assistance programs, propaganda efforts, and repeated attention by the President and other high-level American officials. Under the Alliance for Progress, American power was to be used to promote and sustain democratic government and greater social equity in the rest of the Western Hemisphere. This high point in the exercise of United States power in Latin America coincided with the high point of democracy in Latin America. This period witnessed, in Tad Szulc's phrase, "the twilight of the tyrants": it was the age in which at one point all but one of the ten South American countries (Paraguay) had some semblance of democratic government.

Obviously, the greater prevalence of democratic regimes during these years was not exclusively a product of United States policy and power. Yet the United States certainly played a role. The democratic governments that had emerged in Colombia and Venezuela in the late 1950's were carefully nurtured with money and praise. Strenuous efforts were made to head off the attempts of both left-wing guerrillas and right-wing military officers to overthrow Betancourt in Venezuela and to insure the orderly transition to an elected successor for the first time in the history of that country. After thirty years in which (to quote Jerome Slater) "the U.S. government was less interested and involved in Dominican affairs" than at any other time in history—a period coinciding with Trujillo's domination of the Dominican Republic—American opposition to that dictator slowly mounted in the late 1950's. Following his assassination in 1961, "the United States engaged in the most massive intervention in the internal affairs of a Latin American state since the inauguration of the Good Neighbor Policy." The United States prevented a comeback by Trujillo family members, launched programs to promote economic and social welfare, and acted to insure democratic liberties and competitive elections. The latter, held in December 1962, resulted in the election of Juan Bosch as president. When the military moved against Bosch the following year, American officials first tried to head off the coup, and then, after its success, attempted to induce the junta to return quickly to constitutional procedures. But by that point, writes Abraham F. Lowenthal, American "leverage and influence [with the new government] were severely limited," and the only concession the United States was able to exact in return for recognition was a promise that elections would be held in 1965. . . .

Through a somewhat more complex process, a decline in the American role also led eventually to similar results in Chile. In the 1964 Chilean elections, the United States exerted all the influence it could on behalf of Eduardo Frei and made a significant and possibly decisive contribution to his defeat of Salvador Allende. In the 1970 election the American government did not make any comparable effort to defeat Allende, who won the popular election by a narrow margin. At that point, the United States tried to induce the Chilean congress to refuse to confirm his victory and tried to promote a military coup to prevent him from taking office. Both these efforts violated the norms of Chilean politics as well as of American morality, and both were unsuccessful. If, on the other hand, the United States had been as active in the popular election of 1970 as it had been in that of 1964, Allende might well have been defeated again, and the destruction of Chilean democracy in 1973 thus avoided.

All in all, the decline in the role of the United States in Latin America in the late 1960's and early 1970's coincided with the spread of authoritarian regimes in that area. With this decline went a decline in the standards of democratic morality and human rights which the United States could attempt to apply to the governments of the region. In the early 1960's in Latin America (as in the 1910's and 1920's in the Caribbean and Central America), the goal of the United States was democratic competition and free elections. By the mid-1970's, that goal had been lowered from the fostering of democratic government to attempting to induce authoritarian governments not to infringe too blatantly the rights of their citizens.

A similar relationship between American power and democratic government prevailed in Asia. There, too, the peak of American power was reached in the early and mid-1960's, and there, too, the decline in this power was followed by a decline in democracy and liberty.

American influence had been most pervasive in the Philippines, which, for a quarter-century after World War II, had the most open, democratic system, apart from Japan, in East and Southeast Asia. After the admittedly fraudulent election of 1949 and in the face of the rising threat to the Philippine government posed by the Huk insurgency, American military and economic assistance were greatly increased. Direct American intervention in Philippine politics then played a decisive role not only in promoting Ramon Magsaysay into the presidency but also in insuring that the 1951 congressional elections and 1953 presidential election were open and honest elections. In the next three elections the Philippines met the sternest test of democracy: incumbent presidents were defeated for reelection.

In subsequent years, however, the American presence and American influence in the Philippines declined, and with them went support for Philippine democracy. When President Marcos instituted his martial-law regime in 1972, American influence in Southeast Asia was clearly on the wane, and the United States held few effective levers with which to affect the course of Philippine politics.

In perhaps even more direct fashion, the high point of democracy and political liberty in Vietnam also coincided with the high point of American influence there. The only free national election in the history of that country took place in 1967, when the American military intervention was at its peak. In Vietnam, as in Latin America, American intervention had a pluralizing effect on politics, limiting the government and encouraging and strengthening its political opposition. The defeat of the United States in Vietnam and the exclusion of American power from Indochina were followed in three countries by the imposition of regimes of virtually total repression. . . .

The future of liberty in the world is thus intimately linked to the future of American power. Yet paradoxically—and erroneously—proponents of very differing views concerning American foreign-policy relations have often united in seeing a conflict between the two, interpreting American involvement in the world as the outcome of the conflicting pulls of national interest and power, on the one hand, and political morality and principles, on the other. Shortly after World War II, there emerged a significant group of writers and thinkers, including Reinhold Niebuhr, George Kennan, Walter Lippmann, Hans J. Morgenthau, and Robert Osgood, who expounded a "new realism." They criticized what they called the moralistic, legalistic, utopian, and Wilsonian approaches which they claimed had previously prevailed in the conduct of American foreign relations. This new realism reached its apotheosis in the central role played by the balance of power in the theory and practice of Henry Kissinger. In the 1970's, however, the new realism came to be challenged by the "new moralism," and the pendulum that had swung in one direction after World War II now swung far over to the other side.

This shift was one of the most significant consequences of Vietnam, Watergate, and the democratic surge and creedal passion that dominated American politics in the 1960's. It represented the displacement onto the external world of the moralism that had been earlier directed inward against American institutions. The new moralism manifested itself first in congressional action, with the addition to the foreign-assistance act of Title IX in 1966 and human-rights conditions in the early 1970's, and then in the 1976 election when Jimmy Carter vigorously criticized President Ford for believing "that there is little room for morality in foreign affairs, and that we must put self-interest above principle." As President, Carter moved human rights to a central position in American foreign relations.

The lines between the moralists and the realists were thus clearly drawn, but on one point they were agreed: they both believed that the conflict between morality and self-interest, or ideals and realism, was a real one. The truth, however, is that while in some respects the conflict is real, in others, particularly when formulated in terms of a conflict between liberty and power, it is not. So defined, the dichotomy does not reflect an accurate understanding of the real choices confronting American policy-makers in dealing with the external world. Yet the double thrust of the new moralism was, paradoxically, to advocate the expansion of global liberty, and, simultaneously, to effect a reduction in American power.

The relative decline in American power in the 1970's had many sources. One of them assuredly was the democratic surge (of which the new moralism was one element) in the United States in the 1960's and early 1970's. The strong recommitment to democratic, liberal, and populist values that occurred during these years eventually generated efforts to limit, constrain, and reduce American military, political, and economic power abroad. The intense and sustained attacks by the media, by intellectuals, and by Congressmen on the military establishment, intelligence agencies, diplomatic officials, and political leadership of the United States inevitably had that effect. Imbued with the myth of American repression, the new moralists, without seeing the contradiction, welcomed the end of American hegemony in the Western Hemisphere and, at the same time, deplored the intensification of repression in Latin America.

It is also paradoxical that in the 1970's those Congressmen who were most insistent on the need to promote human rights abroad were often most active in reducing the American power that could help achieve that result. In key votes in the 94th Congress, for instance, 132 Congressmen consistently voted in favor of human-rights amendments to foreign-aid legislation. Seventy-eight of those 132 Representatives also consistently voted against a larger military establishment, and another 28 consistent supporters of human rights split their votes on the military establishment. Only 26 of the 132 Congressmen consistently voted in favor of both human rights and the military power whose development could help make those rights a reality.

The new realism of the 1940's and 1950's coincided with the expansion of American power in the world and the resulting expansion of American-sponsored liberty and democracy in the world. The new moralism of the early 1970's coincided with the relative decline in American power and the concomitant erosion of liberty and democracy around the globe. By limiting American power, the new moralism promoted that decline. In some measure, too, the new moralism was a consequence of the decline. The new moralism's concern with human rights throughout the world clearly reflected the erosion in global liberty and democratic values about the world.

Paradoxically, the United States thus became more preoccupied with ways of defending human rights as its power to promote human rights diminished. Enactment of Title IX to the foreign-assistance act in 1966, a major congressional effort to promote democratic values abroad, came at the midpoint in the steady decline in American foreign-economic assistance. Similarly, the various human-rights restrictions that Congress wrote into the foreign-assistance acts in the 1970's coincided with the general replacement of military aid by military sales.

When American power was clearly predominant, such legislative provisions and caveats were superfluous: no Harkin amendment was necessary to convey the message of the superiority of liberty. The message was there for all to see in the troop deployments, carrier task forces, foreign-aid spending, and intelligence operatives. When these faded from the scene, in order to promote liberty and human rights Congress found it necessary to write more and more explicit conditions and requirements into legislation. These legislative provisions were, in effect, an effort to compensate for the decline of American power. In terms of protecting liberty abroad, they were no substitute for the presence of American power. The reconstitution of that power—political, economic, military—can only have positive effects on the state of liberty and democracy around the world.   focus

Patricia Derian and Samuel Huntington suggest fundamentally different visions of the appropriate human rights focus of American foreign policy. Derian takes the view that change was necessary: In order for the United States to reclaim its historic mission, the problems of human rights had to be tackled from the perspective of the victim. Thus, the U.S. worked to secure the release of individuals held by repressive regimes all over the world. Derian argues that the alleviation of human suffering on a person-by-person basis illustrated the accomplishments and the pragmatism of the Carter administration's approach. For Huntington, human rights can be meaningfully secured only through the politics of strength. He admits this is often a slow, difficult, and frustrating process, but contends the historic results of American foreign policies throughout the world illustrate its wisdom and successes. It should be noted that neither of the approaches suggested by Derian or Huntington speak to the most basic Third World demands that economic and social human rights be achieved before the attainment of civil liberties are addressed.

CHAPTER 8

The United States and the Third World

The 1970s witnessed the emergence of the Third World as a major political, economic, and ideological force in world politics. Third World countries have called for greater levels of economic and political participation in world politics since the 1950s. However, it was not until the early 1970s that the Third World presented the United States and other developed societies (including the Soviet Union) with a systematic set of proposals to establish a new international economic order. The Third World argued that the problems of economic development and poverty were so great that in order to overcome them existing political and economic relations between rich and poor states had to be restructured. One of the most important political alignments in world politics today is that between the wealthy developed countries of the northern hemisphere (the North) and the poor developing states of the southern hemisphere (the South). Their fundamental conflicts are expressed through the term "North-South relations."

Third World demands for the creation of a new international economic order were largely ignored by the United States and the developed countries. With the successful embargo of oil to the United States, Western Europe, and Japan by the Organization of Petroleum Exporting Countries (OPEC) during the winter of 1973-74, a change in United States foreign policy appeared to be in the making. In 1975, Secretary of State Henry Kissinger addressed the United Nations' Seventh Special Session examining issues of international trade and development, where he promised that a constructive American response to the proposals advanced by the South would be forthcoming. The demonstration of OPEC's power and what appeared to be a new American willingness to consider seriously Third World proposals raised expectations throughout the South. Yet, as of 1982, American foreign policy has failed to achieve even minimal success in coming to terms with the proposals put forward by the South. Despite the Carter administration's apparent openness to Third World perspectives, American foreign policy has remained essentially unchanged for over a decade. It is not surprising, therefore, that United States' relations with the Third World have been characterized by increasing bitterness and alienation. Some critics maintain the United States has never really entered into a meaningful dialogue with the South. In this chapter, we will examine two clashing philosophies about the central issues confronting United States foreign policy toward the Third World.

One perspective calls for the United States to implement the Third World proposals for the creation of a more equitable global economic order. This faction argues that the North is responsible for the historic exploitation of the South. Through the conquest and colonization of Latin America, the Middle East, Asia, and Africa, European nations established a system of political, economic, and cultural dominance. The countries of the North continued to exert overwhelming control over the Third World even after the end of colonialism and the establishment of independent Third World states. The North (led by the United States) created a global economic, political, and military system so powerful that it guaranteed the obedience of Third World states, thus continuing the historic process of economic and political exploitation of the South. The cohesiveness of Third World demands for the creation of a more equitable economic system in the 1970s illustrates the intensity of the South's perceptions of its exploitation by the North. Advocates of this position maintain the United States has a moral obligation to remedy the past abuses of a corrupt global system through its foreign policy. Those favoring American support for the South also point to pragmatic objectives. World politics is experiencing a period of profound transition. Not only has American power declined since its peak following World War II, but the influence of the Third World has steadily increased; the economic power of OPEC is only one example of a larger process. The interdependence of all nations has reached global levels, binding all states more closely together. In such an interdependent world, Third World states now have the ability to influence the United States directly in both positive and negative ways. While many Third World states do not possess strategic natural resources like oil, the United States and the North, nonetheless, have a vested interest in the political and economic stability of the entire global system. Thus, this interdependence makes the United States more vulnerable to political and economic upheavals anywhere in the world. Problems of malnutrition, overpopulation, urban congestion, underemployment, and inadequate health care in the South make political stability difficult to achieve. The likelihood of unrest, civil war, revolution, and regional conflicts increases. Those who support active American participation in the North-South dialogue argue that unless a comprehensive attempt is made to restructure North-South economic relations and, thus, to begin solving the most basic aspects of Third World poverty, long term global peace and security cannot be assured. They claim global survival demands a fundamental alteration in the objectives of American foreign policy.

An alternative perspective denies that the United States and the North are responsible for the relative poverty of the South. Opponents of the North-South dialogue argue that no causal link can be established between the legacies of colonialism and imperialism and contemporary Third World poverty. They maintain the economies of the North and the South are so fundamentally different that the alleged exploitation of the South by the North simply does not occur. Moreover, the Third World's emphasis on the external aspects of poverty masks the real causes of its impoverishment—internal obstacles to development. For these critics, a stagnant internal economic system, political corruption, the absence of democracy, the repression of minorities, and cultural values that do not support economic activities better explain the absence of economic growth in many Third World countries than do accusations of exploitation. Finally, this approach argues that the economic growth of the Third World since World War II has been remarkable. Rather than exploiting the South, the North's capitalist economies have assisted Third World development by providing investment opportunities, technology, capital, and managerial skills, they contend. Indeed, the economic gap between the North and the South is growing smaller as both factions grow more affluent.

When analyzing U.S. foreign policy toward the South, it is helpful to define a number of characteristics representative of the Third World. The diversity among its states and societies is extraordinary. Many are former colonies that achieved statehood in the 1950s, 1960s, and 1970s; others have long established histories of independence—as, for example, the countries of Latin America. A few possess vast wealth based on oil (Saudi Arabia, Kuwait), while many confront desperate poverty and imminent starvation (Bangladesh, Sudan, Haiti). There are even vast differences among the members of OPEC, from Saudi Arabia's extraordinary wealth to the far poorer and more populous countries of Indonesia and Nigeria which have limited oil reserves. Every kind of political system is represented in the South, ranging from democratic capitalist societies to right-wing and left-wing dictatorships. Some Third World countries have made impressive strides forward in economic growth—for example, Singapore, Argentina, Brazil, Korea, and Algeria. Because of the vast diversity of the South, it is useful to distinguish between the Third World and the Fourth World. The Third World represents countries that exhibit some level of economic growth; the Fourth World, in contrast, is characterized by the absence of economic growth and the presence of absolute poverty. While the distinction between the Third World and the Fourth World is somewhat arbitrary, it is important to point out the range of circumstances confronting members of the South. For example, Fourth World countries generally possess low levels of natural resources, huge populations, unemployment rates that are among the highest in the world, poor road systems, and increasing rates of migration from the country to the city. The Fourth World countries experience the most basic, or absolute, forms of poverty. Often one person in five is illiterate. All Fourth World societies are characterized by low public expenditures on education. Infant mortality is high; as many as two children in every ten die in some countries. Life expectancy is among the lowest in the world; the average life span is often below 50 years of age. Living conditions are so bad in the Fourth World that the nutritional intake for most of the people is below the absolute minimum necessary to sustain life. Birth rates are the highest in the world. Population growth continues at an alarming pace, despite horrendous living conditions and the absence of food.

The great diversity of the South, especially the extremes in wealth from Kuwait to Bangladesh, illustrate the complexity of the entire Third World. However, it is the cohesiveness of the South's demands for the creation of a more equitable global economic and political system that is most remarkable. Indeed, Southern solidarity despite these extreme variations in affluence, poverty, culture, history, and political systems illustrates the intensity of the proposals for global change.

The countries of the South share the belief that they have been exploited by the North in three ways. First, the North has robbed the South of great endowments of natural resources through the process of colonialism and later by buying raw materials at ridiculously low prices. Since the North established the markets and the economic conditions under which world trade would take place, the Third World had no opportunity to break free of the global system of exploitation first established in the sixteenth century. Second, with the end of colonialism in the twentieth century, the North continued to exploit the South by controlling international trade in the global markets which the North established for its own benefits. Thus, raw materials were extracted from Third World countries and purchased at unreasonably low prices. The North used these raw materials to create manufactured products which were then sold to the South at exorbitantly high prices. Thus, the cycle of exploitation continued even after colonialism ended and Third World states achieved independence. Third, the United States dominated global economic relations after World War II, establishing an economic system that maximized free trade and, thus, providing the U.S. with the ability to penetrate all Third World societies. Through the Bretton Woods System and the General Agreement on Tariffs and Trade, GATT (See Chapter 4), the United States perpetuated the unfair exchange of over-priced manufactured goods for under-valued raw materials. By establishing the U.S. dollar as the global currency, the United States perfected a system of exploitation first begun in the sixteenth century. American control of global politics and economics following World War II provided U.S. multinational corporations with the capability to dominate the world's economy. The U.S.'s containment doctrine and the domino theory (See Chapters 1 and 7) were further means of protecting American investments overseas. Thus, the Third World urges that the existing global economic and political institutions must be substantially changed to end the unfair advantage exercised over international trade by the capitalist states of the North under the leadership of the United States.

Third World proposals for a more equitable economic system emphasize two major types of changes. The first calls for the *structural reform* of the world's central political and economic institutions.[a] For example, the South calls for a change in the structure of world trade, proposing that Northern countries lower trade barriers to Southern exports. Similarly, the South asks for codes of conduct for multinational corporations (MNCs) and the transfer of important technology from the MNCs to the host country. Southern proposals also call for the reform of the international monetary system to provide Third and Fourth World countries with greater monetary resources. Other proposals ask that the value of Southern products (exports) be tied to the rate of inflation of manufactured goods. This system is called indexing. Thus, Southern proposals for the restructuring of world economics call for a revision of the existing rules of international trade. These range from raising the price of Third World exports to direct transfers of economic resources to assist the South in the difficult task of economic development. One proposal calls for the direct transfer of .70 percent of the Gross National Product of Northern countries to assist the South's economic development and to alleviate the slow death through malnutrition and disease of millions of human beings.

A second broad area of change emphasizes reform of Northern *institutions*. These proposals ask that the South be granted greater influence in the world's central economic and political institutions, including the International Monetary Fund, the Organization of Economic Cooperation and Development (OECD), and the World Bank. Demands for institutional reforms also call for the expansion of the power of organizations already dominated by the South, for example, the United Nations General Assembly's new Commitee of the Whole. In addition, the South requests the creation of new institutions to protect Third and Fourth World interests—a Deep Seabed Authority and a Common Fund (to support Third World commodities). These proposals would account for the vastly expanded involvement of the South in every significant area of international trade and finance.

The United States has rejected the thrust of Southern demands for structural and institutional reforms. Yet, despite U.S. assurances that it would deal constructively with the South's proposals, no progress has occurred. The U.S. and other Northern countries steadfastly have failed to accept the South's contention that the North is responsible for the impoverishment of the South. Thus, North-South issues have been stalemated. Moreover, North-South relations have increasingly been polarized by strident rhetoric on both sides. Amid the polarization of positions, American foreign policy has emphasized three tactics. The first has attempted to fragment Southern unity by underscoring the differences separating the vastly different societies of the South. Second, the United States has tried to woo the most powerful regional countries of the South. Thus, the U.S. has attempted to improve relations with OPEC and Mexico, Argentina, Nigeria, Saudi Arabia, Korea, and Pakistan in order to co-opt them. Third, the United States has consistently opposed every major proposal by the South for structural change.[b]

The politics of the United States and the North toward the South have resulted in a deterioration of relations with Third and Fourth World societies. In the following article by Barbara Ward—"Another Chance for the North?"—the implication of Northern policies are examined in terms of both human and political costs. Professor Ward emphasizes the fundamental interdependence of all people and all states in the world of the 1980s. The economic crisis of the southern hemisphere is directly tied to the economic crisis of Northern countries. Under such a condition of interdependence, no part of the world's economy can continue to remain healthy when another is on the verge of destruction. For Ward, the challenge for the North is to restructure global political and economic relations so that all sectors of the world will benefit. Without major institutional and structural changes, the human costs of underdevelopment will translate into political conflicts that will negatively affect all sectors of the world. Time is running out, however, she warns.

References

[a]My analysis of North-South issues is indebted to the work of Roger Hansen, in particular, "North South Policy— What's the Problem?", *Foreign Affairs*, Vol. 58, No. 5 (Summer, 1980), pp. 1104-1128.
[b]Ibid., pp. 1107-1119.

ANOTHER CHANCE FOR THE NORTH?

Barbara Ward, *Foreign Affairs,* Winter 1980-81

Barbara Ward was president of the International Institute for Environment and Development from 1973 to 1980.

If one thing more than any other was made abundantly clear by the whole series of international negotiations in the 1970s, it is that the industrialized democracies—which, with Australia and New Zealand as appendages, and with the Soviet bloc, make up "the North"—have no strategy and no vision when it comes to their dealings with the three-quarters of the human race that lives in the developing "South." For over a decade, the North has been discussing with the South the problem of their long-term economic re-lations—the so-called New International Economic Order. But wherever the focus has been—the five meetings of the United Nations Conference on Trade and Development (UNCTAD), the various special sessions of the U.N. General Assembly, the fumbling and finally negative two-year talks of the Commission for International Economic Cooperation (the ironic name given to a series of North-South consultations in Paris), the fiasco of the latest conference called by UNIDO (the U.N. Industrial Development Organization), or the virtually nonexistent outcome of the so-called Economic Summit of Western leaders in Venice—wherever the place, whatever the context, whoever the parties, the outcome has been virtually the same. In short, it has been nothing.

There are tiny exceptions: the ludicrously inadequate amounts promised to underpin more stable world commodity prices; the guarantees limited to one group of developing states under the Lomé Convention, negotiated by the European Community; the £1.2 billion pledged by the wheat producers (in wheat and long-term low-interest loans) for food relief. But these minor and unrelated acts only throw into clear perspective the utter lack of strategy on a worldwide and sufficient scale.

This is the difficult and discouraging background to the publication early this year of the Report of the Brandt Commission entitled *North-South: a Program for Survival.* The Commission, with West Germany's former Chancellor, Willy Brandt, as Chairman, was composed of distinguished citizens drawn from North and South and from the widest spectrum of interest—former prime ministers, finance ministers, bankers, publishers, the oil producers, trade unions. Its very composition, spanning a range from a young radical leader in Algeria to the chairman of Lehman Brothers Kuhn Loeb of New York, suggested to more cynical observers that the chance of a unanimous report was virtually nil. The fact that the recommendations were unanimously accepted is at the very least a factor of encouragement in the generally dreary international scene.

But the character of the recommendations is more remarkable still. The temptation faced by all such potentially divided and conflicting groups is that of the lowest common denominator—the shuffling, half-muffled, half-uncommitted, half-arguments stretched as far as they will go to cover the basic failure to achieve consensus. There is little sign of this in the Brandt Report. Its general philosophy is quite simply that Planet Earth is a community of peoples in need of the underpinnings of any genuine social order—a floor under poverty, sufficient food, access to education, participation in decision-making, the promise of work. The need for unity expressed in these common purposes should far outweigh the warring interests of nations, cultures and beliefs. The Report's particular recommendations cover the "underpinnings" of unity and are best summed up in its four-point program of immediate action, which expresses a profound sense of the "common good" in practical fashion. The policies cumulatively reinforce each other and in essence extend to the whole of mankind the principles and priorities now largely accepted *within* civilized nation-states.

II

The four priority points, briefly summarized, cover a large-scale transfer of resources to the developing countries, an international strategy for dealing with the energy crisis, a global food program and the first steps in transforming today's chaotic international economic system into a workable and reliable monetary and commercial order. Clearly, the proposals overlap at many points just as they do within a nation: farmers' support prices depending upon governmental revenue, revenue depending upon tax levels, tax levels reflecting economic restraint or expansion as a government objective. The domestic range is vast. An international version must be vaster. But if priorities are correct and action is secured, positive results are as possible at the international level as at the national level.

But it is, of course, at this point that the critics move in on the Report and attack either its general direction or its particular proposals as utterly irrelevant to the "realities" of the 1980s. The concept of a planetary community must surely be left on the back shelf of contemporary idealism— with the Russians in Afghanistan, the Vietnamese in Cambodia, the Middle East in turmoil and Soviet spokesmen making it clear that the vital point today is not New International Economic Orders or more stable North-South relations but the spread of communism throughout the developing world. Abandon capitalism, go communist, and appropriate development toward "unity" may follow. True, China and its rejection of Soviet communism are left out. But this is only one more reminder of division. What is the use of even thinking of world community when the facts amount to violent hostility between groups of nations or, at best, an uneasy oscillation between deterrence and détente?

The critics are equally determined in their attack when they turn from the general principles to particular proposals. We can include the separate principle of food aid in the general proposals for transferring resources, since aid to Third World food production is coming to be one of the highest priorities in many aid strategies, replacing the almost exclusive attention to industrialization, export promotion and infrastructure of earlier decades. There is wide derision at the Commission's general recommendation that the level of official aid, at the present at 0.35 percent of gross national product (GNP) for the industrial democracies, should be raised to the already promised 0.70 percent by 1985 and widened to one percent by the year 2000. This would imply an annual transfer of $50-$60 billion in aid by 1985. Yet, honorable exceptions apart—the Dutch, the Scandinavians—aid has either fallen in absolute terms or barely kept pace with inflation. Most of the industrialized countries are members of the Development Assistance Committee (DAC) and its latest figures show there was very little increase in the flow of official aid between 1965 and 1977, when inflation is taken into account. Yet during this period, the Committee members' GNP actually doubled.

Perhaps the most unfortunate example of delinquency comes from the largest and internally wealthiest of all the democratic states. Official aid from the United States has fallen from just under 0.50 percent of GNP in 1965 to about 0.20 percent in 1980, an exemplary action highly unlikely to put fresh heart into other, poorer donors. If this is the pattern, say the critics, what folly it must be to stress higher aid giving. They do admit that the goals may be desirable. Few critics, for instance, attack the new emphasis on agriculture, which would entail additional annual aid expenditures of some $13 billion a year (in 1980 dollars) as part of the $30-$40 billion needed annually to expand food output to feed the six billion human beings who will be on the planet by the year 2000. But it has to be seen in terms of realism. The trend is the other way. And would it not be the course of wisdom to try to understand why, and examine the reasons?

III

The governments of the industrialized democracies have no doubts about the fundamental cause of their retreat from their promises of greater aid—it is the action of OPEC (the Organization of Petroleum Exporting Countries) in quadrupling the cost of crude oil in 1973. (That the great Soviet "grain raid" on American reserves tripled world grain prices at about the same time is conveniently forgotten.) Since that vast and sudden upheaval, it has proved impossible to bring the industrialized democracies back to anything like the rhythm of growth which prevailed for over two decades after the spectacular postwar recovery originally fired by the Marshall Plan.

After OPEC's action, the Northern balance of payments fell from a surplus of nearly $20 billion in 1973 to an almost equal deficit in 1974. Internally, the determination of large pressure groups—unions, conglomerates—to keep their incomes at the old levels allowed the external pressure of at least $35 billion less in real income to permeate the whole economic system with an inflationary bias. Profits were squeezed, investment fell, governments deflated. Annual variations in per capita incomes changed dramatically from four percent a year growth to an actual fall in value in 1974, and unemployment grew from three to over five percent.

But prices went on rising. Between the onset of the oil price rise (and the grain raid) and the beginning of 1975, inflation rates doubled. There was a small measure of recovery after 1975, but inflation, unemployment and the levels of world trade all remained in uncomfortable contrast with the "golden" 1950s and 1960s. The growth in world trade, for instance, was only half its earlier average, although the industrialized democracies were a little helped by their ability to pass some of the real costs on to Third World nations, which had to pay 40 percent more for their "Northern" imports (mainly of manufactured goods) between 1973 and 1975 alone. But it was basically a very unstable economic system in which the next round of OPEC oil price increases (not agreed to but reached nonetheless) coupled with the turmoil in Iran drove average oil prices in 1979 from $12.90 to $22.70 a barrel. One thinks with incredulity of the less than two dollars a barrel of the earlier decades.

The year 1979 also brought with it a virtual certainty of an erratic but fairly predictable and continuing upward movement in oil prices. Oil prices are now around $30 a barrel. How, then, say the critics, can governments escape the resulting unsupportable inflationary pressures if they add more aid to all this growth of income? How can they check inflation? To propose more aid is like pouring a bucket of water over a drowning man. As all Northern leaders represented at the Venice Summit agreed, controlling inflation is, virtually, the sole aim of governmental policy. So why even talk about aid? . . .

Lack of contact and trust between the North and OPEC is also in some measure responsible for the Northern failure to take any significant action to strengthen international monetary and commercial institutions. At one point, it seemed all but certain that the industrialized democracies would seriously discuss ways in which OPEC surpluses, over and above those spent in developed markets, could be deposited not in uncertain currencies but in an internationally secured "substitution account" probably under the aegis of the International Monetary Fund (IMF) and, with strict guarantees of maintained value and returnability, judiciously lent for development in the most productive areas for investment (many of them, by definition, in the Third World). But all the steam ran out of the proposal in 1980, and the OPEC surpluses have begun to overhang the financial markets as ominously as wild foreign lending helped to precipitate the Wall Street crash of 1929. . . .

It is perhaps a valid criticism of the Report that it underestimates the difficulties with which Northern governments feel themselves confronted. Northern concepts of their own interests do not much enter the debate and may prove a real bar to the persuasiveness of the recommendations. Yet to be without a forward policy for three-quarters of humanity, to expect that what is is in essence the continuance of a semi-colonial relationship can be passively endured, that the degree of solidarity achieved in the emergent South will in some convenient way remove itself—all these assumptions which must underpin the "policy of no policy" are simply examples of an unrealism to which "realists" may too easily succumb. No one can claim that the Brandt strategy solves all conflicts and reconciles all differences. But for each of the criticisms, it has at least a partial answer and the sum of its proposals would give the North a renewed sense of the direction and purpose which proved to be the most notable victims of the troubled 1970s.

Take first the criticism that a greater transfer of resources, a sustained strategy for food and energy, and the beginnings of structural economic changes in monetary and commercial policies are irrelevant because local political differences, communist pressure and Soviet "expansionism" are what is really at stake. No one denies the pressure. But if Third World leaders in political and popular difficulties knew that they could count on resource transfers from the North, might not this be an argument for avoiding a much more arduous and irremovable Soviet involvement?

The revolution in Nicaragua may be lost to the Marxist Sandinistas because Congress held up U.S. aid proposals for over a year. A vital land reform in El Salvador may be undermined by the same arbitrary behavior. One factor in Robert Mugabe's readiness to accept an open election in Zimbabwe and remain nonaligned was the degree of disillusion Samora Machel displayed over Soviet "aid" and farming models in Mozambique. Yet the paradox is that in these critical months when both nations must rebuild economies devastated by war, the needed financial support to do so has not been forthcoming. The chance of their genuine nonalignment (which should be the Northern goal) may be lost for the equivalent of less than one-thousandth of the United States' annual military expenditure. What the Brandt Report in fact proposes is to institutionalize the availability of Northern resources—which, in turn and by definition, increases the measure of choice of Third World leaders, parties and movements.

One could perhaps take the argument a step further and suggest that if the superpowers can reach a SALT III stage of negotiation, the transfer of a percentage of arms spending to international aid transfers might be separately on the agenda. The Soviets' pitiful 0.03 percent of GNP in aid to countries other than Cuba would be seen in a new perspective, and the percentage proposed would only have to reach 25 days of the world's military spending to equal the whole extra $30 billion proposed by the Commission.

IV

All this does not argue that Third World governments—or indeed, the superpowers—*will* make the constructive choices. It merely suggests that a sustained, accepted and certain transfer of Northern resources would greatly increase the elbow room within which all our disturbed and unquiet systems have to work and that this wider area of choice is itself a worthwhile objective. It becomes even clearer when we look at other elements of the Brandt package for, here, to the factor of widening choice is added the near certainty that many of the proposals are actually to the direct advantage of the North, quite apart from their "Southern" value.

The order in which these issues are taken is relatively unimportant. To a very real extent, each supports the other. The food strategy, for instance, is from certain points of view one aspect of the wider plan for more stable primary produce prices. The somewhat imprecise concept of a World Development Fund is intimately bound up with increases in aid. An oil strategy is essential to any degree of monetary stability. This in turn is a critical part of the proposed development and funding of more effective international monetary systems. And their expansion would assist in sustained investment in Third World food, energy and mineral resources; in the uncertain 1970s, each tended to slip below the level needed for actual maintenance, let alone to meet the prospects of expansion in a hoped-for revival in the world economy as the 1980s advance. But this interdependence should not seem surprising. It is embedded in the underlying reality of a planetary economic system, however much governments may still believe in the short-term benefits of carving the larger slice from the shrinking pie. . . .

Price stability is at the center of three of the Brandt proposals—the food program the joint energy approach and support for a measure of stabilization of primary product prices, still the Third World's main exporting sector. Northerners too easily forget that the price rise in 1973 grain (when the Russians cleared out the American reserve) affected North and South alike. Indeed, since a Northerner can consume nearly a ton of grain a year, mainly in meat equivalent, to India's average of some 400 pounds, there can be little argument about Northern interest in stable prices. Yet given the combined certainty and unpredictability of droughts (either in Northern America, the only major surplus area, or the monsoon belt) the basic elements of a good program are inescapable—a reserve regularly maintained for "the lean years" and a big increase in Third World agricultural productivity. . . .

The Northern need for a more stable flow of resources is not confined to food. If one takes America's imports of vital materials—aluminum, chromium, nickel, tin, cobalt to name only a few—dependence on external supplies is never less than 77 percent. Chromium and nickel are in the 100-percent class for the Common Market and Japan. The troubled 1970s meant inadequate investment in future supplies, which in turn will mean a new inflationary spurt as economies recover and the demand for materials revives. An agreed strategy, using aid and recycled currencies for adequate investment, together with a new distribution of processing facilities to favor the South, could give greater stability to the whole world's industrial sector and at the same time increase the Southern states' derisory nine percent of world industrial production. There is no reason why the "multinationals" should not include this transfer in their long-term planning.

Could there be a comparable "bargain" for the most critical of all resources—oil? Here only one thing is certain. It must be better to try to approach OPEC with constructive and cooperative proposals than to leave the whole issue to the uncertainties of confrontation. The essence of the Brandt proposals is that supplies and prices should be given a greater chance of stability and as a result both sides will benefit by the change. So much is obvious. But it entails subsidiary action which the Brandt proposals recognize more frankly than the critics, who, however insensibly, slip into the adversary position. In political terms, it means a new effort to work out a Palestinian compromise. In Northern states, it requires an entirely new seriousness in the priority given to energy conservation. . . .

That oil as a wasting resource will rise in price is certain, OPEC or no OPEC. But there could be a mutual interest in steadier and longer term Northern demand and a longer duration for the international oil market. At the same time, investment in new sources of oil and in the whole range of alternatives—coal, synthetic fuels, nuclear energy (with proper caution), direct and indirect ways of utilizing solar power—could be part of the new resource transfer and be applied with special energy to the world's "sun belt," which happens to include some of the world's poorest peoples. There are already solar pumping stations at work in irrigated agriculture.

Once again, we see the interconnectedness of the Brandt proposals. No one can guarantee their success, but we can and must guarantee the failure of the alternative which, at present, is quite simply not to have one. Even if the Brandt proposals are no more than an insurance policy, it is worth paying the premiums. There is nothing else in sight that works.

V

Even if it is no more than insurance, the program goes some way to meet the most fundamental criticism—that Northerners should be concerned with their own economic crisis. With nearly 20 million unemployed and perhaps $300 billion worth of unused capacity, surely the stimulus and the spending should be undertaken in the North. But this overlooks two final considerations. The first is that the Third World is already a vast market for Northern goods. The figure for merchandise trade for North America and Western Europe is already over one-third of all exports. For Japan, it is nearer one-half. To increase the wealth, stability and opportunity of countries where only relatively few of their population enter fully into the monetary economy will increase their scale as markets and hence their stimulus to Northern expansion and employment. The whole boom of the 1950s and 1960s would have been inconceivable without the launching pad of the Marshall Plan, which in giving away for over five years a goodly *two* percent of a much poorer America's GNP, ensured its own prosperity along with that of its neighbors in the North.

The memory of the Marshall Plan is a reminder of one last point. True, the Plan was in part fueled by the cold war, just as today limits to Soviet adventurism could reasonably be invoked for the Brandt proposals. But another element was quite simply compassion—ordinary Americans feeling the good fortune of surviving so appalling a holocaust and ready to share with fellow survivors the means of rebuilding their lives. Is this feeling of compassionate responsibility entirely dead in the North? When recently Americans were polled on foreign aid, their paradoxical answer was that "aid is too high," but the vast majority were ready to give in terms of their own personal incomes a higher percentage than any aid proposed at any official level. When it comes to choosing between starving children, stunted lives, unemployment in filthy shantytowns and general despair on the one hand, or on the other the kind of cooperative Brandt program that at least begins to meet the scale of both disaster and opportunity, most Northern citizens have not forgotten the moral imperative.

It remains true that although they are only a quarter of the world's peoples, they have over 70 percent of the wealth, over 80 percent of the trade, some 90 percent of the industry and nearly 100 percent of advanced centers of learning and technology.

These stark contrasts can be brought down to a personal level. Northern citizens can compare their average of $6,000 to $7,000 a year per capita incomes with the $150 of the world's poverty belt. They can reckon the Brandt costs—which, including present aid flows, are the equivalent of about a dollar a week per Northerner. And they know where not only justice but survival lies. The task is to bring the mutual interests and the moral impulse together. Auden's words remain true: "We must love one another or die."   focus

Barbara Ward calls for a transformation of Northern policies based on both self-interest and humanitarian concerns. It is certainly plausible that United States foreign policy would be more effective in the Third World if existing levels of Southern opposition to the U.S. declined. Ward argues that it is in the interest of all states to move beyond the North-South stalemate. However, the United States still confronts increasing Southern opposition to U.S. diplomatic objectives based on current United States economic policies. Thus, Ward maintains, the interests of American foreign policy might be advanced more readily if it offered real support for Southern needs. In her view, the support of Third and Fourth World countries seem particularly important during a period when perceptions of Soviet subversion throughout the South are increasing. Barbara Ward's perspective is sharply criticized by Peter Berger's essay "Speaking to the Third World." Professor Berger denies that the U.S. is responsible for Third World poverty. Moreover, he argues that a "Third World" does not exist except in a rhetorical and ideological sense. He believes American foreign policy must resist the self-interested rhetoric of the Third World countries blaming the United States for their internal inadequacies. Berger argues that there is little the United States can do to assist the economic development of the world's poorer countries because economic development is the result of internal obstacles that must be overcome (for example, economic stagnation, corruption, and cultural values that do not encourage economic growth). Until these barriers to development are overcome, contends Berger, the affluent countries of the West will have negligible effects on the poverty or affluence of the Third World.

SPEAKING TO THE THIRD WORLD
Peter L. Berger, *Commentary*, October 1981
Peter L. Berger is University Professor of Sociology at Boston University.

"Third World." The very phrase by now evokes a multitude of images, positive as well as negative. Empirically, of course, the words bear little resemblance to reality—except, perhaps, at the United Nations, where the so-called Group of 77 does possess a real political form. But what, after all, do Brazil and Bangladesh have in common, or Singapore and the Seychelles, not to mention the oil-rich nations of the Gulf and the starvation-ridden countries of the Sahel? The so-called Third World includes countries of astronomically diverse economic, social, political, and cultural characteristics.

There are alternative terms. Within the United Nations, parlance has shifted from "underdeveloped countries" to "developing" to "less developed," each creating difficulties of its own. There is also the currently fashionable term "South," as in the "North/South dialogue" or "North/South global negotiations" urgently propagated by the Brandt Report and other voices for reform of the international system. This terminology, if nothing else, suffers from geographical absurdity. India is "South" and Australia "North," while the industrial societies of the Soviet bloc are in a never-never land left out of the "dialogue" altogether.

Political language is rarely an exercise in scientific logic, however, and chances are that we are stuck with the terms we have. The Third World, whatever else it may or may not be, is a rhetorical reality, and when Americans speak to the poorer nations of Asia, Africa, and Latin America (and even to some of the less poor nations in those regions), they are indeed addressing the Third World.

The phrase itself originated in the early 1950's, and was solemnly proclaimed as a reality at the Bandung conference of 1955, when a number of "non-aligned" countries (including Sukarno's Indonesia, Nehru's India, and Tito's Yugoslavia) asserted their right to pursue a path independent of the two superpower blocs. But already more was implied with respect to the American and Soviet systems than simple non-alignment. There was also the notion of a "third way" of development, different from the allegedly flawed models of American-style capitalism and Soviet-style Communism. Just what the third way might be was never spelled out with much precision. Presumably it was more socialist than the American model and more democratic than the Soviet one—some sort of social democracy, yet not simply a copy of Western models, rather an indigenous construction doing justice to the cultural traditions of the countries first gathered at Bandung. . . .

Just because so much nonsense has been spouted about the Third World, it is useful to step back and try to gain some perspective on a phenomenon which is, at bottom, nothing less than the entry onto the stage of history of vast masses of people who until now have lived in a situation that can be accurately described as pre-historical.

Immense anguish and pain, physical as well as moral, have been associated with the entry of these people into the common history of our age. There is a timeless dignity to the forms of human existence provided by tribe, village, and other traditional structures, and the disturbance of these life-forms by the turbulent forces of modernity has hardly been an unambiguous boon. Yet many if not most of the images of anguish turn out, upon closer scrutiny, to be superimposed upon images of hope. . . .

If one asks *why* so much of the Third World is so crowded, the reason is not high birth rates; it is the dramatic lowering of death rates, and particularly of the rates of infant mortality. This change begins to take place even at very rudimentary levels of economic development, with the introduction of quite modest improvements in nutrition and hygiene. The human consequence of this change is extraordinarily simple: whereas, previously, most children died, now more and more children survive. In this there is joy and hope, and it is precisely these emotions that fuel the energy with which much of the Third World seems to overflow. No amount of skepticism about the blessings of modernity can nullify the human and moral progress which this change signifies.

It cannot surprise us that politics in these cataclysmic circumstances should be volatile, often violent, often irrational. But the politics of the putatively more developed West have not exactly been a model of order and rationality in this century. . . .

It is all too easy to denigrate the nascent nationalisms of the Third World, to ridicule such practices as the investment of scarce capital in the "empty symbolism" of, for example, a national airline. But this self-affirmation of people who only yesterday, so far as the rest of the world was concerned, were silent, must also be part of our understanding of the Third World. It is something to be affirmed, even celebrated.

If the ideology of the Third World consisted only in proclaiming these realities, we should have no serious difficulty with it. Even if that ideology insisted that it was our obligation, humanly and morally, to help, we should assent. The eradication of starvation and of degrading misery is a moral imperative for states and for the international community, as well as for concerned citizens and non-governmental groups in rich countries. Unfortunately, Third World ideology has gone considerably beyond such propositions, and it is not possible, either intellectually or morally, to assent to it as a whole. . . .

To be sure, even within the United Nations different states proclaim this ideology with different nuances and varying forcefulness. Singapore does not speak like India, Senegal says different things from Ethiopia, Brazil from Mexico. But one interesting and unifying aspect should be noted: the construction that one may call the Third World ideology is, broadly speaking, leftist—indeed, in important intellectual respects it depends on elements of Marxist theory—and it is given lip service by states that are anything but leftist in their domestic arrangements. If one asks why that should be, the answer, one must surmise, is that these states expect to gain, politically or economically, from a rhetorical adherence to positions which happen to contradict their own internal strategies. This is distressing—but also hopeful, for it shows the fragile basis of the Third World consensus and provides openings for dissenting points of view.

With these qualifications, it is possible to point to a series of propositions as the common core of the Third World ideology:

• Development is not just a matter of economic growth. Rather, one can only regard as development those processes of change in which the dynamism of economic growth is harnessed to transcendent social purposes—to the progressive rescue from degrading poverty of masses of people and to a more egalitarian distribution of the benefits of growth.

• The causes of Third World poverty must be sought primarily outside the Third World itself—historically in the depredations of colonialism and imperialism, today in the consequences of an unjust international economic system which is heavily weighted in favor of the rich countries of the West (or "North") against the poor countries of the Third World (or "South").

• The West owes "compensation" or "reparations" to the Third World for past acts of exploitation. Also, the West owes the Third World a redress of the unjust international economic system through a variety of juridical, political, and economic measures. This, in the long run, will be of benefit to all countries as it will result in a more stable world order.

• The establishment of a just international system is a prerequisite for all aspects of development, not only economic but political and human as well. For that reason economic and social rights must be accorded parity with civil and political rights within the general conception of human rights espoused by the international community.

These propositions constitute an intellectual and moral whole. That is, they are based on a set of presuppositions about the nature of the world and they also put this view of the world into a moral context, a view of what the world *ought* to be. Moreover, this ideology, culled from a variety of sources (most of them, incidentally, of Western provenance), is not an abstract intellectual enterprise. Rather it is a political instrument, used to legitimate specific objectives. Thus the broad acceptance of this ideology by Third World governments has gone hand in hand with various political initiatives, almost all of them within the United Nations system.

These initiatives have not only been aimed at securing favorable treatment for Third World countries in terms of trade and aid, but have also sought to enshrine some of the features of Third World ideology in international law. In 1974, the United Nations General Assembly adopted a Charter of Economic Rights and Duties of States. This was meant to forge into a juridical instrument the calls for a New International Economic Order, which, first issued by Mexico in the early 1970's, had increasingly become a rallying point for the Group of 77.

This thrust to establish a legal foundation for Third World demands continues today in efforts to change the structure of international monetary institutions, to set in motion a multilateral process of "global negotiations," and to recognize the "right to development" as a fundamental human right (individual as well as collective). A French commentator on this process, Alain Pellet, has aptly described it as one in which "recommendations" are progressively transformed into "obligations." The United States and other Western states have continually resisted these efforts to make the United Nations into a quasi-legislative body on behalf of Third World concerns, but the Group of 77 has been able to override most of the resistance within the United Nations system. (The real world outside the United Nations enclaves of New York, Geneva, and Vienna has been less tractable.) . . .

What I should like to do here is to formulate a possible American response to the main themes of Third World ideology.

It is clear that, with one or two exceptions, such a response must be mainly negative—as, indeed, it has been when American spokesmen have confronted elements of the ideology in the United Nations. Maintaining such a negative stance is not comfortable—not for the individuals who must appear in international forums where the emotional temperature is often very high, and not for a people that historically has an idealistic image of itself and a strong psychological need to be liked. . . .

But we must dissent from the fundamental idea of economic relations that underlies the Third World ideology. This is a vast elaboration of Proudhon's dictum that property is theft. Economic relations are seen here as a zero-sum game. The gain of one is necessarily the loss of another. Wealth is acquired at the expense of the poor. Resources are owned by one and taken away by the other. To be sure, there are such cases, and they can be appropriately characterized as exploitation, but they are the exception rather than the rule. More to the point, this exploitation "model" does not fit the relations between the Third World and the advanced societies of the West either in the past or today.

The thesis that colonialism and imperialism impoverished and hampered the development of Third World societies is highly questionable, to say the least. As P.T. Bauer has pointed out repeatedly, the poorest countries tend to be those whose economic relations with the West have been minimal, while many ex-colonies have done very well indeed. There is no way in which the affluence of a long list of Western countries, including the United States, can be causally explained by colonial exploitation. As for the great colonial powers themselves, such as Britain and France, historians will argue for a long time whether they in fact profited more from their colonies than they put into them.

It is also very questionable whether the contemporary international system can be described as exploitative in the sense that "Northern" wealth is extracted from "Southern" poverty. With the exception of some natural resources, among which oil is paramount, the economies of the "North" are quite independent of the "South." Indeed, that is precisely the problem for Third World economies, which, in order to develop, must seek to enter the "rich" system under favorable conditions. This is a very real problem and a difficult one, and one with a moral dimension. Recognition of that dimension, however, stems from our common humanity and from the solidarity between nations. It is not something that can be optimistically proclaimed in various international instruments; it cannot stem from distorted history, bad law, or pathological guilt feelings.

The demand for "compensation" or "reparations" is thus spurious—historically, juridically, and morally. It is also absurd: one need only ask whether it recognizes any statute of limitations or how the putative debtors are to be defined. Can Hungary demand compensation from Mongolia for the depredations of Genghis Khan? Are black Americans to sue the states of West Africa for the collusion of past political authorities with the slave trade?

There is an even more serious distortion of economic reality in Third World ideology. That is the emphasis on external rather than internal "obstacles to development." These external obstacles are recurrently invoked in what has by now become a litany of exorcism—"imperialism, colonialism, neocolonialism, racism, *apartheid*," to which catalogue, for good measure, "Zionism" is occasionally added. The litany is mostly malicious nonsense.

Let it be stipulated that there are, in fact, situations where external forces serve to impede the development of a country. In these situations the character and strength of such forces must be assessed, and the country in question is fully entitled to seek relief by whatever means. I would contend, though, that such situations are quite rare—except in the massive case of Soviet imperialism, which, for reasons that are patently political, is hardly ever mentioned in this context.

The most frequent "obstacles to development" are internal to the societies in quest of development. Among such obstacles are economic systems that stultify growth and impede productivity; political corruption; oppression of people to the point where they cease to be economically active; persecution of economically productive minorities (such as the Asians in eastern Africa and the Chinese in southeast Asia); and, in some cases, indigenous social patterns and cultural values that are not conducive to economic activity. The fixation on external villains is a convenient stratagem for Third World elites who are either unable or unwilling to face up to internal obstacles. There is no reason, however, why we should fortify them in this evasion.

One may note here as well the tendency of Third World spokesmen and their sympathizers in the West to stress the allegedly growing gap between rich and poor nations and the deteriorating condition of the Third World as a whole. Both propositions are dubious. It is not at all clear that the gap is broadening, especially in recent years when Western economies have faced serious difficulties, many of them caused by the astronomical rise in energy costs (OPEC is virtually never mentioned in Third World pronouncements as a cause of poverty in these countries—roughly for the same reasons Soviet imperialism is not mentioned). And while the condition of some countries has deteriorated, there have also been phenomenal success stories in the Third World, such as those of South Korea, Taiwan, and some of the ASEAN states.

What with all the emphasis on juridical instruments and agreements between states, one gets the impression that many Third World representatives look upon development as something to be wrested from others— namely, the industrialized countries of the West, or rather their governments. It is to be development by fiat, following upon a political struggle in which concessions are won by moral suasion or by pressures of various sorts. . . .

All of this, however, obfuscates the fact that development, in any meaning of the term, cannot be the result of juridical and political arrangements between states (though such arrangements can be useful in particular instances). Development is the result of the sustained economic activity of large numbers of people, the result of effort, hard work, and ingenuity. It cannot be wrested from someone else, like a chunk of valuable matter. Indeed, such a view masks a paternalism of its own, for if development is something that can be wrested from us in the West, then it is we who grant it.

This stands in curious contradiction to the oft-repeated Third World principles of self-reliance and freedom from dependency. Whatever development may mean, it should not mean the establishment of an international welfare system.

The bias in Third World statements about development derives from the fact that many Third World regimes follow some variety of socialism both in theory and practice, while many others, if not socialist, are heavily statist in their economic system. Although a detailed discussion of socialist models of development would take many pages, suffice it to say that among the socialist regimes of the Third World there is not a single success story—defining success not in "our" terms but, precisely, in the Third World terms of victory over the more wretched forms of poverty and a reasonable degree of egalitarian distribution. The typical record of Third World socialism is one of economic stagnation, often perpetuating abject poverty if not outright starvation; the species of egalitarianism that prevails among the "masses" is one of an equality among serfs, lorded over by a privileged elite of party bureaucrats and managers. Shmuel Eisenstadt has called this sytem "neo-patrimonialism"; Pierre Bourdieu's term, "socialo-feudalism," is also apt. The vast panorama of "different paths to development" in the contemporary world only reinforces the conclusion that socialism is incapable of producing in terms of its own promises.

In non-socialist cases, too, it is quite clear that the state as such is not the bearer of development. At best, states can institute policies that *leave room* for the real agents of development—enterprising individuals, families, clans, *compadre* groupings, and other traditional units, and more modern associations such as cooperatives or credit unions.

The moral aspect of this ought to be stressed. A heavy moral responsibility rests on those who impose unproductive and inefficient economic arrangements on developing societies, doubly so when these arrangements are adhered to in the face of hunger, disease, and degrading poverty. It is obscenely inappropriate when the very people who propagate this criminal waste of human and material resources claim to be or to represent the "party of compassion."

Official United Nations declarations and position papers are reassuringly clear on one point: economic, social, and cultural rights are to be thought of as an indivisible whole with civil and political rights, and neither set of rights is to be given priority over the other. This would seem to be official Secretariat doctrine and, on the face of it, would preclude the notion that civil and political rights can be set aside until certain economic and social goals have been achieved (in the manner of both Marxist and other "development dictatorships"). Unfortunately, Third World spokesmen are not always so clear. There is often the suggestion that civil and political rights are devoid of real meaning unless or until economic and social rights have been secured. Worse, the securing of the latter set of rights is now often identified with the establishment of the New International Economic Order, an eschatological event comparable to the final passage to Communism in Marxist thought. This facet of Third World ideology, which offers a pretext for legitimizing sundry violations of human rights in the unredeemed present, is but another version of a gambit favored by many tyrants of our age.

There is one last element of Third World ideology to which we may give at least qualified assent—that is the proposition that Third World development is in the long-term interest of the industrial societies of the West. This proposition is often advanced on economic grounds (as in the Brandt Report), reflecting a Keynesian view of economics that many in the West will not find persuasive today; if Keynesian economics has not worked very well within societies, one may be skeptical about its working between societies. On political grounds, however, there is much to be said for the proposition. A permanently impoverished, politically turbulent Third World cannot be in the interest of the industrial democracies of the West, and steps to forestall such a situation can be seen as expressions of self-interest.

It is appropriate to appeal to people to do things out of self-interest; it is difficult to do so while at the same time denouncing them. In their stance toward the West, Third World spokesmen will have to choose between statesmanship and evangelism; both cannot be plausibly exercised simultaneously. Of the two, statesmanship would appear to be the more promising course.

Given the adversary posture of Third World ideology vis-à-vis the United States, it is inevitable that Americans will have to adopt a critical stance. At the same time, Americans must have the confidence to present a positive model of development that is properly their own—to present, that is, an American ideology of development. Americans had such confidence before the recent period of national self-criticism, and some of it, let it be conceded, was overconfidence. The idea that the American experience could be directly transplanted to the Third World and emulated there in all its details was dubious even in the 1950's. It is both intellectually dubious and politically ineffective now. What we must rather do (and this is by no means an easy task) is to isolate certain key elements of the American experience which are not necessarily dependent on the peculiar historical and cultural features of our society, and define the manner and degree to which they can be transplanted to different societies.

Two such elements stand out: democracy and capitalism. At the heart of any American ideology of development must lie the concept of democratic capitalism, to use the felicitous phrase which Michael Novak has introduced. Specifically, what needs to be shown is that the human benefits associated with the democratic ideal are linked empirically (and perhaps linked necessarily) with societal arrangements that, minimally, leave important sectors of the economy to the free operation of market forces.

We do not, at this point, possess a comprehensive theory of capitalism, but one thing we know is the empirical correlation between capitalism and political liberty (as well as the correlation between political liberty and the whole gamut of human rights). That correlation can be stated with great precision: every democracy in the contemporary world has a capitalist economy; no society with a socialist economy is democratic. The fact that a sizable number of countries, all now in the Third World, are capitalist *and* non-democratic does not negate the correlation between democracy and capitalism, which can be theoretically explicated in terms of the brakes on state power that a private sector *tends* to produce.

Another thing about which we know a good deal is the relationship between economic systems and success in the achievement of development goals. As I noted above, there is not a single socialist success story; all the success stories have occurred in countries with capitalist systems. We do not as yet know enough about the reasons for the failure of some capitalist systems. Obviously all societal decisions entail risks; there are no guarantees. But if the goal is *both* development *and* institutions protecting liberty and human rights, capitalist economic arrangements are the better bet. . . .

The practical implication is that American advice and assistance on development (by government as well as by non-governmental bodies) should emphasize the private sector and private entrepreneurship wherever possible. Such an emphasis by no means implies focusing on the large transnational corporations (though the demonological view of these institutions should be repudiated). Rather, the focus should be on indigenous enterprise, much of it small and precarious. Most important of all, the focus should be on the privately owned and operated family farm, which virtually everywhere has been the agent of successful agrarian development. . . .

It must also be a part of the American position on development that democracy, with its panoply of protections for individual rights, is not a luxury of the rich. On the contrary, it is the poor who need democracy much more urgently than the rich. In most places, certainly in most places in the Third World, the rich manage to protect their interests. It is the poor who need the institutional protections of liberty the most—protection against the arbitrary powers of local police, against employers who would deny them the right to organize, against those who would prevent a journalist from writing about conditions of poverty, and so on.

The proposition that democracy is a luxury of rich *countries* is also false. Democracy and development may not be invariably linked phenomena, but most countries in which democracy has been suppressed in the name of development have not attained their development goals, either. On the other hand, in authoritarian regimes, as development gains the pressures for democracy increase. . . .

One of the most intractable problems of modern life concerns the fate of those institutions ("mediating structures" in sociological parlance) which stand between the individual and the macro-structures of the state. These are the institutions that provide meaning and identity to individuals. Paramount among them in all societies are the family and the religious community. In Third World societies other groupings of a traditional character have to be added—clan, tribe, caste, village, ethnic and regional subcultures. Superimposed on these, and existing often in a symbiotic relation to them, are a variety of local economic, social, and political associations of modern provenance.

A good case can be made that development strategies which ignore or run roughshod over such mediating structures are unlikely to succeed. This case should be made strongly by Americans, as against the totalitarian tendencies in much thinking about the Third World. But the case should be related to the argument for democratic capitalism. Capitalism "leaves room" for mediating structures, while socialist development models almost always try to suppress, regiment, or (perhaps worst of all) "mobilize" them. Indeed, this tendency is causally related to the failures of socialist development; the record is particularly clear in the area of agriculture. What we now know about the fiasco of Maoist policies in China may serve as the *exemplum horribile* of such strategies.

Already in the 1950's the idea was prevalent that traditional values and institutions were "obstacles to development." But development strategies which defy tradition at all points run into great peril. Iran offers an important example. A counter-example is Japan, where, apparently to date, the society has successfully modernized while leaving traditional values and institutions intact over large areas of life. Similarly successful "creative schizophrenia" seems to be a factor in the development of Asian societies with a strong foundation in Confucian or neo-Confucian morality. Recent events in India are also instructive in this regard. Hinduism, more than any other traditional culture, has been characterized by development analysts as an "obstacle"; in the 1960's and 1970's India was always compared unfavorably with China. We now know, beyond a shadow of a doubt, the dismal reality of China's Maoist experiment. In India, in the meantime, there has taken place what may yet come to be seen as an agricultural miracle. The causes of this, as far as one can tell, have been a combination of technological innovation (the "Green Revolution") and imaginative government policies on credit and technical assistance to small farmers. It did *not* involve an attack on traditional Hindu values and social patterns. On the contrary, development has taken place within the traditional forms of Hindu village life.

Once again, Americans should speak for a view of modernity which does not regard traditional ways of life as something to be despised and discarded. And once again, the case should be made that for such purposes democratic capitalism provides the model.

The individuals who purport to speak in the name of the Third World are, typically, unelected and unrepresentative of anything but the tiny group that happens to hold state power at a particular moment. Even when they do represent elected governments, they typically belong to a very small elite with Western education and an international outlook. Most of them have as little knowledge of or contact with "the masses" of their own people as a Harvard professor purporting to represent "the masses" of America (happily, few Harvard professors make such a claim). We should not disguise our awareness of this fact. In addressing the Third World, we may often have to try and speak to people over the heads of their governments. . . .

It has often been said that the United States is a conservative or counterrevolutionary power in the contemporary world. There is truth in this—*if* one looks at the world in purely political terms. American foreign policy has indeed been dominated by the desire to stabilize, while the other superpower has aimed to destabilize. But if one looks at the world in economic, social, and cultural terms, nothing could be farther from the truth. The Soviet Union represents economic stagnation, social conservatism, and cultural sterility. By contrast, the Western world, and the United States above all, brims over with economic, social, and cultural vitality. Whether one considers technological innovation, industrial and agricultural productivity, or the vast array of social and cultural experiments, it is America that is in the lead.

One can ascribe this vitality to a number of factors, but at the core of it is, precisely, the gigantic transforming power of democratic capitalism, that power which Joseph Schumpeter once called "creative destruction." Put simply: the only real revolution going on in the world today is that of democratic capitalism. Its adversaries represent counterrevolution and re-action.

The most important evidence for this elementary fact is the irresistible attraction of American culture—the culture *par excellence* of democratic capitalism—even in, indeed especially in, countries where anti-Americanism dominates political rhetoric. From the realm of ideas to the trivia of everyday living, from high culture to the least appetizing pop fashions, and across the entire range of material and non-material furnishings of what is considered a desirable "life-style" (itself a deeply revealing term, of American origin), it is the symbols and the substance of American civilization that are sweeping the world. There seems to be no letup in this process, and no viable competitors have appeared on the scene. What is more, this revolutionary culture has the unique ability to thrive under conditions that foster freedom and that allow expression to a plurality of values, including many of the values of tradition.

Just as it is preposterous that the international Left, with its miserable and misery-creating record, still arrogates to itself the status of the "party of compassion," so it is preposterous that it pretends to be the party of revolution. In creating an American mode of address to the Third World, we should remind ourselves that we represent the only revolution in the world today that can credibly promise economic development, political liberty, and respect for the dignity of human beings in their infinite variety.   **focus**

The North-South confrontation is the centerpiece of one of the most significant political realignments of world politics in the twentieth century. As the articles by Barbara Ward and Peter Berger argue, it is crucial to understand the implications of North-South relations in order to formulate an effective response by the United States. For Barbara Ward, United States foreign policy lacks vision and sophistication. She argues that, the planet earth is in need of a new social structure that will guarantee four basic areas of life— food, shelter, education, and work—for the remaining three-fourths of humanity. The magnitude of the problems of economic and social development are so great and urgent that all members of the world community must work to find solutions, she says. Ward contends that the interdependence of North and South in economic relations, industrial and agricultural production, and humanitarian concerns demands the creation of a truly global perspective, and that the countries of the North have a special responsibility based on their wealth and power. In order for solutions to come about, she says, the North must begin to respond to the South's proposals for institutional and structural change; the countries of the Third and Fourth Worlds must be granted a role in helping to determine the future. According to Ward, both humanitarian concerns and the self-interest of Northern countries demand new solutions to insure global stability before it is too late to act.

Peter Berger rejects the assumption that the United States is responsible for the economic and social inadequacies of Third World states. Moreover, he argues that global political and economic policies will not cure the impoverishment of the Third and Fourth World. Thus, he believes, United States foreign policy must distance itself from the ideology of development that obscures the real reasons why the countries of the South are poor. U.S. indulgence of Third World demands will accomplish little, he maintains, and the United States cannot base its foreign policy to the Third World on feelings of guilt. Indeed, he says, Americans do an injustice to themselves and the political and economic accomplishments of the United States if Third World accusations are accepted. The United States does not exploit the countries of the Third World, argues Berger, rather, the capitalist system (especially under American direction since World War II) provides the poor of the world with unprecedented opportunities to grow economically, socially, and, most important of all, politically. The self-serving rhetoric of the South cannot alter American contributions, he contends. Indeed, Berger describes American-dominated capitalism as an engine pulling the Third World from its poor past to a more affluent future. Although he agrees that all citizens of the earth must be concerned with the human consequences of poverty and suffering in the Third World, humanitarian concerns, Berger argues, cannot dictate foreign policies that are historically and ideologically incorrect. Thus, he concludes that Third World assumptions must be denied.

It is significant to note that a Marxist interpretation would reject both Ward and Berger's perspectives. Berger's approach would be rejected as the typical rhetoric of American capitalism; Ward's emphasis on reform would be dismissed because it works within an existing global framework defined by capitalism. Thus, the Marxist vision calls for the creation of a new economic order that would eliminate the inequities inherent in capitalism.

CHAPTER 9

Reflections on Nuclear Weapons

On November 22, 1982, President Ronald Reagan announced his decision to deploy a MX missile system in a "Dense Pack" formation on desolate government-owned land in Wyoming. The president's decision was greeted with mixed emotions. Those supporting the president argued that the MX missile system is essential to the defense of the United States, that drastic Soviet military build-ups of nuclear weapons during the 1960s and 1970s has placed the United States in a position of inferiority in terms of both conventional and nuclear weapons, and that Soviet expansionism throughout the world is amply illustrated by its determination to achieve nuclear (or strategic) superiority over the United States. According to this view, the goal of Soviet world dominance is the principal force motivating the U.S.S.R.'s nuclear policy. Thus, it is argued the United States must insure that the threat of Soviet expansion is met by a revitalized nuclear and conventional military establishment, and that the deployment of the MX system is an important step in insuring the defense of the United States and its allies. Moreover, supporters of the MX system argue that the missiles would provide the U.S. with a *second strike capability* in the event of a Soviet nuclear attack. In other words, an attack on the MX system would not result in the complete destruction of all of the missiles. Under the Dense Pack formation, the huge MX missiles would be placed in specially reinforced silos between one thousand and two thousand feet apart in a narrow strip of territory. In the case of a Soviet attack, it is presumed that in-coming Soviet missiles would be destroyed by the explosions of the first missiles reaching the target. Thus, the surviving MX missiles would be ready to be launched in a retaliatory attack or second strike against Soviet targets.

The conventional assumptions of nuclear war maintain that an attack will be deterred if two countries possess the ability to inflict unacceptable losses on each other through a second strike capability. Thus, holds this philosophy, the likelihood that either country would resort to nuclear war is lessened. This idea is called *mutual deterrence*. United States nuclear policy is premised on the *strength* of its nuclear arsenal and the *credibility* of its threat to use nuclear weapons. The Reagan administration argues that the vastly expanded number of Soviet missiles endanger the second strike capability of the United States. The emphasis of President Reagan's defense policies has been to achieve a strong and invulnerable military capability in both nuclear and conventional forces. Reagan argues that American national security can only be assured through strength, particularly in nuclear weapons. Thus, for the president, the MX missile system is a significant attempt to redress a nuclear balance of power that now favors the Soviet Union.

Opponents of the MX system argue that its deployment would contribute to an *arms race* between the United States and the Soviet Union. These critics argue that rather than insuring peace through strength, an arms race heightens the likelihood of war by increasing economic, military, and psychological insecurities. Scarce economic resources are squandered by the huge military-industrial complexes of both the U.S. and the U.S.S.R., they say, and the determination to achieve nuclear invulnerability demands the continual search for technology that will create even more deadly weapons. The danger, maintain critics, is that a technological breakthrough may result in a weapon or weapons system capable of neutralizing an enemy's defenses, thus providing a country with a *first strike capability*. Thus, the ability to launch a successful first strike and, therefore, destroy an adversary's weapons creates the possibility for a preemptive nuclear attack. Opponents of current U.S. nuclear policies contend that rising anxieties and the possibilities of unstable technological breakthroughs or accidents will dramatically increase the chances of war. Rather than enhancing national security, critics of the MX missiles see them as a further step on a road leading to nuclear confrontation. Moreover, many opponents of the MX system suggest that the system would not be able to survive an attack. Several of the underlying assumptions of U.S. nuclear policies are being questioned. From this viewpoint arms races result in insecurity, fear, and instability. The inherent danger is that a new nuclear arms race makes nuclear war more likely in the near future.

Debate over the MX missile system illustrates the intensity of the clashing interpretations of U.S. nuclear policies. It also illustrates the vast gulfs separating supporters and opponents of MX missiles. The growing divergency in outlook between those favoring peace through strength and those calling for an immediate freeze in the production of all nuclear weapons has shattered a long standing consensus in the United States. Both positions are firmly based in changing perceptions of global politics and of the Soviet Union in particular.

Ronald Reagan's election documents a basic shift in American perceptions of the Soviet Union. The brief years of détente underscored the need for compromise and coexistence with the U.S.S.R. in some of the most vital areas of domestic and foreign policy. The U.S.S.R.'s creation of a viable economic sector emphasizing consumer goods and the need to achieve stability in the production of nuclear arms symbolized a changing Soviet posture. The process of détente was an attempt to come to grips with a new, more mature Soviet state. By 1976, however, the rhetoric of détente had evaporated— although the Carter administration pushed hard to achieve ratification of the second round of Strategic Arms Limitations Talks (SALT). The Carter administration withdrew the SALT Treaty in 1979, following the Soviet invasion of Afghanistan. Between 1979 and 1982, American perceptions of Soviet intentions deteriorated further. The Reagan administration both reflected and, in turn, shaped more hostile and fearful perceptions of Soviet motivations throughout the world. These perceptions concerned three areas. First, the Soviet build-up of nuclear and conventional arms was viewed by Reagan as relentless. The Soviet military build-up was not an attempt to catch-up with the United States and attain parity or equilibrium, as the logic of détente suggested, he argued. Rather, it was designed to achieve superiority in order to further the ambitions of an expansionistic ideology. Détente suggested that cooperation and coexistence could exist despite the two nations' conflicting interests; these assumptions were wrong and dangerous, contended Reagan. Soviet intentions to achieve global dominance "posed a mortal threat" to the United States and the West, he said.[a] Reagan believed the Soviet invasion of Afghanistan could only be interpreted as the initial phase of a sophisticated strategy aimed at the seizure of Middle East oil fields. The enormous increase of Soviet military capabilities was the first step in the U.S.S.R.'s strategy of global dominance, contended the president.

Second, Reagan maintained that the decline of American power throughout the world stimulated Soviet expansion.[b] The Vietnam experience unleashed criticism of the U.S. Defense Department and the Central Intelligence Agency that weakened American national security, he claimed. Drastic cuts in the Pentagon's budget damaged the United States nuclear arsenal. Not only had the United States suffered a major defeat in the

Vietnam War, but, said the president, American foreign policy lacked coherence and vision. A period of economic and psychological retrenchment characterized the years of détente, according to Reagan. He believed that more than any other factor, American complacency and fear of involvement in another Vietnam War crippled the U.S.'s ability to act in a decisive manner. The declining power of the United States provided the Soviet Union with the opportunity to achieve nuclear superiority, he said; détente was an illusion created by an American elite fearful of another Vietnam-like disaster. The rejection of the "containment of communism" thesis, which détente implied, was simply incorrect and unfortunate, maintained Reagan, because the U.S.S.R. quickly moved into the vacuum left by the United States.

Third, in Reagan's view, the Soviet invasion of Afghanistan and the capture of American hostages in Iran helped to create the climate necessary to overcome the "illusions" of détente and the legacies of Vietnam. The election of Ronald Reagan in 1980 can be viewed as a reaction to the history of the mistakes of American foreign policy in the 1970's. For Reagan, Soviet motivations are clearly apparent. Under his presidency, the United States began rebuilding national security through increases in Pentagon spending and a more active role for the Central Intelligence Agency. Reagan believes the security of the United States and the West must rest on a tough U.S. foreign policy to the Soviet Union; only when the U.S.S.R. is persuaded that the United States is willing and prepared to defend its interests throughout the world will the global balance of power be stabilized. According to the president, the most basic strategy for the defense of American national interests is a secure foundation of American nuclear strength. The mistakes of the 1970s can never be forgotten, he says: Soviet expansion must be stopped. This, Reagan contends, can only occur through American nuclear power and the willingness to defend U.S. national interests (including the Middle East and Western Europe) with nuclear weapons in order to stop relentless Soviet expansion.

The following is the text of President Reagan's broadcast to the nation on November 22, 1982. The president explains his reasons for recommending the deployment of the MX missile system. The speech underscores Reagan's perceptions of Soviet expansion throughout the 1960s and 1970s, particularly in the development of nuclear weapons.

References

[a]My analysis draws heavily on Norman Podhoretz's "The Future Danger," *Commentary* (April, 1981) pp. 29-41, especially, p. 31.
[b]*Ibid.*, p. 29-31.

NUCLEAR STRATEGY TOWARD THE SOVIET UNION

Ronald Reagan, Address to the Nation, November 22, 1982
Ronald Reagan is the 40th president of the United States.

The week before last was an especially moving one here in Washington. The Vietnam veterans finally came home once and for all to America's heart. They were welcomed with tears, with pride and with a monument to their great sacrifices. Many of their names, like those of our Republic's greatest citizens, are now engraved in stone in this city that belongs to all of us. On behalf of the nation, let me again thank the Vietnam veterans from the bottom of my heart for their courageous service to America.

Seeing those moving scenes, I know mothers of a new generation must have worried about their children and about peace. And that is what I would like to talk to you about tonight—the future of our children in a world where peace is made uneasy by the presence of nuclear weapons.

A year ago I said the time was right to move forward on arms control. I outlined several proposals and said nothing would have a higher priority in this Administration. Now, a year later, I want to report on those proposals and on other efforts we are making to insure the safety of our children's future.

The prevention of conflict and the reduction of weapons are the most important public issues of our time. Yet, on no other issue are there more misconceptions and misunderstandings. You, the American people, deserve an explanation from your Government on what our policy is on these issues. Too often the experts have been content to discuss grandiose strategies among themselves, and cloud the public debate in technicalities no one can understand. The result is that many Americans have become frightened and, let me say, fear of the unknown is entirely understandable. Unfortunately, much of the information emerging in this debate bears little semblance to the facts.

U.S. After World War II

To begin, let's go back to what the world was like at the end of World War II. The U.S. was the only undamaged industrial power in the world. Our military power was at its peak, and we alone had the atomic weapon. But we did not use this wealth and this power to bully, we used it to rebuild. We raised up the war-ravaged economies, including the economies of those who had fought against us.

At first, the peace of the world was unthreatened, because we alone were left with any real power, and we were using it for the good of our fellow man. Any potential enemy was deterred from aggression because the cost would have far outweighed the gain.

As the Soviets' power grew, we still managed to maintain the peace. The U.S. had established a system of alliances with NATO as the centerpiece. In addition, we grew even more respected as a world leader with a strong economy and deeply held moral values. With our commitment to help shape a better world, the U.S. always pursued every diplomatic channel for peace. And for at least 30 years after World War II, the United States still continued to possess a large military advantage over the Soviet Union. Our strength deterred—that is, prevented—aggression against us.

This nation's military objective has always been to maintain peace by preventing war. This is neither a Democratic nor a Republican policy. It is supported by our allies. And most important of all, it has worked for nearly 40 years.

Nuclear Deterrence

What do we mean when we speak of nuclear deterrence? Certainly we do not want such weapons for their own sake. We do not desire excessive forces, or what some people have called overkill. Basically, it is a matter of others' knowing that starting a conflict would be more costly to them than anything they might hope to gain. And, yes, it is sadly ironic that in these modern times it still takes weapons to prevent war. I wish it did not.

We desire peace, but peace is a goal, not a policy. Lasting peace is hat we hope for at the end of our journey; it does not describe the steps we must take, nor the paths we should follow to reach that goal. I intend to search for peace along two parallel paths—deterrence and arms reduction. I believe these are the only paths that offer any real hope for an enduring peace.

And let me say I believe that if we follow prudent policies, the risk of nuclear conflict will be reduced. Certainly the United States will never use its forces except in response to attack. Through the years, Soviet leaders have also expressed a sober view of nuclear war; and if we maintain a strong deterrent, they are exceedingly unlikely to launch an attack.

Now, while the policy of deterrence has stood the test of time, the things we must do in order to maintain deterrence have changed.

U.S. and Soviet Arms Spending

You often hear that the United States and the Soviet Union are in an arms race. The truth is that while the Soviet Union has raced, we have not. . . . In constant dollars our defense spending in the 1960's went up because of Vietnam and then it went downward through much of the 1970's. Soviet spending [has] gone up and up and up. In spite of a stagnating Soviet economy, Soviet leaders invest 12 to 14 percent of their country's gross national product in military spending, two to three times the level we invest.

I might add that the defense share of our United States Federal budget has gone way down, too. In 1962, when John Kennedy was President, 46 percent, almost half of the Federal budget, went to our national defense. In recent years, about one-quarter of our budget has gone to defense, while the share for social programs has nearly doubled. And most of our defense budget is spent on people, not weapons.

The combination of the Soviets' spending more and the U.S. spending proportionately less changed the military balance and weakened our deterrent. Today, in virtually every measure of military power the Soviet Union enjoys a decided advantage. . . .

Comparison of ICBM's

. . . For example, the Soviet Union has deployed a third more land-based intercontinental ballistic missiles than we have. Believe it or not, we froze our number in 1965 and have deployed no additional missiles since then.

The Soviet Union put to sea 60 new ballistic missile submarines in the last 15 years. Until last year we had not commissioned one in that same period.

The Soviet Union has built over 200 modern Backfire bombers—and is building 30 more a year. For 20 years, the United States has deployed no new strategic bombers. Many of our B-52 bombers are now older than the pilots who fly them.

The Soviet Union now has 600 of the missiles considered most threatening by both sides—the intermediate-range missiles based on land. We have none. The U.S. withdrew its intermediate-range land-based missiles from Europe almost 20 years ago.

The world has also witnessed unprecedented growth in the area of Soviet conventional forces; the Soviets far exceed us in the number of tanks, artillery pieces, aircraft and ships they produce every year. What is more, when I arrived in this office I learned that in our own forces we had planes that could not fly and ships that could not leave port, mainly for lack of spare parts and crew members.

Soviet Arms Buildup

The Soviet military buildup must not be ignored. We have recognized the problem and together with our allies we have begun to correct the imbalance. . . .

If my defense proposals are passed, it will still take five years before we come close to the Soviet level. Yet the modernization of our strategic and conventional forces will assure that deterrence works and peace prevails.

Our deployed nuclear forces were built before the age of microcircuits. It is not right to ask our young men and women in uniform to maintain and operate such antiques. Many have already given their lives in missile explosions and aircraft accidents caused by the old age of their equipment. We must replace and modernize our forces, and that is why I have decided to proceed with the production and deployment of the new ICBM known as the MX.

Three earlier Presidents worked to develop this missile. Based on the best advice I could get, I concluded that the MX is the right missile at the right time. On the other hand, when I arrived in office, I felt the proposal on where and how to base the missile simply cost too much in terms of money, and the impact on our citizens' lives.

Closely Based Silos

I have concluded, however, it is absolutely essential that we proceed to produce this missile, and that we base it in a series of closely based silos at Warren Air Force Base near Cheyenne, Wyo.

This plan requires only half as many missiles as the earlier plan and will fit in an area of only 20 square miles. It is the product of around-the-clock research that has been under way since I directed a search for a better, cheaper way. I urge the members of Congress who must pass this plan to listen and examine the facts, before they come to their own conclusion.

Some may question what modernizing our military has to do with peace. Well, as I explained earlier, a secure force keeps others from threatening us and that keeps the peace. And just as important, it also increases the products of reaching significant arms reductions with the Soviets, and that is what we really want. The United States wants deep cuts in the world's arsenal of weapons.

But unless we demonstrate the will to rebuild our strength and restore the military balance, the Soviets, since they are so far ahead, have little incentive to negotiate with us. If we had not begun to modernize, the Soviet negotiators would know we had nothing to bargain with except talk. They would know we were bluffing without a good hand because they know what cards we hold— just as we know what is in their hand.

'One-Sided Arms Control'

You may recall that in 1969 the Soviets didn't want to negotiate a treaty banning antiballistic missiles. It was only after our Senate narrowly voted to fund an antiballistic missile program that the Soviets agreed to negotiate. We then reached an agreement.

We also know that one-sided arms control doesn't work. We have tried time and again to set an example by cutting our own forces in the hope that the Soviets will do likewise. The result has always been that they keep building.

I believe our strategy for peace will succeed. Never before has the U.S. proposed such a comprehensive program of nuclear arms control. Never in our history have we engaged in so many negotiations with the Soviets to reduce nuclear arms and to find a stable peace. What we are saying to them is this: We will modernize our military in order to keep the balance for peace, but wouldn't it be better if we both simply reduced our arsenals to a much lower level?

Let me begin with the negotiations on the intermediate-range nuclear forces that are currently under way in Geneva. As I said earlier, the most threatening of these forces are the land-based missiles, which the Soviet Union now has aimed at Europe, the Middle East and Asia.

Warheads on Soviet Missiles

In 1972 there were 600 [Soviet warheads on these missiles]. The United States was at zero. In 1977 there were 600. The U.S. was still at zero. Then the Soviets began deploying powerful new missiles with three warheads and a reach of thousands of miles—the SS-29. Since then [the] Soviets have added a missile with three warheads every week. Although the Soviet leaders earlier this year declared they had frozen deployment of this dangerous missile, they have in fact continued deployment.

Last year, on Nov. 18, I proposed the total, global elimination of all these missiles. I proposed that the U.S. would deploy no comparable missiles, which are scheduled for late 1983, if the Soviet Union would dismantle theirs. We would follow agreement on the land-based missiles with limits on other intermediate-range systems.

The European governments strongly support our initiative. The Soviet Union has thus far shown little inclination to take this major step to zero levels. Yet I believe and I am hoping that, as the talks proceed and as we approach the scheduled placement of our new systems in Europe, the Soviet leaders will see the benefits of such a far-reaching agreement.

This summer we also began negotiations on strategic arms reductions, the proposal we call Start. Here we're talking about intercontinental missiles—the weapons with a longer range than the intermediate-range ones I was just discussing. We are negotiating on the basis of deep reductions. I proposed in May that we cut the number of missiles themselves to an equal number, roughly one-third below current levels. I also proposed that we cut the number of missiles themselves to an equal number, about half the current U.S. level. Our proposals would eliminate some 4,700 warheads and some 2,250 missiles. I think that would be quite a service to mankind.

Ballistic Missiles

. . . In 1977, when the last Administration proposed more limited reductions, the Soviet Union refused even to discuss them. This time their reaction has been quite different. Their opening position is a serious one, and even though it doesn't meet our objective of deep reductions, there's no question we're heading in the right direction. One reason for this change is clear. The Soviet Union knows that we are now serious about our own strategic programs and that they must be prepared to negotiate in earnest.

We also have other important arms control efforts under way. In the talks in Vienna on mutual and balance force reductions, we've proposed cuts in military personnel to a far lower and equal level. And in the 40-nation Committee on Disarmament in Geneva, we're working to develop effective limitations on nuclear testing and chemical weapons. The whole world remains outraged by the Soviets' and their allies' use of biological and chemical weapons against defenseless people in Afghanistan, Cambodia and Laos. This experience makes ironclad verification all the more essential for arms control.

There is, of course, much more that needs to be done. In an age when intercontinental missiles can span half the globe in less than half an hour, it's crucial that Soviet and American leaders have a clear understanding of each other's capabilities and intentions.

Accident and Misunderstanding

Last June in Berlin, and again at the U.N. Special Session on Disarmament, I vowed that the U.S. would make every effort to reduce the risks of accident and misunderstanding and thus to strengthen mutual confidence between the U.S. and Soviet Union. Since then, we've been actively studying detailed measures to implement this Berlin initiative.

Today, I would like to announce some of the measures which I've proposed in a special letter just sent to the Soviet leadership and which I've instructed our ambassadors in Geneva to discuss with their Soviet counterparts. They include but also go beyond some of the suggestions I made in Berlin.

The first of these measures involves advance notification of all U.S. and Soviet test launches of intercontinental ballistic missiles. We will also seek Soviet agreement on notification of all sea-launched ballistic missiles as well as ballistic missiles of the type we're currently negotiating. This would remove surprise and uncertainty at the sudden appearance of such missiles on the warning screens of the two countries.

Exchange of Data

In another area of potential misunderstanding, we propose to the Soviets that we provide each other with advance notification of our major military exercises. Here again, our objective is to reduce the surprise and uncertainty surrounding otherwise sudden moves by either side.

These sorts of measures are designed to deal with the immediate issues of miscalculation in time of crisis. But there are deeper, longer-term problems as well. In order to clear away some of the mutual ignorance and suspicion between our two countries, I will propose that we both engage in a broad-ranging exchange of basic data about our nuclear forces. I am instructing our ambassadors at the negotiations on an expanded exchange of information. The more one side knows about what the other side is doing, the less room there is for surprise and miscalculation.

Probably everyone has heard of the so-called hot line, which enables me to communicate directly with the Soviet leadership in the event of a crisis. The existing hot line is dependable and rapid—with both ground and satellite links.

But because it is so important, I've directed that we carefully examine any possible improvements to the existing hot line system.

Now, although we've begun negotiations on these many proposals, this doesn't mean we've exhausted all the initiatives that could help to reduce the risk of accidental conflict. We'll leave no opportunity unexplored, and we'll consult closely with Senators Nunn, Jackson and Warner, and other members of the Congress who've made important suggestions in this field.

We are also making strenuous efforts to prevent the spread of nuclear weapons to additional countries. It would be tragic if we succeeded in reducing existing arsenals only to have new threats emerge in other areas of the world.

'Peace Above All Else'

Earlier I spoke of America's contributions to peace following World War II, of all we did to promote peace and prosperity for our fellow man. Well, we are still those same people. We still seek peace above all else.

I want to remind our own citizens and those around the world of this tradition of American good will because I am concerned about the effects the nuclear fear is having on our people. The most upsetting letters I receive are from schoolchildren who write to me as a class assignment. It's evident they've discussed the most nightmarish aspects of a nuclear holocaust in their classrooms. Their letters are often full of terror. This should not be so.

The philosopher Spinoza said, "Peace is a virtue, a state of mind, a disposition for benevolence, confidence, justice." Those are the qualities we want our children to inherit, not fear. They must grow up confident if they are to meet the challenges of tomorrow, as we will meet the challenges of today.

I began these remarks speaking of our children and I want to close on the same theme. Our children should not grow up frightened. They should not fear the future. We are working to make it peaceful and free. I believe their future can be the brightest, most exciting of any generation. We must reassure them and let them know that their parents and the leaders of this world are seeking above all else to keep them safe, and at peace. I consider this to be a sacred trust.

My fellow Americans, on this Thanksgiving, when we have so much to be grateful for, let us give special thanks for our peace, our freedom and our good people. I've always believed that this land was set aside in an uncommon way, that a divine plan placed this great continent between the oceans to be found by a people from every corner of the earth who had a special love of faith, freedom and peace. Let us reaffirm America's destiny of goodness and good will. Let us work for peace, and, as we do, let us remember the lines of the famous hymn, "O God of love, O King of peace, make wars throughout the world to cease."

Thank you, good night, and God bless you.

Debate continued in the weeks that followed President Reagan's decision to deploy the MX system. The House of Representatives rejected the Dense Pack formation and requested the president to develop a new MX system. Toward that end, President Reagan appointed a commission—headed by General Brent Scowcroft and including former Secretary of State Alexander M. Haig, Jr. and former Defense Secretary Harold Brown— to study alternative patterns of deployment. Opposition to the MX system, whether in the Dense Pack formation or earlier proposals put forth by Jimmy Carter, continues. It raises a number of fundamental issues concerning nuclear weapons and illustrates radically different perspectives.

For Ambassador George F. Kennan and others, the nuclear arms race must be eliminated before nuclear holocaust occurs. Their perceptions of the Soviet Union clash with those of President Reagan's supporters, and, not surprisingly, they interpret the history of the 1970s in vastly different ways. Ambassador Kennan argues that subjective American perceptions of the Soviet Union account for the deterioration of U.S.–U.S.S.R. relations from 1974 onward. Kennan finds no significant changes in the objectives of Soviet foreign policy throughout the 1960s and 1970s. More importantly, he sees *no gains* in increasing Soviet influence in world politics.[c] For example, Kennan's assessment disputes the assertions of Ambassador Jeane Kirkpatrick and others who suggest that Soviet inroads in the Third World have been enormously successful. The methods of Soviet involvement may have changed, says Kennan, but there is no evidence to suggest that they have been more successful than in the past. Secondly, Kennan sees the Soviet invasion of Afghanistan as "a crude, bungled operation."[d] Not only is the Soviet presence in Afghanistan a mistake, but it does not directly affect American interests, he contends. A far more threatening alternative might have been the establishment of a rabidly anti-American regime similar to Khomeini's fanaticism, believes Kennan; therefore, the Soviet invasion of Afghanistan is no more important to American foreign policy than the Soviet domination of Outer Mongolia in the 1920s.[e] Third, Kennan asserts that the situation in Poland is not the creation of the 1970s although it is a tragedy for the Polish people. He believes it is significant that Moscow has not invaded the country after repeated requests for refrainment were made by the United States. Yet, he says, American foreign policy continues to punish the Soviet Union even after the latter has shown some restraint.[f] Fourth, the arms race gripping the Soviet Union is real enough, agrees Kennan. However, he adds, arms races do not occur in a vacuum: Undoubtedly, Moscow is responding to rising hostility and fear in Washington. It was the United States that failed to ratify the second SALT agreement, points out Kennan; thus, both sides share the blame for heightening insecurities.[g] The climate will abate only when both sides begin to negotiate in a serious manner, he says, but for such a process to begin, the anti-Soviet rhetoric of the Reagan administration must be toned down. George Kennan views Soviet foreign policy as the product of the history of the twentieth century, believing that that history has been characterized by a fundamental Soviet need to achieve a secure standing in world politics. The conspicuous failures of Soviet expansion throughout the Third World demand a more objective American perspective, claims Kennan.[h] Soviet influence in Cuba has not resulted in the explosion of communism in Latin America notwithstanding the leftist tilt of Nicaragua's ruling elite, he says; indeed, Castro's Cuba has been a disastrous drain on the resources of the U.S.S.R. Moreover, Kennan believes Soviet foreign policy has failed in Egypt and the Middle East in general; the Soviet occupation of Afghanistan will be a huge failure; and Soviet involvement in Africa has resulted in few payoffs.

According to this view, the people of the United States must reject the anti-Soviet biases of the U.S. foreign policy elite because the dangers of nuclear holocaust demand that a sober, unemotional vision of the Soviet Union replace hysterical fear and uncertainties. Thus, George Kennan argues that the United States must look critically and objectively at its perceptions of the Soviet state. "Only a thorough, open-minded, bipartisan re-examination of this whole problem, and a determined imaginative promulgation of the results of such a re-examination," Kennan argues, can save the world from extinction.[i]

References

[c]George F. Kennan, "America's Unstable Soviet Policy," *The Atlantic Monthly,* December, 1982), pp. 77-78.
[d]*Ibid.,* p. 79.
[e]*Ibid.*
[f]*Ibid.*
[g]*Ibid.*
[h]*Ibid.*
[i]*Ibid.,* p. 80.

NUCLEAR WAR: CONFRONTING THE HORROR

George Kennan, Address at Dartmouth College, November 15, 1981

George F. Kennan is a former ambassador of the United States.

The recent growth and gathering strength of the anti-nuclear-war movement here and in Europe is to my mind the most striking phenomenon of this beginning decade of the 1980s. It is all the more impressive because it is so extensively spontaneous. It has already achieved dimensions that will make it impossible for the respective governments to ignore it. It will continue to grow until something is done to meet it.

Like any other great spontaneous popular movement, this one has, and must continue to have, its ragged edges, and even its dangers. It will attract the freaks and the extremists. Many of the wrong people will attach themselves to it. It will wander off in many mistaken directions. It already shows need of leadership and of organizational centralization.

But it is idle to try to stamp it, as our government seems to be trying to do, as a Communist-inspired movement. Of course, Communists try to get into the act. Of course, they exploit the movement wherever they can. These are routine political tactics. But actually, I see no signs that the Communist input into this great public reaction has been of any serious significance.

Nor is it useful to portray the entire European wing of this movement as the expression of some sort of vague and naively neutralist sentiment. There is some of that, certainly, but where there is, it is largely a reaction to the negative and hopeless quality of our own Cold War policies, which seem to envisage nothing other than an indefinitely increasing political tension and nuclear danger. It is not surprising that many Europeans should see no salvation for themselves in this sterile perspective and should cast about for something that would have in it some positive element—some ray of hope.

Nor does this neutralist sentiment necessarily represent any timorous desire to accept Soviet authority as a way of avoiding the normal responsibilities of national defense. The cliche of "better red than dead" is a facile and clever phrase, but actually, no one in Europe is faced with such a choice, or is likely to be. We will not be aided in our effort to understand Europe's problems by distortions of this nature. Our government will have to recognize that there are a great many people who would accept the need for adequate national defense but who would emphatically deny that the nuclear weapon, and particularly the first use of that weapon, is anything with which a country could conceivably defend itself.

No—this movement against nuclear armaments and nuclear war may be ragged and confused and disorganized, but at the heart of it lie some very fundamental, reasonable and powerful motivations: among them a growing appreciation by many people for the true horrors of a nuclear war, a determination not to see their children deprived of life, and their civilization destroyed, by a holocaust of this nature; and finally, as Grenville Clark [who wrote, with Louis B. Sohn, *World Peace Through World Law*] said, a very real exasperation with their governments for the rigidity and traditionalism that causes those governments to ignore the fundamental distinction between conventional weapons and the weapons of mass destruction and prevents them from finding, or even seriously seeking, ways of escape from the fearful trap into which the nuclear ones are leading us.

Such considerations are not the reflections of Communist propaganda. They are not the products of some sort of timorous neutralism. They are the expression of a deep instinctive insistence, if you don't mind, on sheer survival—on survival as individuals, as parents and as members of a civilization.

Our government will ignore this simple fact at its peril. This movement is too powerful, too elementary and too deeply embedded in the human instinct for self-preservation, to be brushed aside. Sooner or later, and the sooner the better, all the governments on both sides of the East-West division will find themselves compelled to undertake the search for positive alternatives to the insoluble dilemma that any suicidal weaponry presents, and can only present.

Do such alternatives exist?

Of course they do. One does not have to go far to look for them. A start could be made with deep cuts in the long-range strategic arsenals. There could be a complete denuclearization of Central and Northern Europe. One could accept a complete ban on nuclear testing. At the very least, one could accept a temporary freeze on the further build-up of these fantastic arsenals. None of this would undermine anyone's security.

These alternatives, obviously, are not ones that we in the West could expect to realize all by ourselves. I am not suggesting any unilateral disarmament.

Plainly, two—and eventually even more than two—will have to play at this game.

And even these alternatives would be only a beginning. But they would be a tremendously hopeful beginning. And what I am suggesting is that one should at least begin to explore them—and to explore them with a good will and a courage and an imagination the signs of which I fail, as yet, to detect on the part of those in Washington who have our destinies in their hands.

This, then, in my opinion, is what ought to be done—what will, in fact, have to be done. But I must warn you that for our own country the change will not come easily, even in the best of circumstances. It is not something that could be accomplished in any simple one-time decision, taken from one day to the next. What is involved for us in the effort to turn these things around is a fundamental and extensive change in our prevailing outlooks on a number of points, and an extensive restructuring of our entire defense posture.

What would this change consist of?

We would have to begin by accepting the validity of two very fundamental appreciations.

• The first is that there is no issue at stake in our political relations with the Soviet Union—no hope, no fear, nothing to which we aspire, nothing we would like to avoid—that could conceivably be worth a nuclear war, that could conceivably justify the resort to nuclear weaponry.

• And the second is that there is no way in which nuclear weapons could conceivably be employed in combat that would not involve the possibility—and indeed the prohibitively high probability—of escalation into a general nuclear disaster.

If we can once get these two truths into our heads, then the next thing we shall have to do is to abandon the option of the first use of nuclear weapons in any military encounter. This flows with iron logic from the two propositions I have just enunciated. The insistence on this option of first use has corrupted and vitiated our entire policy on nuclear matters ever since such weapons were first developed. I am persuaded that we shall never be able to exert a constructive leadership in matters of nuclear arms reduction or in the problem of nuclear proliferation until *this* pernicious and indefensible position is abandoned.

And once it *has* been abandoned, there will presumably have to be a far-reaching restructuring of our armed forces. The private citizen is of course not fully informed in such matters; and I make no pretense of being so informed. But from all that has become publicly known, one can only suppose that nearly all aspects of the training and equipment of those armed forces, not to mention the strategy and tactics underlying their operation, have been affected by the assumption that we might have to fight—indeed, would probably have to fight—with nuclear weapons, and that we might well be the ones to inaugurate their use. A great deal of this would presumably have to be turned around—not all of it, but much of it, nevertheless. We might, so long as others retained such weapons, have to retain them ourselves for purposes of deterrence and reassurance to our people. But we could no longer rely on them for any positive purpose even in the case of reverses on the conventional battlefield; and our forces would have to be trained and equipped accordingly. Personally, this would cause me no pain. But let no one suppose that the change would come easily. An enormous inertia exists here and would have to be overcome; and in my experience there is no inertia, once established, as formidable as that of the armed services.

But there is something else, too, that will have to be altered, in my opinion, if we are to move things around and take a more constructive posture; and that is the view of the Soviet Union and its peoples to which our governmental establishment and a large part of our journalistic establishment have seemed recently to be committed.

On this point, I would particularly like not to be misunderstood. I do not have, and have never had, sympathy for the ideology of the Soviet leadership. I recognize that this is a regime with which it is not possible for us to have a fully satisfactory relationship. I know that there are areas of interaction where no collaboration between us is possible, just as there are other areas where one can collaborate. There are a number of Soviet habits and practices that I deeply deplore, and that I feel we should resist firmly when they impinge on our interests. I recognize, furthermore, that the Soviet leadership does not always act in its own best interests—that it is capable of making mistakes, just as we are, and that Afghanistan is one of those mistakes, and one that it will come to regret, regardless of anything we may do to punish it.

Finally, I recognize that there has recently been a drastic and very serious deterioration of Soviet-American relations—a deterioration to which both sides have made their unhappy contributions. And this, too, is something that it will not be easy to correct, for it has led to new commitments and attitudes of embitterment on both sides. The almost exclusive militarization of thinking and discourse about Soviet-American relations that now commands the behavior and the utterances of statesmen and propagandists on both sides of the line—a militarization that, it sometimes seems to me, could not be different if we knew for a fact that we were unquestionably to be at war within a matter of months; this in itself is a dangerous state of affairs, which it is not going to be easy to correct. So I don't think I underestimate the gravity of the problem.

But, all this being said, I must go on and say that I find the view of the Soviet Union that prevails today in our governmental and journalistic establishments so extreme, so subjective, so far removed from what any sober scrutiny of external reality would reveal, that it is not only ineffective but dangerous as a guide to political action. This endless series of distortions and oversimplifications; this systematic dehumanization of the leadership of another great country; this routine exaggeration of Moscow's military capabilities and of the supposed iniquity of its intentions; this daily misrepresentation of the nature and the attitudes of another great people—and a long-suffering people at that, sorely tried by the vicissitudes of this past century; this ignoring of their pride, their hopes—yes, even of their illusions (for they have their illusions, just as we have ours; and illusions, too, deserve respect); this reckless application of the double standard to the judgment of Soviet conduct and our own; this failure to recognize the communality of many of their problems and ours as we both move inexorably into the modern technological age; and this corresponding tendency to view all aspects of the relationship in terms of a supposed total and irreconcilable conflict of concerns and aims; these, believe me, are not the marks of the maturity and realism one expects of the diplomacy of a great power; they are the marks of an intellectual primitivism and naivety unpardonable in a great government—yes, even naivety, because there is a naivety of cynicism and suspicion just as there is a naivety of innocence.

And we shall not be able to turn these things around as they should be turned, on the plane of military and nuclear rivalry, until we learn to correct these childish distortions—until we correct our tendency to see in the Soviet Union only a mirror in which we look for the reflection of our own superior virtue—until we consent to see there another great people, one of the world's greatest, in all its complexity and variety, embracing the good with the bad—a people whose life, whose views, whose habits, whose fears and aspirations, are the products, just as ours are the products, not of any inherent iniquity but of the relentless discipline of history, tradition and national experience. Above all, we must learn to see the behavior of the leadership of that people as partly a reflection of our own treatment of it. Because if we insist on demonizing these Soviet leaders—on viewing them as total and incorrigible enemies, consumed only with their fear or hatred of us and dedicated to nothing other than our destruction—that, in the end, is the way we shall assuredly have them—if for no other reason than that our view of them allows for nothing else—either for us or for them.

These, then, are the changes we shall have to make—the changes in our concept of the relationship of nuclear weaponry to national defense, in the structure and training of our armed forces, and in our view of the distant country that our military planners seem to have selected as our inevitable and inalterable enemy—if we hope to reverse the dreadful trend toward a final nuclear conflagration. And it is urgently important that we get on with these changes. Time is not waiting for us. The fragile nuclear balance that has prevailed in recent years is being undermined, not so much by the steady build-up of the nuclear arsenals on both sides (for they already represent nothing more meaningful than absurd accumulations of overkill), but rather by technological advances that threaten to break down the verifiability of the respective capabilities and to stimulate the fears, the temptations and the compulsions, of a "first strike" mentality.

But it is important for another reason, too, that we get on with these changes. For beyond all this, beyond the shadow of the atom and its horrors, there lie other problems—tremendous problems—that demand our attention. There are the great environmental complications now beginning to close in on us: the question of what we are doing to the world oceans with our pollution, the problem of the greenhouse effect, the acid rains, the question of what is happening to the topsoil and the ecology and the water supplies of this and other countries. And there are the profound spiritual problems that spring from the complexity and artificiality of the modern urban-industrial society—problems that confront both the Russians and ourselves, and to which neither of us has as yet responded very well. One sees on every hand the signs of our common failure. One sees it in the cynicism and apathy and drunkenness of so much of the Soviet population. One sees it in the crime and drug abuse and general decay and degradation of our city centers. To some extent—not entirely but extensively—these failures have their origins in experiences common to both of us.

And they, too, will not wait. Unless we both do better in dealing with them that we have done to date, even the banishment of the nuclear danger will not help us very much. Can we not cast off our preoccupation with sheer destruction—a preoccupation that is costing us our prosperity and pre-empting the resources that should go to the progress of our respective societies—is it really impossible for us to cast off this sickness of blind military rivalry and to address ourselves at long last, in all humility and in all seriousness, to setting our societies to rights?

For this entire preoccupation with nuclear war—a preoccupation that appears to hold most of our government in its grip—is a form of illness. It is morbid in the extreme. There is no hope in it—only horror. It can be understood only as some form of subconscious despair on the part of its devotees—a readiness to commit suicide for fear of death—a state of mind explicable only by some inability to face the normal hazards and vicissitudes of the human predicament—a lack of faith, or perhaps a lack of the very strength that it takes to have faith, where countless generations of our ancestors found it possible to have it.

I decline to believe that this is the condition of the majority of our people. Surely there is among us, at least among the majority of us, a sufficient health of the spirit—a sufficient affirmation of life, of its joys and excitements together with its hazards and uncertainties, to permit us to sluff off this morbid preoccupation, to see it and discard it as the sickness it is, to turn our attention to the real challenges and possibilities that loom beyond it, and in this way to restore to ourselves a sense of confidence and belief in what we have inherited and what we can become.   **focus**

Ronald Reagan and George Kennan present radically different interpretations of nuclear weapons, American foreign policy, and Soviet ambitions. It is important to recognize the full extent of their clashing perspectives. Ronald Reagan sees peace as attainable only through strength. The MX missile system (which the President has labeled the "peace keeper") and a strong nuclear arsenal are the only means of guaranteeing American survival, he believes. His call for the reduction of nuclear weapons, therefore, is premised on the belief that the Soviet Union will respect only a secure and tough opponent. The history of the 1970s illustrates the need for American vigilance and strength, contends Reagan. Thus, according to the president, America's nuclear arsenal guarantees U.S. national security.

George Kennan argues that the threat of nuclear annihilation is so great that the United States must radically alter traditional assumptions about nuclear security. This is a difficult process but the imminent possibilities of nuclear holocaust demand a new perspective, he claims. Thus, contends Kennan, the urgency of the threat of nuclear war must force the U.S. to reappraise a badly distorted image of Soviet motivations. For Ambassador Kennan, no political conflicts or rivalries with the Soviet Union justify nuclear war. American foreign policy, especially the assumptions about conventional and nuclear war, must change to ensure our survival, he says.

CHAPTER 10

The Future Is Now

The articles in this concluding chapter point to conditions of interdependence that challenge traditional notions of the sovereignty of states. The rise of transnational, or non-state, actors under conditions of interdependence affects the ability of *all* states to act independently. Indeed, the power of the United States since the Second World War has been eroded in military, economic, political, and ideological areas. Global economic relations and the existence of nuclear weapons clearly limit the actions of the United States. The United States' global responsibilities make the implementation of a coherent foreign policy difficult. In the 1960s and 1970s, evidence of the declining influence of the United States in world politics emerged. Three painful events underscore the limitations of future American involvement in global politics: the Vietnam debacle, the OPEC oil embargo, and the seizure of American hostages in Iran. Today, the United States confronts a world of such complexity that long-standing assumptions of U.S. foreign policy have been questioned or proven wrong. The Vietnam War illustrated the failure of the cold war policies of the containment of communism. The U.S.'s defeat in Vietnam was a staggering blow to political and military assumptions, to be sure. However, the ideological consequences of the war destroyed the foundations of a twenty-five year foreign policy consensus. It underscored the importance of non-involvement in Third World conflicts. Despite the rhetoric of the Reagan administration, the U.S. is reluctant to become involved in the present conflicts in Central America. Reports of CIA activities in Honduras, aimed at destabilizing Nicaragua's Sandinista regime, are being carefully scrutinized by the U.S. Congress. The Nuclear Freeze Movement challenges the nuclear weapons policies of the Reagan administration. Concern over the wisdom and safety of America's nuclear arsenal has never been greater. Despite the Reagan administration's emphasis on U.S. power, there exists significant skepticism and doubt about the safety and security of nuclear deterrence. A coherent foreign policy agenda does not seem to exist; it is fragmented among a number of competing perspectives ranging from the left to the right of the American political spectrum. The limitations of U.S. foreign policy in the 1980s suggest a sobering new perspective for many Americans. These trends indicate that Reagan's foreign policy will be scrutinized carefully and, in fact, limited by Congress, the foreign policy bureaucracies, and public opinion.

Second, the economic effects of OPEC price rises and the disastrous economic consequences of the Vietnam War have significantly limited the U.S.'s economic influence in world politics. The devaluation of the U.S. dollar in 1971 and 1973 was an explicit indication of a severely troubled domestic economy. Successive economic summits among the countries of the West underscore the interconnectedness of economic relations and the need for collective action. The expanded role of the International Monetary Fund, the Organization of Economic Cooperation and Development, and other ad hoc committees document the need for collective solutions to the economic problems confronting the United States and its allies.

The International Monetary Fund has been the principal international organization confronting global economic instability. The OECD, the central institution of the wealthy capitalist countries of the West, has attempted to stabilize global economic relations among advanced industrial countries by serving as a forum on international trade and related issues.[a] Both organizations have largely reacted to global economic circumstances while providing stop-gap solutions to problems confronting the advanced industrial societies of the North and the poorer developing countries of the South. The United States remains the most important member of the world's economy but its power is largely derived from the complexity of a global capitalist system which the U.S. no longer dominates. The rise of OPEC also documents the radical transformation of the global political agenda confronting the West. Demands for the creation of a new international economic order have largely been ignored by the United States and its allies. The stalemate that comprises North-South relations has alienated and embittered the countries of the South. The polarization of North and South, however, does not alter the pervasiveness of the ties that bind rich and poor nations together in one world. Indeed, North-South relations may be one of the most important areas of future confrontation in terms of politics, economics, ideology, and military concerns. OPEC's power illustrates both the political and economic vulnerability of the North. Demands for the creation of a new international economic order underscore the totality of the interdependence of the world in fundamental human terms as well.

Third, the Iranian revolution and the seizure of American hostages illustrate the frustrations that global responsibilities entail. Despite the rhetoric of the American political right, U.S. foreign policy options in Iran were limited by the goal of securing the safe release of the hostages. The seizure of the U.S. vessel *Pueblo* by the North Koreans in 1967 dictated a similar posture of patience and negotiation. The American nuclear arsenal provides an aura of invulnerability, perhaps even omnipotence. Most world leaders agree the use of nuclear weapons must be limited to the most desperate situations, however. The irony is that American's extraordinary military power is essentially unusable. It is likely that the United States and other countries of the North will be confronted with even more troubling and painful situations as the South continues to exert its influence. Global levels of interdependence increase the vulnerability of the United States to future Iran-like situations, and raises disturbing questions of global political and economic stability. These questions must be confronted in the future.

The articles that bring this book to a conclusion point to the subtle, but pervasive, conditions of interdependence that challenge the traditional ideas of state sovereignty. James Nathan's "The New Feudalism" and Norman Meyers' "The Exhausted Earth" underscore the importance of *global* solutions to current foreign policy problems. Nathan documents the activities of such transnational actors as multinational corporations (MNCs) and terrorist groups, and shows how they are helping to transform contemporary world politics. As Nathan points out, terrorist groups pose a real threat to the property and personnel of MNCs throughout the world. In order to protect the interests of multinational corporations, private security firms have begun to usurp the police powers of states, he states. These security firms ignore domestic and international laws, effectively by-passing a state's sovereignty, in order to negotiate directly with terrorists, explains Nathan. He believes the willingness of multinational corporations to employ private vigilantees who negotiate with terrorists by paying huge amounts of ransom encourages further terrorist attacks. Nathan argues that many multinational corporations see this form of extortion as just another cost of doing business. The situation outlined by Nathan results in the further erosion of the power of states because it rewards the lawlessness of terrorists while creating a range of private security forces directed by multinational corporations. Nathan refers to this process as the new feudalism, and says it underscores the complexity and vulnerability of the contemporary state system.

Reference

[a]Joan Spero, *The Politics of International Economic Relations* New York: St. Martins, 1977, p. 82. David H. Blake and Robert S. Walters, *The Politics of Global Economic Relations* (Englewood Cliffs, NJ: Prentice-Hall, 1976, p. 70).

THE NEW FEUDALISM

James A. Nathan, *Foreign Policy,* Spring 1981

James A. Nathan is a professor of Political Science at the University of Delaware.

A Texas-based company called Oil Field Security Consultants recently notified potential corporate clients that it had its "own SWAT team of professionals who can be deployed on location to anywhere in the world within 24 hours." Another company, based in London, wired the major U.S. oil companies that "we stand ready . . . [as] a last resort . . . [to] conduct 'search and destroy' missions," against those who would harm company property, lives, or operations.

The business of countering terrorists has never been better. Approximately 40 counter-terrorist firms offer an impressive panoply of services. Some provide protection through chauffeur training and electronic perimeter defenses. Firms may also supply information on specific terrorists and even negotiate with terrorists for the release of kidnaped company personnel. In addition, counter-terrorist businesses may assume a more aggressive role—assisting in the identification of terrorists, engaging in paramilitary operations to release kidnap victims, and ferreting out terrorists in pre-emptive missions.

Large overseas corporations that deal with counter-terrorist businesses should be aware of the extraordinary implications of this commerce. If the international corporate sector seeks protection by private counter-terrorist security firms, a medieval situation may emerge in which the security function of the state is usurped by private contractors. To the extent that this trade prospers, it may be a portent of a new kind of feudalism.

From 1968 to October 1980, between one-third and one-half of terrorist attacks abroad were directed against business executives and commercial property. There have been about 7,000 overseas terrorist incidents since 1970. During that same decade, multinational corporations paid $150-250 million in ransom. U.S. corporations have been the target of many of these attacks, suffering 25 per cent of all kidnapings, explosions, and bombing incidents in 1979. During the last decade, U.S. companies paid $125 million in ransom. Throughout Western Europe, South America, and especially

Central America, U.S.-owned and -managed firms are encountering increased terrorist activity. Since the success rate for terrorist efforts is extraordinarily high—more than 70 per cent of the time ransom is paid or political prisoners released or both—terrorism appears to be a growth industry.

Yet if a multinational business does negotiate with terrorists and ransoms a kidnaped employee, it may be subject to other penalties. In March 1980, five years after Exxon Corporation paid $14.2 million to Argentine terrorists in return for the release of an abducted executive, a stockholder lawsuit was filed demanding that officials responsible for the payment reimburse the company for a decision taken "beyond the lawful powers and the authority of Exxon."

In Colombia, a counter-terrorist firm—Control Risks—that negotiated with kidnapers on behalf of corporations had its operatives jailed, and, in Venezuela, Owens-Illinois had its property expropriated. Italian magistrates who have uncovered corporate dealings with kidnapers have frozen the assets of the companies involved. Recently, Beatrice Foods was sued for $185 million by an employee who had been held in a South American cave for eight months during 1976, while Control Risks bargained his ransom down from $5 million to $450,000.

Faced with government inability or unwillingness to cope with the growing problem of terrorism, many multinational corporations have come to view terrorism as part of the cost of doing business. In fact, the U.S. Internal Revenue Service allows some ransom payments to be deducted as business expenses. To some extent, corporations expect that after they have paid a ransom they will not be bothered by terrorists again. Paying one ransom is a means of insuring the company's interests against future terrorist incidents. Other companies see terrorism as a continuing business expense and are prepared to accept the demands of terrorists even to the point of breaking the law. More than one executive has stated that if local law prohibits ransom payments his company will make a deal in other countries, ignoring customs rules if necessary.

Even if the government does take action against terrorists, it may not resolve the matter to the satisfaction of the corporations. A company's priority is to rescue its employee and pay as little ransom as possible. The concern of the government, in contrast, is to detain or kill the terrorist, with the fate of the victim not infrequently a secondary consideration.

Usurping Police Power

Given this situation, many companies have found it necessary and practical to enlist the services of security firms established specifically for the purpose of helping corporations cope with terrorist incidents. Because companies are usually not experienced in dealing with terrorist threats, these firms—staffed largely by individuals formerly involved in government covert operations—

provide necessary protective and negotiating services. They also undertake to lessen the financial burden of terrorism for the companies. The life and well-being of international business employees are not always uppermost in the minds of executives. Hence, the sales pitch of the counter-terrorist business to the multinational corporation is not centered only on the health and morale of employees. For example, Motorola Teleprogram's *Executive Protection Manual* stresses the responsibility of corporations to avoid draining profits by spending assets on terrorism.

Most firms in the international security business were established recently. One of the oldest, Control Risks, was organized in Britain in 1974 as a division of the Hogg Robinson insurance group. Since then, it has been involved in 60 hostage negotiations and claims to have saved its clients more than $10 million. Control Risks charges $500-800 a day plus expenses while negotiating victim releases. The fees for these services can be as high as those of Payne International, of Miami, Florida, which charges up to $3,000 a day plus expenses.

The security services not only negotiate with terrorists, but they also maintain extensive information files. Risks International claims that its records on individuals are more complete than those of the Central Intelligence Agency and can be displayed on the simplest home computer. For a $960 yearly fee, Risks International will identify suspected terrorists, at home or abroad and, if needed, negotiate with abductors. Another firm, International Management and Resource Corporation, claims to have the most comprehensive and up-to-date file of its kind in private hands, containing 10,000 items concerning terrorism and political violence throughout the world.

It is difficult to judge the effectiveness of these security firms in countering terrorism. The fact of their existence implies that they have succeeded, at least on occasion, when government security agencies have failed. Yet the security firms usually keep the procedures and results of their previous operations secret. Advertising on the basis of past operations could provide terrorists with information needed to resist successfully the efforts of these firms. Sometimes security firms admit they are unsure of their effectiveness, for it is difficult to know whether the absence of a terrorist attack results from preventive action by the security firm or lack of interest by the terrorists. As a result, corporation managers trying to decide whether to enlist the services of a counter-terrorist firm must invariably rely upon brochures, promises, and reputations almost impossible to validate.

Luring kidnapers to capture by the police is acceptable; making a citizen's arrest of foreign nationals using substantial fire-power in a foreign country is another matter. In countering terrorism, the firms may employ para-military forces that usurp the role of the host country's police. For example, when one multinational firm's senior officer in Latin America was threatened with kidnaping, an International Security Group team, disguised as his family, moved into the executive's house. When the suspected kidnapers attempted to gain entry into the house, the security team opened fire and captured eight of them.

A Radical Response to Terrorism

The actions of Texas industrialist H. Ross Perot raise a plethora of these issues. In 1978 Perot financed a commando operation that freed two of his employees from an Iranian prison. Perot assembled a team of 15 men recruited from his firm, Electronic Data Systems. They were led by a retired U.S. Army colonel who had directed an unsuccessful attempt to free U.S. prisoners of war held in a camp outside of Hanoi in 1970.

The action was admittedly precipitated by a desperate turn of events: Civil authority in Iran had broken down; armed mobs were outside the jail; and no group was willing to accept the large ransom that had already been negotiated. Perot's explanation to Richard Shenkman of the *Washington Post* seemed compelling on a human basis, if not on a legal one:

> The government wouldn't do anything for us. . . . The State Department wasn't really interested. . . . Protecting American citizens is a role that our government should perform. Private companies, private individuals shouldn't be involved in this sort of thing. But if your government is not willing to protect American citizens, and if you have people in your company imprisoned in a country, you have an obligation to get them out of there.

If Perot's effort had been a unique affair, it could perhaps be ignored. Because others are now systematically organizing a permanent capability to imitate Perot's response to terrorism, there is cause for concern.

Perot's incursion of 15 armed men into another country—albeit one on the verge of anarchy—was a violation of that nation's sovereignty and, according to international law, a belligerent act. Furthermore, in using military force Perot exercised a power that in the United States is reserved to the government.

The counter-terrorist business is currently unregulated. Indeed, it is even encouraged by many international corporations and governments. Those regimes whose security forces lack adequate resources may find private security firms to be effective allies against political terrorists who threaten the government's survival. Those governments whose citizens are subjected to terrorism in foreign countries are quite likely to view the counter-terrorist firms as an effective means of protection that the host country has failed to provide. If this situation continues, the current international order may dissolve into a new medievalism in which private firms perform the security functions of the state, and citizens are left with little capacity to redress their grievances. Clearly, reform in this area is required.

Not all private security firms offer questionable services. Designing strategies and technologies for chauffeur training, perimeter defense, and risk analysis are merely common sense. It is also prudent to examine a company's possible responses to extortion and kidnaping. Corporate managers should think through the issues of insuring personnel and counseling families. However, when security firms undertake actions normally reserved to public authority, they become a problem for public policy.

Ultimately, the rise of private security firms is the result of feeble municipal police or of police cooperation with terrorists. If the civil order of the host country were secure, there would be little need for private security firms and less chance of abuses by them. In the United States, the rate of capture and successful prosecution of kidnapers is about 90 per cent. The average rate of apprehension overseas is much lower: Of all terrorists abroad, 80 per cent escape death or capture. Of those arrested, less than half serve prison terms.

Cooperative Security

Two areas of reform are commonly suggested. First, assistance could be given to local police and security forces in order to make them more effective against terrorism. This would reduce the need for private counter-terrorist firms and thus lessen the chance of abuses by these firms. The Carter administration tried to provide this type of assistance in spite of a general congressional ban on aid to foreign police departments. The administration encouraged local U.S. police to offer training to Caribbean police. The United States also urged those European countries with historical ties in the Caribbean—Denmark, Britain, and France—to increase their training assistance to police forces there. Suggestions were made that an all-Caribbean police force should be created and assisted by the U.S. Navy and Coast Guard.

Proposals that the United States help other countries strengthen their security forces in order to protect U.S. commercial interests from terrorism raise some of the most sensitive issues in current U.S. foreign policy. Should Washington assist the most hated and feared agents of those regimes under siege by their own citizens? If Washington is publicly linked to the infamies committed by these regimes, terrorists will be encouraged rather than deterred in their attacks on U.S. property. U.S. association with repression does little to weaken the terrorist cause and perhaps strengthens its ideological case.

The second suggested reform, advanced in a report by the American Society of International Law, involves the creation of an international penitentiary for terrorists. This would have the advantage of reducing the exposure of police officials to demands for the release of prisoners whose detention is considered political. However, the obstacles facing the creation of such a penitentiary are tremendous. It would require that a universal definition of political terrorism be established. So far, only the meaning of air piracy has received universal acceptance. The other multilateral treaty that deals with terrorism is a West European convention. Its definition of what is proscribed is very narrow, covering diplomatic and other specially protected people and property, and specified methods of attack, such as bombing. In the United Nations, a U.S.-sponsored treaty that would enlarge that definition to include innocent people and property has been consistently blocked by a coalition of Third World states. But even if a treaty defining terrorism were to be signed and ratified, a penal colony for terrorists would confront seemingly insurmountable procedural difficulties with respect to due process, conflicts of municipal laws, and responsibility of supervision.

Another means of curbing the abuses of private counter-terrorist firms would be through the founding of a universally respected international organization that would offer reputable security services to subscribers for a fee. Indeed, the establishment of an international information clearing-house to combat terrorism is a fairly common suggestion within the private security industry. Certainly the larger security firms would not be averse to a plan that would allow them to corner permanently a large share of the market. One suggested plan calls for the involvement of the United States in the charter of such an information clearing-house. A cooperative venture in private international security would probably reduce the profits of many current counter-terrorist firms and perhaps cause the most dubious among them to collapse.

Such an information clearing-house, however, would endanger the civil liberties of individuals by peddling the names of suspected terrorists. If individuals are concerned that they have been wrongfully identified as terrorists by a U.S. government agency, they can request their file under the Freedom of Information Act or file for an injunction. However, if an individual's name is sold or released by a private firm, recourse is much more difficult. The potential for abuse by an information clearing-house is such that a reminder by Thomas Paine, colonial pamphleteer, is appropriate: "He that would make his own liberty secure must guard even his enemy from oppression."

The sale of names of suspected terrorists by formerly covert agents is an abuse that could be remedied by a decision to enforce existing U.S. laws. All former covert agents have signed security agreements that the courts have consistently upheld. In Snepp v. the U.S., the Supreme Court decided that no information—classified or unclassified—gathered in the course of work at the CIA could be used commercially without authorization. Various federal statutes also proscribe the unauthorized receipt, delivery, or dissemination of classified information. However, enforcement of federal statutes and contracts may lead to a stringent official secrets act, such as that in the United Kingdom. Enforcement would involve a tradeoff between controlling these abuses and maintaining traditional civil liberties. Yet this is the type of sensitive issue that the activities of the counter-terrorists now pose.

A Return to the Wild West

The matter of paramilitary operations undertaken by private security firms is the issue most amenable to regulation. Participation in operations of this type is essentially a mercenary service and should be legally treated as such.

On December 4, 1980, the U.N. General Assembly adopted a resolution authorizing negotiations to begin on a treaty outlawing mercenary activities. However, when the General Assembly in 1980 passed a resolution merely requesting that assaults on diplomats be reported to the U.N. Secretariat, the United States, United Kingdom, Austria, and France privately objected. Washington feared that the statistics resulting from these reports would make the United States look unsafe because of the number of diplomats in New York and Washington exposed to private crimes against person or property.

Even if a treaty banning mercenaries is successfully negotiated and signed, it is unlikely that it would be ratified by the U.S. Senate. A treaty of this type could be interpreted as proscribing Jewish Americans from volunteering to serve in the Israeli armed forces. Similarly, it might be seen as a bar to Greek Americans and others who are sometimes required to do military service if they wish to claim an inheritance in the country of their ancestors.

In the absence of an international treaty banning mercenary activity, a remedy may be found in U.S. domestic law. Title 18, paragraph 960, of the U.S. Criminal Code prohibits participation in any group that takes armed action against foreign nationals or foreign property within the United States and abroad, except under conditions of war. It also forbids the rendering of any form of assistance to "armed expeditionaries." This statute and others similar to it provide the means for controlling the involvement of U.S. citizens in counter-terrorist and mercenary activities. Despite repeated urging by the State Department, the U.S. Department of Justice has never brought an indictment against anyone engaging or assisting in mercenary activity. Inaction on the part of Justice may be indicative of its priorities and of a concern that such prosecutions will have to be initiated against those who fight for Israel, as well as those who fight for profit. The use of presidential waivers, specifying those countries in whose armed forces U.S. citizens could legally enlist, might resolve this difficulty.

Enforcement of these statutes may simply cause the counter-terrorist firms to move their offices abroad while still providing services for U.S. corporations. But an active U.S. policy might place some inhibition on Americans contemplating involvement in this activity and may give pause to firms considering enlistment of mercenary services. If corporations are aware of legal penalties attached to the use of paramilitary services by the private sector, they might consider more carefully the security of the environment in which they are planning to locate.

It will not be easy to design and implement the reforms needed to control effectively counter-terrorist security firms. Yet reforms are important, not only for the safety of the people and corporations involved, but also for the future of international order. International efforts to define and prohibit such activities should be vigorously pursued in the United Nations and other forums, as should official efforts to counter terrorism. Pending international agreement, the United States should enforce existing domestic legislation that outlaws participation by U.S. citizens in the operations of the private security firms engaged in mercenary activities. The international community should understand that unless common action is taken soon against terrorists and counter-terrorists alike, a growing violence by both could signal the beginning of a new international feudalism.   **focus**

In the following article by Norman Myers, "The Exhausted Earth," the problem of the ecological destruction of the planet earth is raised. Rather than noting the threat of nuclear annihilation, global pollution, or overpopulation, Myers reminds us of the extraordinary complexity and fragility of the earth's species. He defines species as the most basic form of genetic differences defining all living organisms. Scientists have explored only about one percent of all species, explains Myers, and these living organisms are crucial to the continuance of the earth's physical environment. The species that Myers points to are the least noted but most crucial building blocks of our natural environment. These species contain the information necessary for overcoming some of the most difficult problems confronting the world: greater agricultural production, the preservation of scarce natural resources, and the development of new forms of energy. As Myers points out, genetic engineering has already created a billion dollar industry. Myers argues that protecting the fragile species in the world's shrinking tropical rain forests may be crucial for the long-term survival of the human race. However, for him, the protection of tropical rain forests is not an isolated problem confronting conservationists. The destruction of the world's most delicate ecosystems—for example, the Amazon region of Brazil—is dictated by the demand of a global market in search of prized hardwoods, he explains. Myers argues that the only way rare genetic species can survive is through comprehensive global agreements. Indeed, the fact that the most valuable genetic materials are located in the endangered tropical forests of the South illustrates the extent of global interdependence. For Myers the only way that tropical forests will survive is through global political arrangements as epitomized in the South's demands for the creation of a new international economic order. He contends, however, that the cumulative effects of global pollution from the North and the South endanger the survival of these delicate genetic materials.

THE EXHAUSTED EARTH

Norman Myers, *Foreign Policy,* Spring 1981

Norman Myers is a senior associate of the World Wildlife Fund.

The welfare of humankind is served by the species that share the earth. Not only do they supply natural products such as rubber, but they also provide germ plasm—living tissue that harbors hereditary codes in the form of genes. These genetic stocks enable human beings, through techniques of bioengineering, to devise new products for agriculture, medicine, and industry.

To date, scientists have explored the utilitarian value of only 1 per cent of all species. Further research will disclose myriad products for everyday use. Indeed, species could rank among humankind's most valuable resources in tackling the challenges of the future. Yet the earth's stock of species is being depleted even more rapidly than several of its most precious mineral deposits. Of the planetary stock of 5-10 million species, one species disappears each day. By the end of the 1980s, the figure could be as high as one an hour. By the year 2000, 1 million species could be extinct, and the rate of depletion could continue to grow.

The earth is currently afflicted with severe forms of environmental degradation, such as desertification and pollution. Whereas these forms of degradation can generally be reversed, extinction of species cannot. It constitutes an irreversible loss of a unique natural resource.

Most extinctions are occurring in the tropics. This single zone, with year-round warmth and often with year-round moisture, has served as earth's main powerhouse of evolution, and it is here that three quarters of all species exist. By contrast, the temperate zones are relatively deficient in species concentrations and gene reservoirs. Most of the developing world is in the tropics; yet it is the developed countries, situated largely in the temperate zones, that possess the technological capacity to exploit species and their genetic resources for economic advantage. This situation raises several issues salient to North-South relations and, in particular, to economic issues addressed in negotiations for a New International Economic Order.

The need to preserve germ-plasm resources is but one of several global resource and environmental issues that emerged in the 1970s that is likely to receive increasing attention during the 1980s. These problems, which often underline differences between the developed and developing worlds, include food, energy, and pollution as well as "environmental commons" issues such as the oceans, Antarctica, the ozone layer, and the carbon dioxide cycle. They highlight the interdependent nature of society at large and the need for collective action on the part of the community of nations. Moreover, many of the problems are interrelated: Progress can be made on one front only by tackling several other problems simultaneously.

No Home-Grown Meals

Because the United States is heavily dependent on foreign supplies of genetic material, it should play an active if not a leading role in proposing and implementing measures to address the problem of disappearing species. This is not simply a biological phenomenon of concern to scientists and wildlife enthusiasts. It is a problem of economic and political significance that must be treated as a matter of public policy.

The problem may eventually impinge on everyday lives as much as will the decline of other natural resources. Thus, the productivity of modern agricultural crops cannot be maintained—let alone expanded—without constant infusions of fresh germ plasm. Without these foreign infusions, Americans would have their diets limited to cranberries, blueberries, strawberries, pecans, sunflower seeds, and little else. There is no such thing as a homegrown meal. The U.S. Department of Agriculture (USDA) estimates that genetic improvements account for at least 1 per cent of agricultural productivity each year, a farm-gate value approaching $1 billion.

The success of U.S. agriculture rests on a disturbingly restricted genetic base. Seventy per cent of the seed corn used in 1970 derived from five inbred lines of corn. As a result, when a leaf blight struck that year, it eliminated 15 per cent of the entire U.S. crop, causing losses to farmers and increased costs to consumers of more than $2 billion. The damage was halted with the aid of a blight-resistant strain of corn whose genetic materials originated in Mexico.

Another species of Mexican corn, a perennial, has been discovered recently. This wild strain, resistant to four of the seven familiar corn viruses and probably immune to sundry insects and other pests, was found in damp, mountainous localities, environments that foster fungus diseases such as the one that caused the 1970 blight. This corn's capacity to grow in wet soil would increase markedly the acreage suitable for the production of corn worldwide. Were its perennial attributes to be crossbred into current commercial forms of annual corn, it could eventually reduce the massive expense of season-by-season plowing and sowing. This wild strain was discovered in just a few acres of common land that were earmarked for alternative activities: A gene reservoir of exceptional potential was on the verge of elimination.

Because U.S. agriculture is essentially an imported agriculture, for the last two decades U.S. agronomists have sought germ plasm in many gene-rich localities outside the country, notably in the tropics and subtropics. They have searched for new varieties of wheat in a crescent extending from Turkey to Afghanistan in order to support U.S. agriculture. Commercial wheat strains now last only about five years before falling prey to new disease hybrids. But a wild form of imported wheat that is resistant to several diseases has boosted U.S. wheat production by about $500 million a year.

Beneficial Foreign Organisms

Exploitation of natural environments is eradicating genetic diversity. In Mexico, many indigenous types of corn have been supplanted by high-yielding varieties, hybrid sorghum, strawberry farms that export to the United States, and an eight-lane highway across the central plateau. Many strains of wild wheat have all but disappeared in their native areas. Even in the remotest valleys, native wheats are becoming rare; in Turkey, wild progenitors of several grains find sanctuary from grazing livestock only in castle ruins and graveyards.

The International Board for Plant Genetic Resources, a coordinating agency under the Food and Agriculture Organization (FAO), has suggested that 10 zones qualify for high-priority germ-plasm collection programs: the Mediterranean basin, West Africa, Ethiopia, Central Asia, Southwest Asia, South Asia, Southeast Asia, Mexico and Central America, the Andes, and Brazil. All of these environments, except for Central Asia and remote parts of Brazil, are subject to misuse and overuse because of expanding human populations and inefficient agriculture. Most of these zones supported extensive gene stocks as recently as 1960; few will have much left in 1990. In the developing tropics, the problem is not so much urban sprawl or pollution of wildlife ecosystems—phenomena that characterize industrial countries—as it is attrition of species' habitats, resulting from increased human populations.

The value of gene reservoirs to the great grain-growing belts of the world is increasing, especially for those areas in the temperate zone extending through North America and Eurasia. The prospect of radically altered climates in the temperate zone during the next half century (owing to a build-up of carbon dioxide in the global atmosphere, leading to warmer and drier weather) increases the need for substantial germ-plasm supplies to support adaptive agriculture. Genetic materials are also required for the booming agro-industry of bioengineering. Technological breakthroughs in this new field may achieve advances for innovative agriculture surpassing those of the Green Revolution, which produced grain that was highly responsive to fertilizer, was less sensitive to growing conditions, and matured early. Yet there is now much less genetic material available for research and innovation than at the outset of the Green Revolution two decades ago.

The new varieties of grain that result from crossbreeding can also be highly resistant to natural enemies such as insect pests. In California, biological control projects have reduced insect-induced crop losses and cut back on the need for pesticidal chemicals, resulting in savings of more than $200 million.

About one-half of the 500 species of insects, which inflict $2 billion worth of damage on U.S. crops annually, have developed resistance to insecticides. Furthermore, 200 of the major insect pests in the United States, accounting for at least half of all crop losses, are of foreign origin; it is against these species that foreign introductions offer the greatest promise. Conservative estimates by the Agricultural Research Service of the USDA suggest that 1,000 species of foreign organisms—not only insects, but also mites and pathogens—could be profitably introduced into the United States at a cost of less than $40 million over a period of 20 years. Past performance indicates that there could be a $30 return for each dollar expended on importation of beneficial organisms.

The commercial value of all medicinal preparations derived from natural origin now surpasses $10 billion a year in the United States alone. The United States is also heavily dependent upon imported plant materials for its pharmaceutical industry. The rosy periwinkle from tropical rain forests yields two drugs that achieve 80 per cent remission of leukemia and Hodgkin's disease, with current commercial sales in the United States amounting to $37 million a year. A small shrub of Asia's tropical forests, the serpentine root, relieves hypertension, the greatest and fastest-growing source of mortality in advanced societies; this first modern tranquilizer now generates sales of $60 million a year in the United States.

In 1972 the United States imported plant products worth $24.4 million for medicines, perfumes, and sundry other uses. Imports by all developed nations totaled $74 million. These plant products contributed $1.5 billion in commercial sales of plant-derived drugs in the United States. Across the developed world, this trade has been growing rapidly: According to the United Nations Conference on Trade and Development, it has increased in recent years by as much as 7 per cent a year.

"New Dimension of National Security"

Wild species have industrial applications as well. Plants supply latex, pectins, resins and cleoresins, dyes, tannins, gums and other exudates, essential oils for flavors and related juices, vegetable fats and waxes, insecticides, and multitudes of other biodynamic compounds.

Exceptional potential appears to lie with those plant species whose tissues contain hydrocarbons such as oil, instead of carbohydrates such as sugar. These hydrocarbons are similar to those in fossil petroleum but are virtually free of sulfur and other contaminants. According to Melvin Calvin, a Nobel Prize-winning biochemist, 12 species of trees from the genus *Euphorbia* seem to be especially suitable for "growing gasoline." These trees, which are found in Brazil, can be grown in areas too dry for conventional agriculture. They can flourish on land that has been made useless, such as strip-mined land. This suggests that land degraded through extraction of hydrocarbons from beneath the surface could be rehabilitated by growing hydrocarbons above the surface.

Genetic resources benefit the U.S. economy through utilitarian applications totaling $20 billion a year. This contribution is possible because of advances in genetic engineering. U.S. dependence on foreign sources of genetic resources may come to be perceived as a strategic interest as technology expands its search for raw materials. On June 5, 1980, World Environment Day, then Secretary of State Edmund Muskie described international issues associated with the environment, including genetic resources, as a "new dimension of national security." Yet the profound implications of the problem of disappearing species are only beginning to be appreciated by political leaders and the general public.

Species become extinct almost entirely through loss of habitat. This loss occurs because of economic exploitation of natural environments; and natural environments are often exploited to meet consumer demand for numerous products. This means that species are eliminated through the activities of millions of people who are unaware of the impact of their consumerist habits on distant areas experiencing environmental degradation. Affluent nations, with one-fifth the earth's population, account for four-fifths of raw materials traded through international markets. Many of these materials come from the tropics, where their extraction disrupts the environment. Thus affluent sectors of the global community are increasingly responsible—unknowingly for sure, but effectively nonetheless—for destruction of species' habitats in far-off lands.

Economic-ecological linkages among the global community are illustrated by the case of the tropical moist forests, which cover only 7 percent of earth's land surface but harbor at least 40 percent of all species. The richest of all ecological zones, they are being rapidly depleted. These forests could be destroyed during the next three to five decades, causing the extinction of at least 1 million species.

These species represent back-up germ plasm for existing agricultural crops, as well as potential sources of new food. They could also be used in developing whole pharmacopoeias of new drugs. Their loss would set back the campaign against cancer, heart disease, and other major scourges, and reduce the prospect of finding a safe and effective contraceptive. Their elimination would remove the source of some of the richest feedstocks of phytochemicals—materials in growing demand as petrochemicals become increasingly expensive.

The destruction of tropical forests stems in part from market demand on the part of affluent nations for hardwoods and other specialty timbers. The disruptive harvesting of tropical timber is often conducted by multinational corporations that supply the capital, technology, and skills without which developing countries could not exploit their forests' stocks at unsustainable rates. Many forests, notably in Latin America, are being cleared to make way for human-established pasturelands, with the aim of producing more beef for export to the United States and other developed countries. This foreign beef, cheaper than that produced within the United States, is valued as a weapon in the campaign against inflation. Thus, many hands are on the saw at work in tropical forests.

Protecting the Common Heritage

The problem of declining tropical forests is intimately related to other major issues of the interdependent global community: food, energy, population, and inflation. The loss of species is one of the problems that arises from integrated living within the global village—and especially between the developed and developing world. Hence the query of former Mexican President Luís Echeverría: How can an advanced-nation conservationist be concerned with the International Union for Conservation of Nature and Natural Resources, without being equally concerned with a New International Economic Order? To date there have been only a few rumblings from developing countries about what they see as an inequitable situation, but consciousness is growing.

A few years ago, Zambia supplied germ plasm to an agricultural seed corporation in Europe at nominal cost. When Zambia subsequently asked for supplies of newly developed hybrids of the crop plant, the corporation responded that abundant supplies of seed could be made available, but at substantial cost. Mexico was once the sole source of a wild yam that supplied virtually all the world's diosgenin, a key component in the manufacture of contraceptive pills and cortisone. Receiving only $5.10 a pound in 1970 for a plant product that led to commercial sales worth hundreds of millions of dollars, Mexico exploited its monopoly position to raise the price until, at $69 a pound, synthetic substitutes became economically competitive. Kenya possesses a *Maytenus* shrub, a leading candidate as a potential source of anti-cancer material, and may try to sell the germ plasm for as much as the international market will bear. Ethiopia, a major center of genetic diversity for many temperate-zone crops, is now denying export of germ plasm in any guise whatever.

Developing countries may eventually devise strategies enabling them to derive greatly increased revenues from their tropical stocks of species, further fueling inflation in the developed countries—the principal consumers. Some Third World countries are considering the possibility of levying substantial charges on their exported germ plasm. Other developing countries, disaffected by North-South relations, may consider using their unique genetic wealth for political leverage as well as for economic gain; already there are occasional remarks about using the survival of tropical wildlife as a negotiating chip in North-South bargaining. Though the political leverage is likely to be ephemeral, the economic damage could be permanent for both sides.

Insofar as everybody bears some responsibility for the species problem and will suffer its consequences, all share the responsibility of relieving the problem. Efforts by national and international institutions are called for on a scale reflecting the increasingly interdependent character and needs of the global community.

The first priority in addressing the issue of disappearing species is to establish the problem on political agendas as a strategic resource issue. Consciousness raising must entail an extensive educational campaign through the mass media, as well as forums for political leaders and policy makers. Formal policy commitments on the part of governments and international forums such as the U.N. General Assembly should then be possible. A two-thirds majority endorsement of a commitment to species preservation by the

United Nations would foster international participation and minimize resistance to collective initiatives.

A species trust convention could be created in recognition of the principle
that species constitute "resources of common heritage, to be maintained on
behalf of the global community now and forever." Collective responsibility for
the common heritage would not mean collective rights to particular resources.
Far from playing down sovereignty, this approach would emphasize it as a
functional concept. Thus, a country would no longer be left to rely on its own
isolated efforts to protect its species, but could expect assistance from the
community at large.

Developing countries often have difficulty keeping their citizens alive, let
alone guaranteeing the survival of their wild creatures. The benefits of efforts
at species conservation tend to accrue to those states with the technological
expertise to exploit species' genetic resources—that is, the developed
countries. Most people in the developing world do not live long enough to
contract cancer or heart disease. To the extent that developing countries are
currently trying to safeguard their species through parks and related measures,
their efforts amount to a resource handout to developed countries.

Trifling Budgets

Several programs designed to maintain the earth's stock of species already
exist, but they are limited in both scope and scale and need to be massively
supplemented. International development organizations, such as the International Bank for Reconstruction and Development (World Bank), the United
Nations, and bilateral aid agencies, could subsidize conservation activities in
developing countries through greatly increased support for national park
networks and similar measures that assist species. The World Bank directs no
attention to species, despite their value as highly diverse stocks of natural
resources. It has, however, supplied substantial funding together with the
Ford and Rockefeller foundations and other major donors to 10 international
agricultural research centers in the tropics, including the International Rice
Research Institute in the Philippines. Of the collective budget for these
centers—$135 million a year—only a small share is allocated to systematic
exploration for germ plasm. The World Bank has recently increased its
lending for tropical forestry by 500 per cent, with the emphasis on protection,
rather than production, forestry.

The FAO's International Board for Plant Genetic Resources devotes a
mere $1.5 million a year to genetic resources, reflecting the low priority
accorded to crop germ plasm by FAO member states.

The United Nations Educational, Scientific, and Cultural Organization
(UNESCO) operates a project on natural areas and genetic resources—
essentially a clearing-house for information—and the World Heritage Fund
supports a handful of exceptional parks around the world. But both these

activities receive trifling budgets. UNESCO also seeks to establish a global system of biosphere reserves representing the earth's 200 biotic provinces that would harbor sample communities of species. But only one-third of the reserves have been set up, even though instituting and operating the rest would cost only about $80 million a year.

The United Nations Environment Programme is still reviewing its options in regard to threatened species, genetic resources, and wild-land habitats, with a total budget of only slightly more than $1 million. As for bilateral agencies, the U.S. Agency for International Development leads the field in recognizing the value of species conservation. To date, however, the agency has hardly begun operational activities in this field.

Although citizen conservation groups have made contributions, they have been unable to attract sufficient funding. The World Wildlife Fund, working in conjunction with its scientific arm, the International Union for Conservation of Nature and Natural Resources, has been able to mobilize only $40 million since its founding 20 years ago.

This dismal record confirms that the species problem tends to be perceived largely in scientific terms and therefore lacks political clout. What is needed is a campaign of sufficient scope to confront the overall problem. International assistance should recognize common responsibility on the part of the community of states for a deteriorating asset of common heritage. An appropriate measure could involve creation of a trust for species to establish an international fund in support of conservation efforts in those countries where the need is greatest and local funds are in shortest supply.

It is difficult to offer more than approximate estimates of funding requirements necessary to make significant progress toward species preservation. There are several seed collections in the United States to support its major crops, but far fewer than required. The budget for the USDA's gene conservation program now totals only $8.5 million a year, a marginal amount compared with the returns realized through genetic investments in the nation's crops. Plant-breeding experts recommended, in a 1978 National Academy of Sciences report, *Conservation of Germplasm Resources—An Imperative*, that the budget should be expanded at least five times forthwith. Were the United States to expand its gene conservation activities in this way, the cost would equal that of a couple of jet fighters. One may speculate on which outlay would offer the greatest contribution to national security.

A number of screening and breeding programs for genetic resources, established to produce pest- and disease-resistant varieties of major crops, have cost less than $100,000 each. This sum contrasts with the cost of developing safe and species-specific pesticides, on the average $5 million each.

Many U.S. agronomists and plant breeders believe that an annual budget of $100 million is necessary to meet U.S. and international requirements for the exploration of gene reservoirs, collection of germ plasm, and maintenance of seed-bank facilities. A comprehensive save-species campaign could probably be done for one-tenth the $10 million that the developed world now spends each day on tranquilizers; and it may reduce the chances that the depletion of the earth's genetic stocks will become a source of anxiety to developed-world citizens.

Paper Parks

At least as important as the matter of funding is the question of norms and procedures with respect to resources issues. The species problem, as one of an emergent category of controversial resource issues that are intrinsically international in nature, will establish precedents for other global-commons questions, such as carbon dioxide, chlorofluoromethanes, and deep-sea mineral deposits. Fortunately, there are some precedents already available.

At least three precedents should be of help: the Convention on Wetlands of International Importance, the Convention on Conservation of Islands for Science—both of which safeguard prime habitats with their species concentrations—and the Convention on International Trade in Endangered Species (CITES), established in 1975 (largely through U.S. instigation) and now ratified by more than 60 nations. CITES seeks to cut down the vast commerce in threatened creatures and their products, and it has had some success in restraining those persons who make money at the expense of declining species. But it does nothing about the great number of people who harbor no malign intent toward wildlife, but who constitute a far greater threat through their disruption of wildlife habitats. For every one species that is endangered because of the poacher's poisoned arrow, hundreds are in trouble because of the cultivator's digging hoe. Nonetheless, CITES could serve as a model for a further convention of comprehensive scope to assist threatened species through extensive networks of protected areas and gene banks.

In order to safeguard the majority of species found in tropical rain forests, scientists believe that at least 10 per cent, and possibly 20 per cent, of total forest expanse needs to be set aside as protected areas. To date, only 2 per cent has been so established, and many of the areas amount to "paper parks," with few effective safeguards on the ground. Indonesia, with one-tenth of the world's rain forest, has announced that it wishes to expand its parks network from 3 per cent to 10 per cent of its national territory and has increased its conservation budget threefold, to $2 million a year. This is an expansive gesture for a country with a per-capita gross national product of only $360. So Indonesia appears a prime case for financial and technical support from the international community. Something similar applies to Zaire and Brazil, both with extensive sectors of tropical rain forest and with ambitious plans and limited institutional capacity to bring undisturbed tracts under protection.

The United States can take many steps to instigate a save-species strategy in the international community. In conjunction with other developed and gene-poor nations, the United States needs to maintain a low political profile, broaching the matter in a way that reinforces consensus and cooperation while playing down politics and reducing divisiveness. It should demonstrate a spirit akin to that with which it is handling the carbon dioxide question—an issue where, as with species, a central concern lies with the distribution of benefits and costs of resource management. Thus, the best role for the United States in a save-species campaign lies with quiet diplomatic activities, plus financial contributions and technical back-up for whatever international measures emerge, leaving other parties to blow clarion calls for action.

Apart from instigating a strategy at the multilateral level, the United States could pursue a number of bilateral measures. For example, it could offer assistance to Mexico in order to protect natural environments that may harbor wild strains of modern crops. Indeed, giving species preservation greater visibility within the U.S. aid program may increase domestic support for development assistance in general.

The means are available to save many species. The funding could be made available if it were given the priority accorded to food, energy, and pollution. The missing element is political will. If nothing is done before the problem becomes all too apparent—for example, through extensive collapse of the world's wheat crop—the process of mass extinction may have generated too much momentum to be halted. As is the case with the carbon dioxide problem, the international community must act ahead of time, before it is too late. The United States has recently taken a lead in drawing attention to the decline of tropical rain forests, a natural resource of exceptional value, and—coincidentally—the earth's major repository of species. The United States could take similar steps through a low-key approach, to the problem of disappearing species.

Given the North-South dimension to the issue, there is a premium on a cooperative endeavor for a save-species campaign. Inasmuch as most species exist in developing countries, developed countries can exercise only indirect influence over their survival prospects. This means that the developed world will derive greater benefit from careful coordination within the international community.

An approach in this spirit is all the more pertinent because developing countries may be less inclined to participate in an international campaign to safeguard the world's wealth of species as long as cooperative relations are lacking in respect to their principal concern, North-South economic issues. However, an increased emphasis by the developed countries on the preservation of species might also help induce the spirit of international cooperation necessary in addressing broader international economic, resource, and security issues. A campaign in support of species could help articulate the common interests of nations. It might even encourage governments to adopt a more collective approach to other international issues, leading to an enhanced world order. **focus**

The articles by James Nathan and Norman Myers illustrate the importance of global solutions to problems confronting individual states. How United States foreign policy would come to grips with a more fully global perspective is difficult to predict, however. The perceptions and direction of American foreign policy are overwhelmingly defined by the history of the United States, the persistence of traditional assumptions (often expressed in the form of an ideology), and a host of long-term and short-term policies often suggesting conflicting interpretations of issues and problems. The contemporary setting of world politics and the post-World War II state system inhibit a truly global perspective. Many of the issues outlined throughout this book call for policies that transcend the frustrations of the present and look toward the future. The success or failure of United States foreign policy depends on the ability of the U.S. to recognize the dilemmas and difficulties that an interdependent world creates for a country that has played such a significant role in world politics during the twentieth century.

Do the realities of an interdependent global environment demand that the United States transcend its historical and political past? Can the United States realistically confront complex global problems that demand subordinance to a global ideal not yet achieved among 167 self-interested states? Is the existing global political system capable of accommodating the nationalism of states and the global concerns of transnational actors? Can the diverse political, economic, ideological, and cultural needs of the peoples of the world be fulfilled? The answers to these and other issues posed throughout this volume depend on one's frame of reference. In the absence of an emerging global consensus on the problems and the central issues confronting humankind, distinctive political, economic, and ideological values will define the possible solutions to these problems. The fragmentation of perspectives and the politicization of issues illustrates the magnitude of the problems confronting all members of the human family. This volume documents the range and diversity of opinion in contemporary American foreign policy among conservatives, moderates, and neo-Marxists. The conflicting ideological perspectives suggest the complexity of the policy-making choices confronting the United States: for example, the clashing economic interpretations of American foreign policy posed by Robert Tucker and Paul Sweezy and Harry Magdoff; the vastly different analyses of the needs of U.S. national security in the Third World addressed by Jeane Kirkpatrick and Michael Klare; the conflicting analyses of human rights policies illustrated by Patricia Derian and Samuel Huntington; and the radically different interpretations of U.S. responsibilities toward Third World development offered by Peter Berger and Barbara Ward. In each issue, the policy choices recommended document the importance of distinctive political, economic, and ideological values. Thus, in analyzing the issues confronting American foreign policy in the 1980s, basic political, economic, and ideological issues must first be addressed. In an age of unprecedented global interdependence in which fragile human institutions may ultimately determine the fate of humankind, it is imperative that the policy choices raised throughout this book be scrutinized from the dual perspectives of American interests and global concerns. Thus, political, economic, and ideological issues must be confronted within the context of contemporary American foreign policy.

Further Readings

Chapter 1. American Foreign Policy in an Era of Transition
Allison, Graham T. *The Essence of Decision: Explaining the Cuban Missile Crisis.* Boston: Little Brown, 1971.
George, Alexander L. *Presidential Decisionmaking in Foreign Policy: The Effective Use of Information and Advice.* Boulder, Colo.: Westview Press, 1980.
Hoffmann, Stanley. *Gulliver's Troubles, or the Setting of American Foreign Policy.* New York: McGraw-Hill, 1968.
_____. *Primacy or World Order.* New York: McGraw-Hill, 1978.
Jones, Walter S. and Rosen, Steven J. *The Logic of International Relations,* Fourth Edition. Boston: Little Brown, 1982.
Kegley, Jr., Charles W. and Wittkopf, Eugene R. *American Foreign Policy, Patterns, and Process,* Second Edition. New York: St. Martin's Press, 1982.
_____. eds. *Perspectives on American Foreign Policy.* New York: St. Martin's Press, 1983.
Morgenthau, Hans J. *A New Foreign Policy for the United States.* New York: Praeger Publishers, 1969.
Perkins, Dexter. *The Evolution of American Foreign Policy,* Second Edition. New York: Oxford University Press, 1966.
Sondermann, Fred A., McLellan, David S., and Olson, William C. eds. *The Theory and Practice of International Relations,* Fifth Edition. Englewood Cliffs, N.J.: Prentice-Hall, 1979.
Spanier, John. *American Foreign Policy Since World War II,* Ninth Edition. New York: Holt, Rinehart, and Winston, 1982.
_____. *Games Nations Play,* Third Edition. New York: Holt, Rinehart and Winston, 1975.
Stoessinger, John G. *Crusaders and Pragmatists,* New York: W.W. Norton, 1979.
Stupak, Ronald J. *American Foreign Policy: Assumptions, Processes and Projections.* New York: Harper and Row, 1976.

Chapter 2. Clashing Assumptions of American Foreign Policy in the 1980s
Barnet, Richard J. *Real Security: Restoring American Power in a Dangerous Decade.* New York: Simon and Schuster, 1981.
Gaddis, John Lewis. "Containment: Its Past and Future." *International Security* 5(Spring, 1981).
Hoffmann, Stanley. "Foreign Policy: What's to be Done?" *The New York Review of Books* 28 (April 30, 1981).
Huges, Thomas L. "Up from Reaganism." *Foreign Policy* 44 (Fall 1981).
Kirkpatrick, Jeane. "Dictatorships and Double Standards," *Commentary* (November, 1979).

Chapter 3. Power and American Foreign Policy
Alperovitz, Gar. *Atomic Diplomacy.* New York: Vintage Books, 1967.
Aron, Raymond. *The Imperial Republic.* Cambridge, Mass: Winthrop Publishers, 1974.
Draper, Theodore, et. al. *Defending America.* New York: Basic Books, 1978.
Halle, Louis J. *The Cold War as History.* New York: Harper and Row, 1967.
Kennan, George F. *American Diplomacy, 1900-1950.* New York: New American Library, 1951.
Morgenthau, Hans J. *Politics Among Nations,* Revised, Fifth Edition, New York: Knopf, 1978.
Pipes, Richard. ed. *Soviet Strategy in Europe.* New York: Crane Russak, 1976.
Steel, Ronald. *Pax Americana.* New York: Viking, 1967.
Tucker, Robert W. *The Purposes of American Power.* New York: Praeger, 1981.

Chapter 4. Economic Interpretations of American Foreign Policy
Barnet, Richard J. *Roots of War.* Baltimore: Penguin Books, 1971.
Cohen, Benjamin J. *The Question of Imperialism.* New York: Basic Books, 1973.
Fann, K.T. and Hodges, Donald C. eds. *Readings in U.S. Imperialism.* Boston: P. Sargent, 1971.
Gardner, Lloyd C. *Architects of Illusion.* Chicago: Quadrangle Books, 1970.
Horowitz, David. *Empire and Revolution.* New York: Random House, 1969.
Kolko, Gabriel. *The Roots of American Foreign Policy.* New York: Random House, 1968.
Maddox, Robert James. *The New Left and the Origins of the Cold War.* New York: Monthly Review Press, 1969.
Tucker, Robert. *The Radical Left and American Foreign Policy.* Baltimore: Johns Hopkins University Press, 1971.
Williams, William Appleman. *The Tragedy of American Diplomacy,* Second Edition, New York: Delta, 1972.

Chapter 5. The Role of Secrecy in a Democratic Society
Barnet, Richard J. *Roots of War: The Men and Institutions Behind U.S. Foreign Policy.* Baltimore: Penguin Books, 1973.
Borosage, Robert L. and Marks, John. eds. *The CIA File,* New York: Grossman Publishers, 1976.
Kirkpatrick, Jr., Lyman B. *The U.S. Intelligence Community: Foreign Policy and Domestic Activities.* New York: Hill and Wang, 1973.
Marchetti, Victor and Marks, John D. *The CIA and the Cult of Intelligence.* New York: A Dell Book, 1974.
Ransom, Harry Howe. *The Intelligence Establishment.* Cambridge, Mass.: Harvard University Press, 1970.
Turner, Stansfield and Thibault, George. "Intelligence: The Right Rules," *Foreign Policy* Number 48 (Fall, 1982).

Chapter 6. The Continuing Legacies of the Cold War
Barnet, Richard J. *Real Security: Restoring American Power in a Dangerous Decade.* New York: Simon and Schuster, 1981.
Draper, Theodore. *The Abuse of Power.* New York: Viking, 1967.
Fitzgerald, Frances. *Fire in the Lake.* Boston: Little Brown, 1972.
Gaddis, John Lewis. "Containment: Its Past and Future." *International Security* 5 (Spring, 1981).
Harrison, Michael M. "Reagan's World." *Foreign Policy.* 43 (Summer, 1981).
Hoffmann, Stanley. *Primacy or World Order.* New York: McGraw-Hill, 1978.
Klare, Michael J. *Beyond the Vietnam Syndrome.* Washington, D.C.: Institute for Policy Studies, 1981.
May, Ernest. *Lessons of the Past.* New York: Oxford University Press, 1973.
Podhoretz, Norman. *Why We Were in Vietnam.* New York: Simon and Schuster, 1982.
Shawcross, William. *Sideshow: Kissinger, Nixon and the Destruction of Cambodia.* New York: Simon and Schuster, 1979.

Chapter 7. American Foreign Policy and Human Rights
Kommers, Donald P. and Loescher, Gilburt D. eds. *Human Rights and American Foreign Policy.* Notre Dame, Ind.: Notre Dame University Press, 1979.
Nanda, Ved P., Scarrit, James R., and Shepherd, George W. eds. *Global Human Rights: Public Policies, Comparative Measures, and NGO Strategies.* Boulder, Colorado: Westview Press, 1981.
Schlesinger, Jr., Arthur M. "Human Rights and the American Tradition," in *America and the World 1978, Foreign Affairs,* Special Issue, 1979.
Thompson, Kenneth. "New Reflections on Ethics and Foreign Policy: The Problem of Human Rights," *The Journal of Politics* 40, No. 4 (November, 1978).
Vogelgesang, Sandra. "What Price Principle? U.S. Policy and Human Rights," *Foreign Affairs.* (July, 1978).

Chapter 8. The United States and the Third World
Bhagwati, Jagdish, ed. *The New International Economic Order.* Cambridge, Mass.: M.I.T. Press, 1977.

Blake, David and Walters, Robert. *The Politics of Global Economic Relations.* Englewood Cliffs, N.J.: Prentice-Hall, 1976.

Frank, André G. *Development and Underdevelopment in Latin America.* New York: Monthly Review, 1968.

Galtung, Johan. "A Structural Theory of Imperialism," *Journal of Peace Research,* (2), 1971.

Hayter, Teresa. *Aid as Imperialism.* Baltimore: Penguin Books, 1971.

Hansen, Roger D. "North South Policy—What's the Problem?" *Foreign Affairs,* 58, No. 5, (Summer, 1980).

Report of the Independent Commission on International Development Issues under the chairmanship of Willy Brant, *North-South: A Programme for Survival.* Cambridge, Mass.: M.I.T. Press, 1980.

Spero, Joan. *The Politics of International Economic Relations.* New York: St. Martin's, 1977.

Tucker, Robert. *The Inequality of Nations.* New York: Basic Books, 1977.

Chapter 9. Reflections on Nuclear Weapons

Atomic Energy Commission. *The Effects of Nuclear Weapons.* Washington, D.C.: U.S. Government Printing Office, 1962.

George, Alexander L. and Smoke, Richard. *Deterrence in American Foreign Policy.* New York: Columbia University Press, 1974.

Kahan, Jerome H. *Security in the Nuclear Age.* Washington, D.C.: The Brookings Institution, 1975.

Kennan, George F. *The Clouds of Danger.* Boston: Atlantic-Little Brown, 1980.

Podhoretz, Norman. *The Present Danger.* New York: Simon and Schuster, 1980.

Schell, Jonathan. *The Fate of the Earth.* New York: Knopf, 1982.

Chapter 10. Toward the Future

Barnet, Richard and Muller, Ronald. *Global Reach.* Simon and Schuster, 1974.

Brown, Lester. *World Without Borders.* New York: Random House, 1973.

Commoner, Barry. *The Closing Circle.* New York: Knopf, 1971.

Galtung, Johan. *The True Worlds.* New York: The Free Press, 1980.

Kahn, Herman, Brown, William and Martel, Leon. *The Next 200 Years.* New York: Morrow, 1976.

Keohane, Robert and Nye, Joseph. *Power and Interdependence.* Boston: Little Brown, 1977.

Mendlovitz, Saul. ed. *On the Creation of a Just World Order.* New York: Free Press, 1975.

Morse, Robert. *Modernization and the Transformation of International Relations.* New York: Free Press, 1976.

Report on the Limits to Growth. International Bank for Reconstruction and Development. Washington, D.C.: 1976.

Toffler, Alvin. *The Third Wave.* New York: Bantam Books, 1980.

Index

Abrams, Elliott, 36
Adenauer, Konrad, 27
Afghanistan, reaction to Soviet invasion of, 9, 13, 20, 22, 28, 32, 69, 70, 71-72, 109, 110, 111, 120, 142, 187, 188, 194, 196, 200
Africa, 77, 216; foreign powers in, 4, 13, 73, 74, 149
agriculture, U.S., 215
Agriculture, U.S. Department of, 215, 216, 221
Alaska, 5
Algeria, 164
Allen, Richard, 27, 43
Alliance for Progress (1961), 8, 156
Allison, Graham, 15
Al-Sabah, Ali Khalifa, 98
American Institute for Free Labor Development, 143
Andes, 216
Angola, and Cuba, 133; and U.S., 29, 30, 32, 46, 74, 103, 104, 105, 120, 122, 123, 124, 149
anti-nuclear war movement, 197-203. See also nuclear freeze movement
Argentina, 9, 37, 148, 164, 165. See also British-Argentine War
Arms Control and Disarmament Agency, 33
arms race, 24, 28, 31, 190, 196. See also MX missile system
ASEAN states, 179
Asia, 158, 183, 216
Atlantic Charter (1941), 8
Austria, 154
Australia, 166, 174

balance-of-payments, 80; of U.S., 75-76, 92, 95, 97, 99
Ball George, 17, 18, 99
Bandung Conference (1955), 175
Bangladesh, 12, 163, 164, 174
banking system, effect of Poland's loans on, 100-01; U.S., 76
Barnet, Richard J., 24, 25, 33, 49, 105
Bauer, P.T., 178
Bay of Pigs, 110
Berger, Peter L., 174, 185, 224
Berlin blockade, 11
bioengineering, 216
biological weapons, 193-94
bombers, Soviet and U.S. compared, 191
Bowdler, William, 135, 139
Brazil, 84, 148, 164, 174, 216
Bretton Woods Agreements (1944), 10, 79, 80, 91, 96, 164
British-Argentine War, 1
Brzezinski, Zbigniew, 13, 36, 70, 123, 127, 134
Buckley, James L., 41
bureaucracies, foreign policy, 44; role of, in foreign policy making, 1, 15, 24, 32, 33, 42, 56, 120, 204
Bush, George, 43
Bushnell, John, 41

Calvin, Melvin, 217
Cambodia, and U.S. foreign policy, 9, 23; U.S.S.R. in, 74, 194; and Vietnam, 120, 142
Canada, 89
Cancun North-South Summit, 46

capitalism, and Third World, 181-82, 185; U.S., 77
Caribbean, foreign powers in, 1, 7, 8, 9, 86, 120, 155, 156, 157; nationalism in, 77, 132
Carlucci, Frank C., 112, 113
Carter, Jimmy, 41; foreign policies of, 4, 5, 6, 8, 9, 13, 14, 19, 20, 22, 23, 25, 33, 38-39, 57, 70, 119, 121, 124, 132, 134, 135, 136, 137-40, 142, 143, 144; and human rights, 146, 148, 149, 151-52, 153, 159; and Nixon-Kissinger policies, compared, 146; and Reagan compared, 27-28, 35, 36, 47, 128-29, 146; and Third World, 62, 69, 138-42, 162. See also human rights; Strategic Arms Limitation Talks (SALT) II
Casey, William, 116-17
Castro, Fidel, 132, 135, 136, 156
Center for Defense Information, 72-73
Central America, germ plasm in, 216; upheaval in, 1, 77, 131, 132, 136-37; and U.S., 4, 7, 9, 20, 22, 26, 86, 142, 155, 156, 157; and U.S.S.R., 4, 20, 24, 119, 120. See also El Salvador; Honduras; Nicaragua
Central Intelligence Agency (CIA), 15, 17, 20, 30, 33, 102, 107-14, 149, 204: Reagan's view of, 115-17; and U.S. foreign policy, 107, 118, 120; effect of Vietnam syndrome on, 123, 146, 187
Central Intelligence Agency Act (1949), 108
chemical weapons, 194
Chiang Kai-shek, 11, 72
Chile, CIA in, 111, 149; and MNCs, 101, 102; Soviet policy toward, 142; U.S. policy toward, 32, 37, 157
China, People's Republic of, 11, 12, 72, 183; and U.S., 24, 31, 77, 121, 147, 148
Chinese doctrine, 71-72
Christopher, Warren, 140
Churchill, Winston, 11
Civil War, U.S., 6, 8
Clark, William P., 43
Clark Amendment, 103, 123
Clemenceau, Georges, 10
cold war, 11, 12, 13, 17, 197. See also Reagan, Ronald
Colombia, 156-57
Commerce, Department of, 33
Commission for International Economic Co-operation, 166
Committee on Disarmament, 193
Common Fund, 165
Common Market, See European Economic Community
Common Sense (Paine), 6
communism, and anti-nuclear war movement, 197, 198; and Carter's foreign policy, 36-37, 47; and Reagan's foreign policy, 36-37, 47; and U.S. foreign policy, 11, 12, 19, 119, 204
Congress, and Central America, 130, 170, 204; and CIA, 107, 109-14, 116; and human rights policies, 146-47, 152, 159-60; and Reagan, 44, 195
conscription, under Carter administration, 70, 123
Conservation of Germplasm Resources—An Imperative, 221

Conservation of Islands for Science Convention, 222
conservativism, 33
Constitution, U.S., 8
containment, role of, in U.S. foreign policy, 23, 40, 41, 47, 119, 121, 165, 204
Control Risks, 207, 208
Convention on International Trade in Endangered Species (CITES), 222
cosmocorps, 99
counter-terrorist firms, 208, 209, 210, 211
Cuba, in Angola, 103, 104, 124, 149; in Ethiopia, 73; and the FSLN, 138, 139, 141; in Latin America, 1, 137; and U.S., 7, 8, 15, 23, 29-30, 39, 57, 132, 133, 148, 151, 156; and U.S.S.R., 29-30, 171
Czechoslovakia, 32, 154, 155

Debayle, Anastasio Somoza, *see* Somoza, Anastasio
Declaration of Independence (1775), 5, 8
decolonization, effects of, 50, 96
Deep Seabed Authority, 165
Defense, Department of, 15, 16, 33, 108, 119, 120, 187
democracy, 181, 182
democratic capitalism, 181, 183
"Dense Pack," *see* MX missile system
Derian, Patricia, 148, 153, 160, 161, 224
desertification, 214
détente, reaction against, 147, 188; U.S.-China, 24, 31, 121; effect of, on U.S. foreign policy, 119; U.S.-U.S.S.R., 12-13, 104, 119, 121, 187
developing countries, *see* Third World
Development Assistance Committee (DAC), 168
dollar, in foreign markets, 96, 164; in world currency, 80, 91, 92, 93, 96, 97, 98, 204
Dominican Republic, 32; U.S. influence in, 7, 155, 156
domino theory, in U.S. foreign policy, 4, 11, 39, 41, 119, 121, 165
Dulles, John Foster, 27, 77

Economic Summit, 166, 169
Egypt, 65, 73, 104, 123
Eisenhower, Dwight D., 11, 115, 123
El Salvador, 1, 130, 132; Carter's policy toward, 28, 142-43, 144, 148; Reagan's policy toward, 25, 28, 41, 129, 170; and U.S.S.R., 120
Enders, Thomas O., 41
environment, and new international economic order, 213-24
Eritrean People's Liberation Front (EPLF), 73, 74
Essence of Decision, The (Allison), 15
Ethiopia, foreign powers in, 73, 74, 104, 120, 124; and germ plasm, 216, 219
Europe, dollars in, 96; Reagan's policy toward, 26-27, 28, 31; U.S. private investment in, 83
European Economic Community (EEC), 12, 172

Falkland/Malvinas Islands, 1. *See also* British-Argentine War
Fate of the Earth, The (Schell), 3
Federal Bureau of Investigation (FBI), 108, 110, 120
first strike, 187, 190, 198, 199, 201

Florida, 5
food production, effect of environmental degradations on, 218; role of, in world stability, 171, 172
Ford, Gerald, and CIA, 107, 109; foreign policy of, 22, 121, 147; and OPEC, 63
Foreign Assistance Acts (1961, 1975), 135, 159, 160
Foreign Corrupt Practices Act, 85
Foreign Intelligence Advisory Board, 108, 116
foreign policy, U.S., 4; role of CIA in, 107-14, 204; role of Congress in, 146-47, 152, 159-60, 170, 204; effect of economics on, 74-78, 79, 101-02; goals of, 14, 29, 54; history of, 2, 4-14, 22, 48, 188, 203, 224; influences in, 1-2, 29, 44-45, 46; during Nixon administration, 13, 22; on nuclear arms, 199, 200-03; effect of OPEC on, 62-65, 162; philosophies of, 16-20, 99; role of power in, 50-77, 203; presidential role in, 1-2, 13, 34; effect of Reagan on, 4, 42-43; and save-species strategy, 222-23; role of Soviet Union in, 4, 17, 22-23, 31, 34, 36-39, 72, 121, 144, 153, 187, 188, 200, 201; and Third World, 162-66, 184, 185, 204. *See also* Carter, Jimmy; human rights; Manifest Destiny; Monroe Doctrine; multinational corporations; national security policy; Reagan, Ronald; Truman Doctrine; Vietnam War
Fourteen Points, 9
Fourth World, 12, 164
France, 15
Franklin, Benjamin, 6
Freedom of Information Act (F.O.I.A.), 112, 113, 211
free trade, 79, 80, 81, 90; role of multinational corporations in, 99
FSLN, *see* Sandinist National Liberation Front

General Agreement on Tariffs and Trade (GATT) (1947), 79, 90, 91, 164
genetic engineering, 217
George, Lloyd, 10
Germany, Nazi, 11; after WWII, 154, 155
germ plasm, 216, 218, 219
globalism, 36, 42, 48, 133, 135, 224
Good Neighbor policy, 156
grain trade, 171
Great Britain, 1
Great Depression, 10
Greece, 154; U.S. policy toward, 150, 151, 155
Green Revolution, the, 183, 216
Grenada, 120, 132
Group of 77, 174, 177
Guam, 8
Guatemala, and U.S. foreign policy, 30, 102, 110, 137, 148
gun boat diplomacy, 9

Haig, Alexander, 25, 27, 36, 38, 39, 42, 43, 47, 129, 130
Haiti, 12, 163; U.S. in, 7, 9, 148, 155, 156
Hawaii, 8
Honduras, 1, 204
Hong Kong, 77, 84
Hormats, Robert D., 79, 81, 90
hot line system, 194-95
Huddleston, Walter, 112, 114
Hughes-Ryan amendment, 111, 112
human rights, 182; and Congress, 146-47; and foreign policy, 13, 35-36, 70, 120, 146, 148, 150-51, 159; in Third World, 20, 26, 135

Human Rights and Humanitarian Affairs, Assistant Secretary of State for, 147, 148
Hungary, 32, 155
Huntington, Samuel, 153, 160, 224

idealism, role of, in shaping foreign policy, 9, 19
immigration, 6, 8, 10
imperialism, 16, 17, 91, 92, 99; Soviet, 71, 72, 73; effect of on Third World countries, 176, 178; U.S., 8, 30, 71, 72, 91, 95, 96, 120
indexing, and Third World, 165
India, 12, 171, 174, 175, 183; and U.S.S.R., 73
Indonesia, 164, 175; Soviets in, 73, 74
industrialization, 8, 10
intercontinental ballistic missiles (ICBMs), Soviet and U.S. compared, 191
Intelligence Identities Protection Act (1982), 107, 114
Intelligence Reform Act (1980), 112, 114
International Bank for Reconstruction and Development (IBRD), establishment of, 11, 79, 86, 91; and species preservation, 220; and Third World, 165
International Board for Plant Genetic Resources, 216
International Development, U.S. Agency for, 221
International Finance Corporation (IFC), 86
internationalism, U.S., 5, 6, 7, 8, 9, 22, 45, 47, 78, 108, 120
International Labor Organization, 88
International Monetary Fund (IMF), 11, 15, 79, 80, 93, 204, 205; and Poland, 101; reform of, 91, 165; and Third World, 170
international money markets, 93
International Rice Research Institute, 220
International Union for Conservation of Nature and Natural Resources, 221
investment, international, 81-90. See also multinational corporations
Iran, oil production in, 60, 61, 62, 66, 67; revolution in, 123, 183; Soviet policy toward, 142; U.S. policy toward, 9, 22, 23, 41, 97, 110, 123, 124, 148, 151
Iran hostage crisis, 14, 20, 22, 70, 109, 111, 123, 128, 188, 204, 205
Iraq, 67, 73
isolationism, 2, 4-7, 35, 51
Israel, 1, 46, 65
Italy, 154, 155

Japan, 172, 173; post-war development of, 12, 154, 155, 183; and U.S., 28, 31
Jefferson, Thomas, 6
Johnson, Lyndon B., 11, 40, 44; and Vietnam, 119-20, 121
Johnson Act (1924), 10
Jordan, 65

Kampuchea, 142
Kegley, Charles W., 33, 49, 57
Kellogg-Briand Pact (1928), 10, 51
Kennan, George F., 196, 197, 203
Kennedy, Edward, 123
Kennedy, John F., 6, 8, 11, 40, 57, 190; and Vietnam, 119, 121
key currency, 94, 95, 96
Khrushchev, Nikita, 57
Kirkpatrick, Jeane, 23-24, 33, 41, 49, 131, 132, 145, 196, 224
Kissinger, Henry, 13, 14, 17, 20, 22, 37, 119, 147, 159, 162
Klare, Michael T., 121, 122, 131, 144, 224
Korean War, 11, 45, 123

Krauthammer, Charles, 79, 99, 100
Kuwait, economy of, 67, 163, 164

Laird, Melvin, 17
Laos, 74, 194
Lardner, Jr., George, 109
Latin America, and U.S. foreign policy, 1, 7, 51, 131, 132, 134, 135, 136, 137, 143, 144, 145, 155, 156, 157, 159
League of Nations, 9
Lebanon, 46
Lefever, Ernest, 44
Lenin, Vladimir, 16
less developed countries (LDCs), 85. See also Third World
liberals, economic ideology of, 79, 80, 81, 99
Libya, oil production in, 67; and superpowers, 27, 43, 104
linkage, agricultural, 218; political, 39-40
Linowitz reports, 133-34
Lome Convention, 166
Louisiana Purchase (1803), 5
Lusitania, 9

Machel, Samora, 170
Magdoff, Henry, 50, 71, 78, 79, 91, 224
Management and Budget, Office of, 108, 112
"Manifest Destiny," 5, 6, 7, 8, 9, 10, 11, 19, 119, 120
Marshall Plan, 16, 169, 173
Marx, Karl, 16
"massive retaliation" doctrine, 77
McKinley, William, 7
McNamara, Robert, 17
Mediterranean basin, 216
Meese, Edwin, 34, 43
Mexico, agricultural resources of, 215, 216, 219, 223; political system of, 137; and U.S., 165
Middle East, 77; oil production in, 67; U.S. investments of, 89; U.S. policy toward, 4, 13, 65, 70, 147. See also Egypt; Jordan; Lebanon; Organization of Petroleum Exporting Countries; Palestine, Saudi Arabia
military, U.S., 43, 50, 187, 189
military spending, U.S., under Carter 28, 70, 121; under Kennedy, 190; Korean War, 45; under Reagan, 4, 28, 45
missiles, Soviet and U.S., compared, 191, 192, 193. See also MX missile system
MNC, see multinational corporations
Mondale, Walter, 111
Monroe, James, 6
Monroe Doctrine (1823), 6, 7, 25
moralism, in U.S. foreign policy, 158-59, 160, 173
Morgenthau, Hans J., 14, 15, 50, 51, 56-57, 78, 153, 154, 158
Most Favored Nation status, 80, 87, 88
Moynihan, Daniel Patrick, 109, 110, 111, 112, 113, 114
Mozambique, U.S.S.R. in, 74, 170
Mugabe, Robert, 102, 170
Muller, Ronald, 105
multinational corporations (MNCs), role of, in economic and political affairs, 75, 99, 106, 172, 205; foreign investment by, 75, 82, 98; and foreign policy, 2, 12, 17, 18, 79, 91, 92, 99-105; regulating, 88, 165, 206; and terrorism, 206-13; in Third World, 30, 164-65
Muskie, Edmund, 217
mutual deterrence, 186
MX missile system, under Carter administration, 70,

121, 196; opposition to, 186-87, 196; under Reagan administration, 186, 187, 188, 191, 192, 196, 203
Myers, Norman, 205, 213, 224

Nathan, James, 205, 206, 224
nationalism, U.S., 8
National Security Act (1947), 108
National Security Council (NSC), 43, 108, 112, 114, 128
National Security Planning Group, 43
national security policy, purpose of, 29, 30, 32
national treatment principle of investment, 87, 88
neo-Marxism, and American foreign policy, 16-20, 24, 33, 78, 79; and global economic relations, 91
Netherlands, The, and Third World, 168
neutralism, and anti-nuclear war movement, 197, 198
Neutrality Acts, 10
neutron bomb, 27, 28, 43
new federalism, 34
new international economic order (NIEO), 46-47, 166, 168, 177, 205; and the environment, 213-14
New Zealand, 166
Nicaragua, and Carter administration, 137-39, 144, 148; civil war in, 123, 132, 170; U.S. in, 7, 9, 22, 28, 122, 134, 137, 151, 155, 156, 204; U.S.S.R. in, 120
Nigeria, 164; and U.S. foreign policy, 65, 165
Nixon, Richard, foreign policy of, 13, 20, 22, 119, 147; and OPEC, 63
North Atlantic Treaty Organization (NATO), 11, 15, 80; and Reagan, 24, 189; Soviet view of, 142
North Korea, 43, 142, 154, 205
North-South: a Program for Survival (Brandt Commission), 167. *See also* Brandt Report
North-South relations, 46, 162-74, 176, 185, 205, 223. *See also* Third World
North Vietnam, 12
Novak, Michael, 181
nuclear freeze movement, 24, 31, 204
nuclear war, and American foreign policy, 1, 4, 187, 202; conventional assumptions about, 186, 203; European view of, 27; Reagan's view of, 31; and superpower power struggle, 74
nuclear weapons, role of, in foreign policy, 50, 147; limiting, 192, 193, 194; Reagan's view of, 186, 187, 189; Soviet policy of, 186, 190, 191; U.S. and Soviet, compared, 190, 191. *See also* anti-nuclear war movement; MX missile system; nuclear freeze movement; Strategic Arms Limitation Talks, I and II

oil trade, 93, 97; and monetary stability, 58-69, 171; effect of, on U.S. foreign policy, 147. *See also* Organization of Petroleum Exporting Countries
Organization for Economic Cooperation and Development (OECD), 83, 84, 85, 87, 90, 204, 205; and Third World, 165
Organization of American States (OAS), 80, 139
Organization of Petroleum Exporting Countries (OPEC), 12, 57, 58, 59, 60, 61, 66, 67, 68, 69, 97, 205; and Brandt report, 172; effect of, on Third World, 169-70, 179; effect of, on U.S. foreign policy, 62-65, 78, 79, 162, 163, 165, 204
Overseas Private Investment Corporation (OPIC), 85, 101

Paine, Thomas, 6
Pakistan, 12, 165
Palestine, 65, 142
Palestine Liberation Organization (PLO), 1

Panama Canal Treaties (1978), 13, 70, 121, 133, 134
Paraguay, 156
Pearl Harbor, 10, 108
Pentagon, and CIA, 108, 118; and U.S. foreign policy, 43, 187
Pentagon Papers, 109
Philippine Islands, U.S. influence in, 7, 8, 9, 158
Platt Amendment (1901), 7, 156
pluralism, *see* liberalism
Poland, 27, 100-01, 154, 155; Soviet intervention in, 13; and U.S. foreign policy, 37, 40, 46, 99, 100, 196
Politics Among Nations (Morgenthau), 51
pollution, 214
Portugal, 154
power, U.S., 158; role of economics in, 74-75, 205; role of, in foreign policy, 14-16, 50, 71, 154; since WWII, 64, 159-60, 204
president, and CIA, 112; and Congress, 146-47; role of, in foreign policy, 1-2, 13, 33, 34. *See also* Carter, Jimmy; Eisenhower, Dwight; Ford, Gerald; Johnson, Lyndon; Kennedy, John F.; Nixon, Richard; Reagan, Ronald; Roosevelt, Franklin D.; Roosevelt, Theodore; Wilson, Woodrow
Puerto Rico, 7, 8, 133

Rapid Deployment Force, 70, 78, 128
Reagan, Ronald, 1, 34, 45, 46, 126; and Carter, compared, 27-28, 35, 36, 153; and CIA, 107, 109, 114, 115; and Congress, 44, 46; economics of, 44, 46-47, 81; foreign policy of, 4, 5, 13-14, 19, 20, 22, 24, 25, 34, 35, 44, 47, 57, 103, 119, 120, 121, 131, 187-88; and military, 31, 41, 42, 43; and nuclear arms, 27, 186, 190, 193, 203, 204; restraints on, 33, 42-43, 44, 45; and Soviet Union, 31, 39, 144, 187, 189
realism, political, 51-56, 78, 158-59, 160
Revolutionary War, 6
"revolving door," 17
Rhodesia, 65, 102
Roosevelt, Franklin D., 6, 8, 10
Roosevelt, Theodore, 7, 9, 14

Saavedra, Humberto Ortega, 141, 142
Samoa, American, 8
Sandinista, 136, 142, 170. *See also* Sandinist National Liberation Front
Sandinist National Liberation Front (FSLN), 138, 139, 140, 141
Saudi Arabia, and Mobil Oil, 105; oil production in, 62, 67, 163; U.S. relations with, 44, 45, 65, 97, 165
Savimbi, Jonas, 103-04
Scandinavia, 168
Schell, Jonathan, 3
Schlesinger, James R., 124
Schultz, George, 17
Selassie, Haile, 73
Singapore, 77, 84, 164, 174
Sino-Soviet rift, 15, 72
Smith, Ian, 102
Solidarity movement, 100
Somalia, 73, 123
Somoza, Anastasio, 134, 138, 139, 140, 141, 156
South Africa, 37, 46, 142
South America, 77, 136
South Asia, 4, 77
Southeast Asia, 216; U.S. in, 12, 109, 158
South Korea, conditions in, 77, 84, 150, 151, 154, 164, 179; and U.S., 9, 23, 37, 165

South Pacific, 7-8
South Yemen, 104
Soviet Union, in Afghanistan, 9, 13, 20, 22, 28, 69, 70,
  71-72, 104, 120, 121; in Africa, 74, 102, 103, 104,
  142, 170; in Eastern Europe, 100, 101, 151; in Latin
  America, 1, 142; military strength of, 50, 189; and
  Reagan foreign policy, 4, 22-23, 31, 34, 38, 144; and
  South Yemen, 104; and Third World, 168, 170, 171;
  and U.S. foreign policy, 9, 11, 13, 47-48, 121, 200;
  U.S. view of, 17, 72, 121, 187, 200, 201, 202, 203;
  and Vietnam War, 12, 120
Spain, 154
Spanish-American War (1898), 5, 7
special interest groups, 1-2
species conservation, 220-24
Stalin, Joseph, 11, 155
Start negotiations, 193
State, Department of, 15, 33, 108, 147
Strategic Arms Limitation Agreement (SALT I) (1972),
  13, 70, 121
Strategic Arms Limitation Treaty (SALT) II, 13, 70, 121,
  148, 187
Strategic Services, Office of (OSS), 108
submarine warfare, 9
Sudan, 163
Sweezy, Paul M., 50, 71, 78, 224

Taft, William H., 7
Taiwan, conditions in, 77, 179; investment in, 84; U.S.
  policy toward, 37
terrorism, in Latin America, 132, 137, 143; and MNCs,
  205, 206-13; U.S. policy toward, 36, 130, 131, 135
Texas, 5
Third World, 174, 175; characteristics of, 163-64, 175-
  76; economies of, 28, 36, 46-47, 69, 90, 91, 104;
  genetic resources of, 219, 223; and human rights,
  148, 161; ideology of, 176-77, 178, 179, 180, 181;
  relations of, with industrialized nations, 84. 85, 162,
  165, 173; Soviet influence in, 72, 73, 74, 121, 170,
  171; superpowers in, 32, 50; and U.S. foreign policy,
  1, 12, 15, 16, 19, 22, 23, 70, 77, 81, 96, 106, 120,
  125, 126, 147, 153, 165, 168, 170, 171, 177-78,
  181, 184, 185
Treasury, Department of, 15, 17, 33
Truman, Harry, 6, 11, 121. See also Truman Doctrine
Truman Doctrine (1947), 8, 11, 80, 121
Tucker, Robert W., 50, 57, 69, 78, 79, 224
Turkey, 146, 155, 216
Turner, Frederick Jackson, 6

Uganda, 148
United Nations, 10, 15; and disappearing species, 219,
  220, 221; and mercenaries, 212, 213; role of Third
  World nations in, 174, 177
United Nations Charter of Economic Rights and Duties
  of States, 177
United Nations Committee of the Whole, 165
United Nations Conference on Trade and Development
  (UNCTAD), 88, 166, 217
United Nations Educational Scientific and Cultural
  Organization (UNESCO), 220, 221
United Nations Environment Programme, 221

United Nations Food and Agricultural Organization
  (FAD), 216, 220
United Nations Industrial Development Organization
  (UNIDO), 166
United Nations Special Session on Disarmament, 194
United States, economy of, 12, 18, 29, 32, 46, 74-75,
  79, 80, 98; foreign direct investment in, 89-90, 97;
  nuclear policy of, 186, 187; effect of WWII on, 15, 76,
  95, 189. See also dollar; foreign policy, U.S.; military,
  U.S.; power, U.S.; Soviet Union
Universal Declaration of Human Rights, 149
urbanization, effect of, on U.S. foreign policy, 7, 8

Vance, Cyrus, 13, 70, 126
Venezuela, 156-57
Versailles, Treaty of, 9
Versailles Summit (1982), 1
Vietnam, and Cambodia, 120, 142; and Laos, 74; and
  U.S., 23, 29, 32, 93, 158. See also North Vietnam
Vietnam Syndrome, 122-31, 187-88; and human rights
  philosophy, 146
Vietnam War, and El Salvador struggle, compared, 26;
  effects of, on U.S. foreign policy, 12, 13, 19, 20, 23,
  25, 45, 119-20, 121, 132, 145, 147, 159, 187, 188,
  204. See also Vietnam Syndrome
Vladivostok Accords (1974), 13, 121

Walsea, Lech, 100
Wake, 8
War, Department of, 108
Ward, Barbara, 165, 166, 174, 185, 224
Warnke, Paul, 126
War Powers Act (1973), 123, 146
Washington, George, 6
Washington Naval Arms Limitation Agreements (1922),
  10, 51
Watergate, 13, 108, 109, 146, 147, 159
Weinberger, Casper, 17, 27, 40, 43, 129
Wetlands of International Importance, Convention on,
  222
Wilson, Woodrow, 6, 7, 9, 10, 14
Wittkopf, Eugene R., 33, 49, 57
World Bank, see International Bank for Reconstruction
  and Development
World Development Fund, 171
World Environment Day, 217
world industries, 83
World War I, 9, 10
World War II, 102, 108; democratic regimes created
  after, 154, 155; economic effects of, 79, 80, 95; U.S.
  after, 15, 76, 189; effect of, on U.S. foreign policy, 5,
  10, 47, 48
World Wildlife Fund, 221

Yamani, Ahmed Zaki, 62
Young, Andrew, 70, 126
Yugoslavia, 175

Zaire, 123
Zambia, 219
Zero Options, 27
Zimbabwe, MNCs in, 102; Soviet policy toward, 74,
  142, 170